THE

Unexpected
Einstein

ALSO BY DENIS BRIAN

THE
Unexpected Einstein

The Real Man Behind the Icon

DENIS BRIAN

WILEY

John Wiley & Sons, Inc.

Copyright © 2005 by Denis Brian. All rights reserved

Published by John Wiley & Sons, Inc., Hoboken, New Jersey
Published simultaneously in Canada

Photo credits: pages iii, 227 third from top: University of Frankfurt; page 8: Courtesy of Stadt Ulm Stadtarchive; pages 28, 60: Courtesy of ETH, Zurich; pages 40, 178, 190: Courtesy of AIP; pages 44, 52, 77, 155, 211: Courtesy of Jamie Sayen; page 48: Alice Kahler; page 51: Courtesy of Luise Rainer; page 53: *Princeton Weekly Bulletin*; page 69: Courtesy of Evelyn Einstein; page 81: Courtesy of Elizabeth Roboz Einstein; pages 117, 118: Courtesy of Dr. Thomas Bucky; page 134: Courtesy of George Wald; page 28: Courtesy of Linus Pauling; page 143: Courtesy of John Kemeny; page 147: Courtesy of Abraham Pais; page 149: Courtesy University of Texas, Austin; page 152: Courtesy of Monique Weston Claque; page 171: Courtesy of Banesh Hoffman; pages 176, 227 second from top, 228: Library of Congress; page 206: Courtesy of Jewish American Archives; page 218: Courtesy of Mrs. Alan Richards, Institute for Advanced Study; page 221: H. Landshoff, FIT; page 227 bottom: Courtesy of Lady Soames; page 229 top: Courtesy of Dr. Lucy Rorke; page 229 bottom: Courtesy of Rocky Raisen; page 230: Courtesy of Pamela Rutter

Design and composition by Navta Associates, Inc.

For general information about our other products and services, please contact our Customer Care Department within the United States at (800) 762-2974, outside the United States at (317) 572-3993 or fax (317) 572-4002.

Wiley also publishes its books in a variety of electronic formats. Some content that appears in print may not be available in electronic books. For more information about Wiley products, visit our web site at www.wiley.com.

Library of Congress Cataloging-in-Publication Data:

Brian, Denis, date.
    The unexpected Einstein : the real man behind the icon / Denis Brian.
        p. cm.
    Includes bibliographical references and index.
    ISBN-13 978-0-471-71840-6 (alk. cloth)
    ISBN-10 0-471-71840-8 (alk. cloth)
    1.   Einstein, Albert, 1879–1955—Biography.   I. Title.
    QC16.E5B7375 2005
    530'.092—dc22   2004025914

Printed in the United States of America

10 9 8 7 6 5 4 3 2 1

To Martine, Danielle, Alex, and Emma,
with love

There have already been published by the bucketful such brazen lies and utter fictions about me that I would long have gone to my grave if I had let myself pay attention to them.

—*Albert Einstein's comment to his friend Max Brod, on February 12, 1949*

CONTENTS

ACKNOWLEDGMENTS

My thanks to the following Einstein experts, scientists, and biographers for helping to counter the attempts to discredit Einstein's life and work: I. Bernard Cohen, Stanley Goldberg, Banesh Hoffmann, Gerard Holton, John Kemeny, Ashley Montagu, Abraham Pais, Linus Pauling, I. I. Rabi, Jamie Sayen, Robert Schulmann, John Stachel, George Wald, Victor Weisskopf, John Wheeler, and Eugene Wigner.

To the following Einstein neighbors, friends, and relatives for their accounts of the man they knew: Andrew Blackwood, Thomas Bucky, Dorothy Commins, Elizabeth Roboz Einstein, Evelyn Einstein, Gillette Griffin, Alice Kahler, Clair Gilbert, Christopher Stone, I. F. Stone, and Jane Leonard Swing Chapman.

To Michele Zackheim, author of *Einstein's Daughter: The Search for Lieserl*, who gives Einstein's admirers and critics a chance to discuss the mystery of Lieserl's disappearance, and to speculate on Einstein's motives and character.

And to Richard Alan Schwartz, who first obtained Einstein's extraordinary FBI file.

My editor, Hana Lane, greatly enhanced the finished product. My wife, Martine, as always, encouraged me and gave invaluable help every step of the way.

Introduction:
Demythologizing Einstein

B ecause of the myths that portrayed Albert Einstein as a superman with unearthly powers and a key to all the secrets of the universe, he was regarded with such awe that a young woman once fainted at the sight of him, and a child asked someone if he was the Lord.

My aim is to reveal, with the help of his colleagues, relatives, friends, and enemies, the often unexpected human being Einstein really was, and to expose the incredible myths about him, many of them published while he was alive. I will present the facts as offered by those who knew him best.

For instance, the story persists that he didn't say his first words until he was four or five, implying that there was something seriously wrong with him as a child. Some claim that he was dyslexic. Speech therapists and those who knew him will present their views. At college he was called a lazy dog. I consider whether there was any truth to that.

And how about the accusation by the Nazis that he stole other scientists' ideas? Now, some fifty years after his death and on the centenary of the four 1905 papers that made him famous, including those elucidating the special relativity theory and the photoelectric effect, the charge of plagiarism has been revived, especially on the Internet. Some writers claim that his first wife, Mileva, was his unacknowledged scientific partner. Experts respond to this charge in the chapter titled "Einstein under Attack—Was He a Plagiarist?"

Others portray him as a heartless egotist who despised and

1

mistreated women. He has been characterized as a terrible husband, an absent father, and a brazen womanizer. Those who know the facts, including close friends and his eldest son, Hans Albert, give their views.

What about the rumors concerning the fate of his daughter, Lieserl? And how did he manage to keep her a secret from the world? Here you will find almost everything that is known about that mystery, based on the latest investigations.

Some say he believed in God, and others, with equal conviction, say he didn't. This book attempts to give a clear answer.

Why did FBI director J. Edgar Hoover suspect Einstein of being a Communist, a spy for the Russians, and secretly at work on a "death ray" even more devastating than the atomic bomb? I will recount the twenty-year-long investigation and Hoover's conclusions.

Nobel physicist Eugene Wigner provides a firsthand account of exactly how Einstein was persuaded to write to Roosevelt proposing the building of an atomic bomb. Nobel biochemist George Wald reveals what Einstein worried and wondered about. Friends and colleagues discuss his foibles and fancies, weaknesses and strengths—the intimate details of his private life. Strangers recall their memorable encounters with him.

Those who knew Einstein intimately at all stages of his life, from his childhood to his death, dispel the myths to reveal the man, explaining as they do their enduring fascination with a complex, flawed, humane, and entertaining genius with a "wicked tongue" and a lively sense of humor. Some material is from my own books, *Genius Talk* and *Einstein: A Life*. Much is new, including an account of his Princeton woman friend, Johanna Fantova, to whom he wrote poetry and who kept notes—only recently discovered—of their frequent conversations until shortly before Einstein died.

Here then are answers to the "brazen lies and utter fictions" which Einstein had deplored but are still in circulation.

1 | Was Einstein Dyslexic, a Late Talker, and a "Lazy Dog"?

Today dyslexia is recognized as a common learning disability. In several countries, it is customary to screen children for the disorder before they start school. Some think that Albert Einstein—along with Michael Faraday (Einstein's idol), Thomas Edison, and Alexander Graham Bell—may have been dyslexic. The symptoms of dyslexia include transposing and omitting letters and numbers and scrambling sentences.

Dyslexics take comfort in the belief that Einstein was one of them—pointing to his many accomplishments.

Was he, in fact, one of them?

The reality is that among the many thousands of documents in the Einstein archives, there is not one thing to indicate that he had the disability. Quite the reverse. His writing demonstrates that he had no trouble expressing his thoughts clearly and understanding, as well as creating, complex mathematical formulas. Only if the term *dyslexia* was to cover a broader range of learning disabilities could Einstein be called dyslexic.

The question remains whether Einstein was a slow learner. Some say that he was four or five before he first spoke. Others even say seven. The implication is that the future genius, far from being a child prodigy, was mentally retarded, and later, so the story goes, he was at best a mediocre student all through his school and college days. Let's consider the facts.

His maternal grandmother, Jette Derzbacher, and her husband, Julius, saw Albert when he was two years and three months old. Immediately afterward she wrote to Albert's mother, Pauline: "He was so good and dear and we talk again and again of his droll ideas." How could he have expressed droll ideas without speaking?

Maja, his younger sister, provides more evidence to dispel the myth that he was silent until he was three or four. She wrote in a memoir—presumably based on what she was told by her parents—that before her birth, when Albert was two and a half, he had been promised a baby to play with. To him, this must have meant a new toy, because, on her appearance, he asked, obviously disappointed, "Where are the wheels?" Quite a quip from someone reputed not to be talking at all.

It is reasonably established, then, that he began talking somewhat late, at about the age of two.

Einstein himself surmised that he kept silent for so long because he wanted his first words to be a complete sentence, which sounds like a wisecrack. He wasn't above contributing to his own mythology. Fellow scientific greats Edward Teller and Richard Feynman and mathematician Julia Robinson are reputed to have been late talkers, too. At two and a half, Teller spoke his first words: "really" and "yes." The delay may have resulted from Teller's growing up in a bilingual home, where Hungarian and German were spoken. Feynman was silent until he was two, then he talked nonstop.

Some have suggested that late talkers may well become superbright in science and math. Author Thomas Sowell called late talking "the Einstein Syndrome," which is also the title of his book. Unfortunately, young Einstein became the late talkers' poster child.

Speech therapist Wendy Grant warns: "The trouble with the Einstein Syndrome is that parents with a child who is a late talker say, 'Oh, he's just another Einstein,' and leave it at that. But if a child hasn't said a word by eighteen months, something should be done about it."

Another speech therapist, Misty Williams, says, "Most children utter their first words like ball, baba, or ada between ten and twelve months. If a child hasn't spoken by eighteen months, that's a red flag. He or she should be taken to a speech therapist. There could be many explanations, such as chronic ear infection, asthma, or being in an environment where the child isn't getting enough mental stimulation. None of those, apparently, explain Einstein's case."

Speech therapist Linda Kuchner defines late talkers as "children between eighteen and twenty months who speak fewer than ten words; those between twenty-one and thirty months who speak less than fifty words and no two-word combinations. Between seven and twelve months, a child should speak one to three words. From thirteen to eighteen months, three to twenty words. From nineteen to twenty-four months, fifty words or more.

"If Einstein wasn't saying a word at twenty-four months he was definitely a late talker. But he was also a genius. Maybe there are different rules for them. Didn't he once say: 'I don't even know my telephone number, because I never bother to remember anything I can look up'?"

Barbara Wolff at the Einstein Archives, the Jewish National and University Library, Jerusalem, comments that the above quote "sounds quite authentic. In order to not contribute to the growing amount of false, twisted and completely forged Einstein quotes, I would suggest you use it 'as quoted by [somebody].' If I am not mistaken the quote was published in J. Sayen's 'Einstein in America.'" What Sayen quoted there was Einstein's answer when asked the speed of sound: "I don't know," he replied. "I don't burden my memory with such facts that I can easily find in any textbook."

The big change in Einstein's behavior manifested itself when he was five. He was ill in bed, and the strange force of the magnetic compass his father gave him intrigued and baffled him. Why did the arrow always point in the same

Albert Einstein, 6, and his sister, Maja, 4. They were not then close friends.

direction, no matter how much he shook it or tried to catch it unawares? This was the sort of mystery he never gave up trying to solve.

Until he was seven Albert was tutored at home. His mother was overjoyed when, instead of his being the backward boy she feared she had produced, the tutor said Albert was exceptionally bright. But later his mother was crushed when she read his first elementary school report, which rated him dull-witted.

What reasons did his teachers give for such an assessment? Apparently he didn't mix with the other boys and couldn't learn by rote, and instead of immediately answering a question, he would hesitate and whisper the answer to himself before saying it aloud.

Einstein had apparently adopted this unique defense mechanism to cope with a system that terrorized students into learning their lessons by rote. The wrong answers got painful raps on the knuckles. Albert simply couldn't learn by rote, especially if the subject bored him. Speech therapist Kuchner thinks that to avoid the pain and humiliation of a wrong answer, Einstein would make a trial run to make sure he had it right.

Speech therapist Williams suggests another motive. "This could be the behavior of a perfectionist," she says. "A bright person who is also a perfectionist might say the answer to himself first, before speaking."

Einstein knew that his teachers had him tagged as mentally slow, unsociable, and adrift forever in his foolish dreams. He told his son Hans Albert about this characterization many years later. In fact, his autocratic teachers resented his attitude and odd verbal behavior so much that even though, at seven, his marks put him at the top of the class, they gave him a low rating.

Einstein's contemporary George Bernard Shaw, by contrast, seems to have been born with the gift of the gab but had an equally miserable time as a schoolboy. Shaw considered school to be even more cruel than prison, because prisoners were not forced to read books written by the warders, and they were not beaten or otherwise punished if they could not remember the utterly unmemorable contents.

Einstein certainly had learning problems in his early years, but later, in a more congenial and stimulating environment, he completely overcame them. Then it was his attitude and odd behavior, not his lack of ability, that caused his teachers to express a low opinion of him. That he did lose himself in his dreams—as they complained—was true. He was also able to rise above the situation, as is illustrated in a wonderful photograph of his Munich class in 1889. Of the fifty-two boys, ten-year-old Albert alone manages a slight smile. All the others look downtrodden, as though auditioning for the lead in *Oliver Twist* or anticipating the next rap over the knuckles.

His contemporaries, too, found his behavior odd. To his grim fellow students, he was a freak because he wasn't interested in sports and shunned their company.

However, his sister noticed that if anything captured Albert's interest, he gave it unusual, sustained concentration. After watching her compete with friends in trying to build the tallest house of cards, Albert decided to have a go. The reigning champion had made a card house four stories high before it collapsed. Albert's collapsed many times, but he persisted until he finally built one of fourteen stories.

Though he hated his Munich school, Einstein (front row, second from right) is the only one of his class smiling in this early 1889 photo.

At twelve, he hit on his life's work, taking an unusual delight in physics and Euclidian geometry. Mathematics, however, especially algebra, didn't appeal to him in the same way. Then came a transformation, after his father's brother Jakob made it fun instead of force-fed. He aroused Albert's curiosity by announcing, with the air of a magician, that algebra "is a merry science in which we go hunting for a little animal we don't know. So we call it X. When we bag the game, we give it the right name." Between twelve and thirteen Einstein's progress in math and physics as well as in philosophy was amazing, as Max Talmey, a family friend and medical student who frequently lunched with the Einsteins, recalled:

Albert was profoundly impressed by Bernstein's *Popular Books on Physical Science* which describes physical phenomena lucidly and engagingly. After a few months he devoted himself to higher mathematics. Soon the flight of his mathematical genius was so high that I could no longer follow. Thereafter philosophy was often a subject of our conversations. Albert was still a child, only thirteen years old, yet Kant's work, incomprehensible to ordinary mortals, seemed to be clear to him. Kant became Albert's favorite philosopher, after he had read through his *Critique of Pure Reason*. Albert also read something by or about Charles Darwin, worked his way through sections of the twenty volumes of *Science for the People* by Aaron Bernstein, and absorbed Alexander von Humboldt's five-volumed *The Cosmos—An Attempt at a Description of the Physical World*.

Albert's inability to adapt well to school continued into his teens. Brilliant at home, he was considered a hopeless case in high school, especially by his seventh-grade teacher of Greek, Dr. Joseph Degenhart, probably because Albert hated Greek grammar and sat at the back during Dr. Degenhart's class, doubtless thinking of something else, like his next violin lesson, or why the sky is blue. Whenever the teacher glanced his way, he caught Albert smiling and finally asked to see him after class. To Albert's dismay, Degenhart suggested that he leave the school, accused him of wasting everyone's time, and predicted that he would never amount to anything. Albert protested that he had done nothing wrong. He had, the exasperated teacher insisted, by sitting at the back and smiling. His mere presence undermined the respect a teacher needed from his class.

But it was a myth that he was a bad student across the board. He showed a special talent for math and Latin. And there were many factors to explain his problems in school. It was a bad time for Albert. His family had moved from Munich to Milan, Italy, where his father, Hermann, hoped to improve his prospects in his electrochemical business. At fifteen, Albert was left in Munich to complete his high school education, looked after by a distant relative. He was miserable at school, where he had no close friends, missed his family, and felt desperate when he thought he might not see them again for three years. He longed to leave the school and join them in Milan, but he was faced with what seemed an insoluble problem. At eighteen, all fit German males were drafted into the German army and could not leave the country until they'd completed their military service. Help came from the family doctor, Max Talmey's older brother. When Albert consulted him about a minor illness, he spoke of his loneliness and despair with such feeling the doctor feared he was on the verge of a nervous breakdown. So he gave him a to-whom-it-may-concern note saying that if Albert wasn't allowed to join his family abroad he might suffer a complete mental breakdown.

Strangely, Einstein didn't show the note to his Greek teacher, who was eager to see the last of him. Nor to the one teacher he really liked, a Dr. Ferdinand Ruess, who taught history and German. In fact, Einstein enjoyed Dr. Reuss's classes and looked forward to being kept after school for some infraction, if Dr. Ruess was to be his supervisor.*

Instead, he handed the note to the math teacher, Joseph Ducrue, who thought well of his work and presumably would want him to stay. It turned out to be a smart move. The math teacher believed the doctor's diagnosis was correct, sympathized with Albert's plight, and gave him another note saying that he was so good at math there was little more he could teach him. The school principal read the two notes, decided a sick fifteen-year-old student was no good for the school or the army, and gave his approval, virtually a passport for Einstein to join his family in their apartment, Via Berchet 2, in Milan.

In Milan, things began to improve for Einstein, academically and otherwise. He flourished in Italy, where he made friends, visited museums and art galleries, and explored the countryside. He also sometimes worked for his father. The years in Italy were among his most beautiful memories.

---

*Many years later, probably in 1909, Einstein returned to the school to call on Dr. Ruess, who did not remember him. Einstein was poorly dressed and assumed that Ruess suspected that he was a stranger down on his luck who had come to beg, borrow, or steal from him. Einstein ended the embarrassing encounter with a quick exit.

Albert, about 14, and sister Maja, 12, when they were becoming friends.

He had decided to become a philosophy teacher, but after a struggle he gave in to his father's insistence that he come down to earth and study to be an electrical engineer. Still, he aimed high, applying for entrance to a world-class technical college, Zurich Polytechnic in Switzerland.

One big attraction of Zurich Polytechnic was that if he passed the entrance exam he would not have to finish high school but could go straight to college. So he studied hard, concentrating so much that he was rarely distracted, even in a noisy room.

His sister, Maja, attests to his "rather strange working methods. Even when we had company and there was quite a lot of noise, he would retire to the sofa, pick up a pen and paper, precariously balance the inkwell on the backrest, and engross himself in a problem to such an extent that the many-voiced conversation stimulated rather than disturbed him. After my brother mastered the violin he and mother played piano duets, mostly Mozart and Beethoven sonatas. He became so adept that he would constantly search for new harmonies and transitions of his own invention. More than once I saw that he had solved a problem after a session on the violin or the piano. He would suddenly stop playing and cry out: 'There, now I've got it.'"

The family now had great hopes for Einstein's academic success. His favorite uncle, Caesar Koch, showed friends an essay in which Einstein described an experiment he had thought up to find out if electricity, magnetism, and the ether were somehow connected. At this time it was conventional wisdom, since discounted, that the ether existed as a rarefied element that completely filled the upper regions of space. Koch was proud of this young original thinker and expected him to go far. If anything, Einstein's uncle Jakob was even more impressed. He and an assistant engineer had been struggling for days over calculations needed to solve a tricky technical problem. Einstein offered to help and solved the problem in about fifteen minutes.

The myth has it that Einstein failed his exam to enter Zurich Polytechnic. While technically this is true, the facts are that at sixteen he was too young to take the exam. The rigid rule was that no one could take the entrance exam until he or she was eighteen. Hoping the authorities would make an exception for him, a family friend, Gustav Maier, wrote to the college principal, Professor Albin Herzog, describing Albert as a child prodigy. Herzog was not impressed. Even if Einstein was a child prodigy, he was against taking him from his high school until he had completed his studies there. But he offered a gleam of hope. If Maier could provide written documentation from the principal of Einstein's high school that backed Maier's opinion of him and confirmed his mental maturity, only then would he take the exceptional step of waiving the minimum-age rule.

It was a long shot. But what seems to have worked is the written testimony Einstein already had from his high school math teacher rating his math knowledge and ability up to graduation standard. With this in hand, Herzog allowed Einstein to take the exam.

But he was doomed to fail, adding to the myth that he was a poor student. Albert had no complaints against the patient and understanding examiners. They certainly weren't the problem. Nor, of course, was his exceptional knowledge of math and physics. But it wasn't enough, as Albert soon realized. The exam covered several other subjects of which he had only a hazy knowledge, especially French, chemistry, and biology. He expected to fail the exam, and did.

However, Einstein's exam results in math and physics were so outstanding that Professor Heinrich Friedrich Weber offered to break the rules—again—for young Einstein and let him attend physics lectures for second-year students. The principal upped the ante with an even better offer: if Einstein went back to high school and graduated, he would be admitted to the Polytechnic without having to retake the entrance exam.

There was no chance that he would return to his high school in Germany. He'd probably have rather gone to work in a bank. Instead, after a family conference, it was decided that he would attend a school with a great reputation in Aarau, Switzerland, twenty miles west of Zurich. Its headmaster, Dr. August Tuchschmid, had been Professor Heinrich Friedrich Weber's assistant at Zurich Polytechnic.

One classmate there, Hans Byland, was among the small

but growing group of people who recognized Einstein not as a hopeless case but as an exceptionally bright and charismatic human being. Byland all but idolized Einstein. As Byland observed:

> His attitude to the world was that of a laughing philosopher and his witty mockery lashed any conceit or pose. He loathed any display of sentimentality, and kept a cool head even in a slightly hysterical atmosphere. Fate decreed that this precise thinker should pitch his tent with the romantically inclined Winteler family where he felt completely happy. Albert did not fit into any mold even as a young man and the school's atmosphere of skepticism suited him. With his gray felt hat pushed back of his mass of silky dark hair, Albert strode energetically up and down in a rapid, almost crazy tempo of a restless spirit. Nothing escaped his large, bright brown eyes, and whoever approached him was captivated by his superior personality. A sarcastic curl of his rather full mouth with the protruding lower lip did not encourage Philistines to tangle with him. Unconfined by conventional restrictions, he confronted the world as a laughing philosopher, and his witty sarcasm mercilessly punished all those who were vain or artificial. We were once on a field trip to the Jura mountains led by the geology professor, Fritz Muhlberg. When the professor asked in his usual gruff way, "Now, Einstein, how does the strata run from here? From below upwards, or vice versa?" Einstein replied, "It's pretty much the same to me whichever way they run, Professor." This showed Einstein's . . . love of truth and gave his whole personality a certain cachet which, in the long run, was bound to impress even his opponents.

But his teachers were still not impressed. He was told that he needed to catch up on chemistry, and to take private coaching in French and natural science. Yet, the liberal atmosphere of the school delighted him, and he was relieved when he learned that singing, physical training, and military training were not compulsory in his case. He opted out of all of them.

His scores in his Christmas school report for 1895 were 6 in algebra and chemistry (the highest possible); 5–6 in physics; 4s and 5s in the others, except for French, for which he got an abysmal 3, the lowest score of anyone.

Albert's father was not at all fazed by the mixed results, accustomed as he was to Albert's bringing home report cards with a mixture of good and bad grades.

Most of his schoolwork gradually improved, partly because of the warm, intellectual atmosphere provided by the Winteler family with whom he stayed as a paying guest. Jost Winteler, the father, taught Greek and Latin at Aarau high school. He and his wife, Pauline, had four sons and three daughters, and treated Albert like another son. Anna Winteler, the eldest daughter, confirmed that he was far from being the solitary and mediocre student reported by the mythmakers. She knew him as a pleasant member of the household who was fond of initiating scientific conversations and had a great sense of humor and a hearty laugh. In the evenings he usually did his homework or sat around the table discussing various subjects with the others. Anna also remembered that he was no spoilsport and rarely went out.

He managed to incorporate his scientific preoccupations into the conversation at Winteler family meals. He was teaching himself calculus, speculating on the possibility of splitting the atom, and wondering what it would be like to run behind a light wave, keeping pace with it as it made its immense journey through space. This, he recalled many years later, was his first mental experiment connected with the special theory of relativity.

But there was little time or inclination for mental experiments when he began his momentous exam to graduate from

Aarau high school at seven in the evening on September 18, 1896. It took him over two hours to complete the first task: to describe the plot of a Goethe play. Perhaps his heart wasn't in it. Fortunately the examiner, Adolf Frey, gave the mediocre performance a generous 5.

His worst mark was for his essay in French titled *My Plans for the Future*. In it he wrote of his hope to attend Zurich Polytechnic for four years, to study mathematics and theoretical physics, for which he felt most fitted. His ultimate aim was to be a philosophy teacher. French itself was obviously not his forte. There was hardly a line in the essay without a mistake. And the examiner gave it a 3–4—just above terrible. Einstein tackled the exams in geometry, algebra, physics, chemistry, and nature study enthusiastically but carelessly, making several spelling mistakes. But the work itself was exceptional and the examiners obviously overlooked the mistakes. For all those subjects he got an average 5½. This was the highest mark any of the nine examiners gave any of the students taking the exam, in which 6 was a perfect score.

Einstein, with an open book in a class conducted by Jost Winteler, the father of his first sweetheart, Marie. He broke her heart.

As promised, now that Einstein had graduated from high school, he was allowed to enter Zurich Polytechnic without retaking the entrance exam. But the old problems resurfaced. His reception there was a far cry from that at Aarau. The teachers soon resented his attitude, his skipping their lectures, and failing to give them the near worshipful respect that they expected as their right. Instead, he spoke to them and the cleaning women in the same easygoing, friendly manner—as equals. He was a natural democrat, and they didn't like it. Sometimes he gave the impression that he thought he knew more about their subject than they did, which was probably occasionally true.

His reputation outside the classroom was mixed. After only a few conversations with Einstein over coffee at the Metropole café, one classmate, Marcel Grossmann, told his parents: "I believe that Albert Einstein will become a very great man."

But Grossmann was the exception. His perceptive prediction was hardly shared by anyone else. And those exposed to Einstein's absentmindedness scoffed when they heard of his high ambition, especially friends with whom he spent one weekend and left, forgetting to take his suitcase. His host predicted that he would never amount to anything. His Zurich landladies, too, suffered from his forgetfulness. But they liked him so much that neither tried to evict him though he frequently woke them late at night to let him in because, once again, he'd forgotten or lost his house keys.

Marcel Grossmann predicted that Einstein would be a great man and helped him to get his first steady job at the Swiss Patent Office.

His autocratic college professors were much less forgiving. Math professor Hermann Minkowski called him a lazy dog. Physics professor Heinrich Weber had expected great things from Einstein but was irritated when he persistently called him "Herr Weber" instead of the more respectful "Herr Professor." Weber also disapproved of his self-selected study habits. Einstein, for his part, was disappointed with Weber for excluding from his physics course the dazzling ideas of James Clerk Maxwell, considered second only to Isaac Newton (another Einstein idol) in his contributions to science. Maxwell, who died in 1879, the year Einstein was born, had produced one of the first color photographs, demonstrated that light is an electromagnetic wave, was the author of a theory of Saturn's rings and a kinetic theory of gases, and did pioneer studies on electricity and magnetism. He had based some work on Faraday's ideas, but his equations were his own. And they became a mathematical key to unlocking the mysteries of electricity that led to radio, radar, and television.

Hermann Minkowski called Einstein "a lazy dog," and later made use of his work.

Einstein often cut Weber's physics classes to read, for example, Maxwell's astonishing theory that light and electricity were different aspects of the same phenomenon and that electromagnetic action moves through space in waves not unlike, and at the same velocity as, light waves. Although Weber put his foot down when it came to cutting his classes, he understood that students were disappointed that his lectures did not include recent scientific breakthroughs, and he encouraged them to read the relevant works for themselves. Einstein, of course, needed no such encouragement.

So much reading meant that he was neglecting lab experiments, and when he was criticized for this, he tried to make amends by quickly setting up an experiment while treating with contempt the printed instructions provided by Professor Jean Pernet, his Zurich Polytechnic physics instructor.

Seeing Einstein dump his official instructions on how to conduct an experiment into a wastebasket, Pernet complained to an assistant. He daringly replied that Einstein's methods were interesting and his solutions always right.

A peeved Pernet disagreed and confronted Einstein. "You're enthusiastic but hopeless at physics," he said. "For your own good you should switch to something else, medicine, maybe, literature, or law."

When Einstein ignored the advice and persisted in doing the experiment his way, it exploded, severely injuring his right hand.

While recovering from the accident, Einstein asked Professor Weber if he might try a more ambitious experiment guaranteed not to explode—to measure Earth's movement against the ether. Professor Weber wouldn't buy it, saying, "You're a clever fellow, Einstein, but you have one fault. You won't let anyone tell you a thing."

This response was one of several hints that Weber had become disillusioned with his protégé and was among those who thought of him as a lost cause. Einstein's colleague and eventual biographer Philipp Frank had a different take on him, knowing that he was mostly teaching himself from his own sources: "Day and night, he buried himself in books from which he learned the art of erecting a mathematical framework on which to build up the structure of physics."

Einstein attended a few math lectures by Carl Geiser and by Hermann Minkowski, who considered him a lazy dog. Einstein found some of their lectures fascinating, but had decided that math was too complicated, with too many distracting aspects, in contrast to physics, for which he was developing a growing passion. With physics he could understand the fundamentals and get to the heart of the matter. Wherever he was, on the veranda smoking his pipe, sipping coffee in a Viennese café, or at a picnic with friends in the nearby forest, he had a book open to study, between breaks in their conversation, the revolutionary theories of contemporary physicists.

Even when sailing on Lake Zurich with his landlady's schoolteacher daughter, Susanne Markwalder, as soon as the wind died, instead of chatting with the young woman, he would turn to the inevitable book in his lap and lose himself in the writings of Maxwell, Hertz, Kirchhoff, or Helmholtz.

In contrast to his lonely existence in Germany, where most classmates had shunned him as an oddity, in Switzerland Einstein made several close college friends—some of whom would be his friend for life. One, Michele Besso, a colleague who was studying electricity, got him to read Ernest Mach's *Science of Mechanics*, which ridiculed Newton's laws of absolute space and absolute motion and suggested that they should be reexamined, updated, and rewritten. Einstein relished Mach's direct, no-nonsense attitude, and Besso believed it was Mach's influence that led Einstein to think about "observables—and to become profoundly skeptical of concepts like absolute space and absolute time."

As a schoolchild, Mach had been regarded by his teachers as backward and difficult. Yet, he, too grew into an intellectual giant, rivaling even Helmholtz for versatility. Einstein admired the charming, unassuming Mach for his independence, incorruptibility, and not least for seeing the world, like himself, as if through the eyes of a curious child. He totally agreed with Mach's view that scientists must use the simplest means of arriving at their results and exclude everything not perceived by the senses.

Einstein's most admiring and enormously helpful friend, his classmate, Marcel Grossmann, rated him in the same league as Mach. What incredible clairvoyance, especially given that the professors thought he was a dud! He, in turn saw Grossman as an ideal and popular student, which he was. Einstein regarded himself objectively as an aloof daydreamer, discontented and unpopular, except among a coterie of adoring friends and the cleaning women.

His classmate, Jakob Ehrat, also a Jew, admired Einstein for his uncompromising honesty and complete lack of pettiness. Another friend, Friedrich Adler, son of the psychiatrist Viktor Adler, founder of the Austrian Social Democratic Party, sympathized with Einstein as a brilliant misfit, who was so disliked by his professors that they locked him out of the library. He believed that Einstein's problem was an inability to ingratiate himself with those in authority.

During the fall vacation Einstein learned the laws of thermoelectricity (electricity produced by heat) and devised a simple way to find out whether an electrically charged body has a heat different from one that's uncharged. After returning to college for the 1889 winter semester, he continued to defy authority, as Adler would have predicted, by deciding for himself which mandatory courses to attend.

Although Einstein believed that we will never know the true nature of things, he shared Spinoza's view that the fundamental secrets of nature were to some extent accessible to human probing. He devoted much of his time trying to unravel those secrets, rather than attending math lectures. This became a problem when the time approached for the math professor to give an exam on those same lectures— about which Einstein knew absolutely nothing.

Fortunately, Marcel Grossmann always came to his rescue. He willingly handed over to Einstein the meticulous notes he had taken, having attended every lecture. Einstein was a quick study: each time he at least got a passing grade.

Without Grossmann, it's unlikely that he would have graduated. Through Grossmann's help he was able both to stay in college and continue the studies that would lead to his monumental discoveries.

Einstein, along with Mileva Maric, who would become his first wife, took the final exam in the summer of 1900. Should they fail, one line of work would be closed to them: they would never be able to teach in college.

Three days before the exam, Heinrich Weber did something that Einstein found difficult to forgive. He made him completely rewrite an article because it had been written on nonregulation paper. His mean-spirited enforcement of a petty regulation so close to the start of the all-important exam took up considerable study time and foreshadowed worse to come. It indicated how much Einstein had antagonized a man who had once been among his most enthusiastic supporters.

Four men and one woman took the final exam: Albert Einstein, Marcel Grossmann, Louis Kollros, Jakob Ehrat, and Mileva Maric.

Kollross came out on top with a score of 60.

Grossmann was second with 57.5.

Ehrat, a close third, got 56.5.

Einstein was fourth with 54.

Maric trailed them all with 44. She was the only one to fail the exam.

Although she had the lowest score, she equaled Einstein's 10 in experimental physics, and got 9 to his 10 in theoretical physics, 4 to his 5 in astronomy, and 16 to his 18 for the diploma thesis.

Despite Weber's animosity, Einstein was confident that he would be one of the two assistants the physics professor was about to hire. Weber had implied as much. But to Einstein's dismay Weber chose mechanical engineers, rather than fellow physicists, for the positions.

*Mileva Maric at 21. She was Einstein's fellow
physics student and his first wife. He was
enchanted by her voice, and she idolized him.*

Einstein's anxiety increased when he learned that all his
male classmates had been hired as assistant professors and
that he alone had been rejected. During the next few weeks
he mailed scores of job applications to professors in different
colleges and countries, including one to Wilhelm Ostwald, a
physical chemist at Leipzig University, whose work Einstein
admired. He also enclosed his paper recently published in the
prestigious *Annalen de Physik*, inspired by Ostwald's own
research. Getting no answer, he sent a follow-up letter.
Apparently Ostwald didn't reply to that either. All those who
did reply to his applications had nothing for him.

As the weeks and months went by, his father saw that
Einstein had become deeply depressed and, without telling
him, decided to act. In a letter to Professor Wilhelm Ostwald
on April 13, 1901, he wrote

My son Albert Einstein is 22 years old, has studied for four
years at the Zurich Polytechnic and last summer brilliantly

passed his diploma examinations in mathematics and physics. Since then he has tried unsuccessfully to find a position as assistant, which would enable him to continue his education in theoretical and experimental physics. Everybody who is able to judge praises his talent, and I can assure you that he is exceedingly assiduous and industrious and is attached to science with a great love. My son is profoundly unhappy about his present joblessness, and every day the idea becomes firmly implanted in him that he is a failure in his career. . . . On top of that he is very depressed by the thought that he is a burden on us since we are not very well-to-do people. Because my son honors and reveres you the most among all the great physicists of our time, I permit myself to apply to you with the plea that you will read his treatise [Deductions from the Phenomena of Capillary, December 13, 1900] published in *Annalen der Physik* and hopefully, that you will send him a few lines of encouragement, so he might regain his joy in his life and work. If you could obtain for him an assistant's position, either now or in the fall, my gratitude would be boundless. I beg your forgiveness in my audacity in sending you this letter and want to add that my son has no idea of this extraordinary step of mine.

It is not known if Einstein ever knew that his father wrote this letter, nor if Ostwald replied to Einstein's father. He certainly didn't give Einstein a job.*

Trying to account for Einstein's jobless state, Mileva Maric wrote to a friend that her sweetheart had a very wicked tongue and was a Jew in the bargain. However, anti-Semitism was hardly the reason Einstein couldn't find a job. By most

---

*Wilhelm Ostwald was the first person—in 1910—to propose Einstein for a Nobel Prize, and Ostwald agreed that Einstein's independence prevented him from being hired by any of his professors.

Einstein's easygoing and unsuccessful father, Hermann, whom he loved.

accounts, there was less overt anti-Semitism in Switzerland than in Germany. Furthermore, Professor Minkowski was Jewish. So were several of Einstein's friends who had been hired by Zurich Polytechnic, Jakob Ehrat among them. It was his wicked tongue, his independent, rebellious spirit, and his inability to kowtow to authority that crippled his chances.

In hindsight Einstein admitted that he was not a model student. Once, in a talk on education, he asserted that teachers who used fear, force, and false authority in the classroom destroyed the students' self-confidence. Not in his case, however, or not for long. What helped him to defy such pressure, he said, was being as stubborn as a mule.

It has been reasonably established that, despite the generally accepted myths, Einstein was not dyslexic, was not a remarkably late talker, and overcame his learning problems such that at seven he got the top marks in his class.

It's true that he failed to get into Zurich Polytechnic on his first attempt. He was, however, two years younger than others taking the exam. And he turned that failure into triumph.

2 | Einstein: Woman Hater or Womanizer?

At times Einstein gave the impression that he despised women, once calling them the sex without brains. Unable to include Marie Curie in that category, he said that she had the soul of a herring and that her daughter, Irène, perpetually grumbled like a soldier throwing hand grenades. And they were women he considered to be his friends.

When he fell out of love with his first wife, Mileva, and in love with his cousin Elsa, his cruel, disdainful treatment of Mileva would have made a misogynist blanch. Einstein even admitted that he had never been able to love his controlling mother, Pauline.

Yet women played an important role in his life. He was rarely without a wife, a lover, or a woman friend—and at times he had more than one of those in his life. Most of them adored him.

Ronald Clark, the first major Einstein biographer, may have been misinformed by Otto Nathan and Helen Dukas, the trustees of Einstein's estate, when he wrote: "Einstein's pleasure in the company of women lasted all his life. But there was little more to it than that. Like most famous men he attracted the hangers-on, the adorers and the semi-charlatans."

In fact, while married to Elsa, and despite her protests, he found several women irresistible. But not if they interfered with his work.

He was attractive to women even before he was famous, but fame brought them on in a steady supply. He certainly enjoyed more romantic interludes in and out of marriage than, say, Isaac Newton, a bachelor of uncertain sexual orientation, or his friend and contemporary, Niels Bohr, the devoted husband. Yet some say that most of Einstein's liaisons were platonic. Readers may judge for themselves.

Einstein's strong-minded mother, Pauline, who bitterly opposed his first marriage. He said that he was never able to love her.

What is remarkable is that no woman who knew him in the flesh, so to speak, ever spilled the beans about the nature of their relationship. And both of his wives were either too discreet or too humiliated to go public. A housemaid, a doctor friend, and letters discovered after his death have given the lie to the official line that he was too obsessed with his hunt for the secrets of the universe to have love affairs.

He knew he had been a rotten husband, admitting during the last year of his life to having failed rather disgracefully to live in peace and harmony with either of his long-suffering wives. Or as noted biographer Brenda Maddox wrote: "It seems pretty clear that Einstein was a terrible husband, a guilt-stricken, absent father, a handsome, sociable man, a superb violinist and a good hiker—in other words, the typical Central European male of the early century. . . . His wife [Mileva] became a caricature of the nag, alternating depression with bursts of jealousy, and fighting with her mother-in-law, who was Jewish as she was not."

Most Einstein experts would agree with Maddox, although some might dispute his musical talent. One man who heard him said that Einstein played the violin like a lumberjack. Others said that his timing was off, because he couldn't count.

His first love was at seventeen. As a high school student in Aarau, Switzerland, living with the Winteler family, Einstein fell for one of their three daughters, the sensitive and affectionate Marie, who at eighteen had just begun her teaching career in the village school. She called Einstein "my darling curly-head" and "my great dear philosopher." With her father as chaperone, they walked through the local flower-filled countryside on bird-watching expeditions, and made music together, with Marie on the piano and Einstein on the violin.

Soon after arriving home in Italy for the spring break, Einstein wrote to her that he was already pining for his beloved sweetheart, his little angel with her dear little eyes and dainty little hands. He told her that she meant more to his soul than the whole world had before he met her.

It was a short-lived but idyllic romance while it lasted. It began to sour when he left to study at Zurich Polytechnic

Einstein, the 17-year-old Swiss high school graduate, when he was briefly in love with Marie Winteler.

twenty miles away and started to take more than an academic interest in a rarity in his physics class, a young woman named Mileva Maric, despite the fact that she was not as attractive as Marie, had one leg distinctly shorter than the other, and so walked with a limp. When friends asked what he saw in Mileva, he said her limp didn't bother him and that he was captivated by her charming, mellow voice.

He never denied that he had been desperately in love with Marie Winteler, and he made an effort to avoid meeting her after their breakup, because he feared not only that it would be too emotionally charged for them both but also that he might not be able to resist her, that she would drive him mad. But did he mean mad with desire or out of his mind? Another Einstein mystery.

Marie's big mistake had been to announce that when she next visited him in Zurich, she intended to rearrange his study so that everything would be the way she liked it, a move that, had she turned up, he would have strenuously resisted. But he still sent her loving letters along with his dirty clothes, which he expected her to wash and mail back to him, while he took an increased romantic interest in her rival.

Devastated when she realized that their romance was over, Marie had a physical and emotional breakdown. Einstein blamed himself for her distress, saying that he had been frivolous and unaware of her delicate nature. She later remembered Einstein as being "as pretty as a picture," and that they had "loved each other sincerely but it was an entirely ideal love."

Einstein had considered her parents as his "second parents" and remained on good terms with them and the rest of the family. His sister, Maja, married Paul, one of the Wintelers' sons, and his close friend Michele Besso married their eldest daughter, Anna.

Ten years after Einstein broke off with her, Marie Winteler married a watch factory foreman, Albert Muller, ten years her junior. They had two sons and were divorced in 1927. She then gave piano lessons and waited tables to support herself and her younger son, and wrote poetry.

Just before the outbreak of World War II, when Einstein was living in Princeton and a widower, she wrote to him from Zurich, reminding him that he had once promised not to forget her, that her mother had done him and his sister, Maja, many favors, and could he lend her a hundred francs? If she got a positive reply, she vowed that her future letters would be of a different kind. She said that she had had a good life, with God's guidance, and recalled how when they were together she had been a good, innocent child who understood neither herself nor life's realities. Marie sent a second letter to him three months later, asking him to send her money so that she and her son could immigrate to the United States. She hadn't eaten lunch for a year, she claimed, and her son, suited for intellectual pursuits, was working as a poorly paid manual laborer. There is no evidence that she received a reply to either letter. Probably his secretary Helen Dukas or his close friend Otto Nathan kept the letters from him in an effort to protect him. Marie died in a mental hospital in Meiringen, Switzerland, on September 24, 1957.

Young Einstein enchanted women of all ages, especially the pianists he accompanied on his violin. But he was so susceptible to the female sex that he preferred older women as his musical partners, especially grandmothers. Or so he said. "He had," according to a friend, "the kind of male beauty that, especially at the beginning of the century, caused such havoc."

Einstein's opinion of women generally was that they were the weaker sex, inferior to men, clinging to them for support and direction, and the few who were bright weren't attractive. Although later in life he admired Marie Curie for her intelligence and character, he ridiculed the rumor that she was having an affair with his married friend Paul Langevin, saying that despite her sparkling intelligence and passionate nature she wasn't appealing enough to be dangerous.

From the summer of 1897 Marie Winteler was out and Mileva Maric was in as the new woman in his life. Einstein had responded to his mother's furious opposition to his new relationship by making Mileva pregnant. (See chapter 4, "Whatever Happened to Einstein's Daughter?") Then, when she was again pregnant, with their son Hans Albert, he married her. A second son, Eduard, was born seven years later.

Early in his marriage to Mileva, Einstein had replied to a letter from Anna Meyer-Schmid, a former girlfriend of his youth, now married, by inviting her to meet him at his workplace. Mileva intercepted the letter and insisted that he call the whole thing off, which he did. But he was humiliated and offended by what he considered her overreaction, and their doomed marriage moved a little closer to its end.

By now Mileva had abandoned her own scientific ambitions, and Einstein began to neglect her for his work, his friends, and, finally, for his cousin and childhood friend, Elsa, after a brief flirtation with her younger sister, Paula. Elsa was a warm, outgoing, motherly woman with no significant intellectual or academic pretensions.

Einstein loved his father but considered his mother to be "perfidious in her hatred," and, as a mother-in-law to Mileva,

Wedding photo of Albert Einstein and Mileva Maric on January 6, 1903.

"a true devil." He now used his "very wicked tongue," as Mileva had once called it—apparently not unlike his mother's—with withering effect on Mileva. He used it both in his efforts to get a divorce and during the aftermath when they were concerned with the future well-being of their sons. Each feared that the other was trying to alienate the boys' affections.

To the man who had once waited for Mileva with open arms and a pounding heart, she had become, he told Elsa, "uncommonly ugly, blinded by jealousy, a typical Slav of strong negative feelings, a cold-blooded schemer, the sourest sourpuss" he'd ever known. And in a letter to Besso, he described her as "an odious smell under his nose, who gave their home the atmosphere of a cemetery."

She complained that she was neglected, lonely, and starved for love. All of which was true, as Einstein became more famous, feted, and focused on his work, not only as a compelling preoccupation but as an escape from private tribulations, while she was left at home to care for their two sons.

In the spring of 1914, when Mileva seemed prepared to stay married to him at any cost, he gave her these incredible conditions: At home, she must do his laundry, serve him three meals a day in his room (which meant he would never eat with her), keep his bedroom and study shipshape, but never let anyone, herself included, touch his desk. They were to have no personal relations except when in public, to keep up appearances. She must not ask him to stay at home, go out, or travel with her. She must promise never to reproach him for his lack of affection, answer him immediately when he spoke to her, and leave his bedroom and study immediately if he asked her to. And she must also promise not to denigrate him by word or action in the eyes of their sons.

Einstein's reputation for modesty took a hit when he concluded the dictatorial demands by describing himself as a great man. Perhaps with tongue in cheek? The "great man" was visibly upset when Mileva left their Berlin home for

Switzerland, taking her sons with her, because he did not know when he would see his sons again.

He soon regained his good spirits, feeling liberated, and for a while led a carefree bachelor's life, working at all hours on his research and neglecting his health. Food was scarce in Germany during World War I, and he often went without food, or forgot to eat, until he became so rundown with life-threatening ulcers that Elsa came to the rescue, nursed him back to health, and had reason to believe—he had already declared his love for her and was calling her daughters his stepdaughters—that the restored invalid would soon become her second husband. What she apparently didn't know is that she had a serious rival in her attractive, twenty-year-old daughter, Ilse.

Einstein's love life attained almost farcical dimensions when he couldn't decide which way to turn, to Elsa or Ilse. In a letter to a friend, George Nicolai, which Ilse asked him to destroy immediately after reading it——but he obviously didn't—she described her dilemma:

Yesterday, suddenly the question was raised about whether A. wished to marry Mama or me. Albert himself is refusing to take any decision, he is prepared to marry either Mama or me. I know that A. loves me very much, perhaps more than any man ever will, he also told me so himself yester-day. But I have never wished nor felt the least desire to be close to him physically. This is otherwise in his case—recently, at least. He himself even admitted to me once how difficult it is for him to keep himself in check. But still I do believe that my feelings for him do not suffice for conjugal life. In the end, I would feel like a slave girl, who has been sold. You must admit, this is a somewhat unnat-ural thing for our sensibilities nowadays. (Although A. asserts that these are social prejudices.) A. also said that if I did not wish to have a child of his it would be nicer for me not to be married to him. And I truly do not have this wish. I do not know whether it really would be fair—after all my mother's years of struggle—if I were to compete with her over the place she has won for herself, now she is finally at the goal. It will seem peculiar to you that I, a silly little thing of a twenty-year-old, would have to decide on such a serious matter. I can hardly believe it myself and it makes me also feel very unhappy. Help me!

Help was unnecessary. Einstein settled on Elsa.

When Mileva realized divorce was all but inevitable, she offered Einstein advice about how to treat Elsa. She suggested, according to biographer Ronald Clark, what "can be inferred from his reply—that if he ever wished to leave his second wife, no power on earth could stop him."

Einstein got his divorce from Mileva on February 14, 1919, and she was given custody of their sons. He had been sending her most of his income as well as supporting his mother after his father's death. Now he promised to send Mileva the money from the Nobel Prize he anticipated—a promise he kept. She told her sons that he "was still their father and wanted their love and respect. He was a strange man in many ways," she explained, "but he was good and kind." According to biographer Peter Michelmore, "Mileva knew that for all his bluff, Albert could be hurt in personal matters—and hurt deeply."

Pressured by her parents, Elsa in turn pressured Einstein to marry her, which he did, somewhat reluctantly, in a registry office on June 2, 1919, four months after divorcing Mileva. Soon afterward Einstein's widowed mother, Pauline, came to live with them.

When he went to Norway at the invitation of Oslo University's Students' Union, Einstein, oddly enough, took his stepdaughter Ilse with him rather than Elsa, because, he told his friend Max Born, "she is healthier and more practical." In fact, Ilse had been working as his secretary for some time.

Life with Elsa did not improve his jaundiced view of women, which he revealed when interviewed by a journalist acquaintance, Alexander Moszkowski. After answering a wide-ranging series of questions, Einstein said that although he believed women should get the same opportunities as men to pursue scientific careers, he doubted if they would reach the same heights as men, being handicapped by their physical makeup. What about Marie Curie? the interviewer asked. A sparkling exception, Einstein replied, and returning to the qualities of women at large, he said: "It is conceivable that nature may have created a sex without brains."

Moszkowski didn't take this grotesque remark seriously, but Einstein's friends and critics did. After reading an as yet unpublished account of the interview, Hedi, the talented playwright wife of physicist Max Born, wrote to him: "The gutter press will get hold of it and paint a very unpleasant picture of you. Your jokes will be smilingly thrown back at you. A completely new and far worse wave of persecution will be unleashed not only in Germany but *everywhere* until the whole thing will make you sick with disgust. . . . It would be the end of your peace, everywhere and for all time." She concluded that his interviewer was to blame for trivializing him and countered Einstein's chauvinistic remarks about women with a witty rejoinder, promising to keep her pleading letter a secret, for "I have heard how much you dislike it when women meddle in your affairs. Women are there to cook and nothing else, but it sometimes happens that they *boil over*." What also made her boil over was Einstein's assertion that women's production centers were not in their brains, and that no woman could have created differential calculus.

Max Born warned him that anti-Semites would triumph if the interview was published, and he accused Einstein of self-promotion (politically incorrect for scientists at that time). "I implore you to do as I say. If not, Farewell to Einstein. . . . In these matters you are a little child. We all love you, and you must obey judicious people (not your wife)." Born believed that Elsa favored publication, because she wanted to help the impoverished interviewer.

Einstein sent Moszkowski a registered letter saying that his splendid work must not appear in print. But it did, in 1921, in a book titled *Einstein the Searcher: His Work Explained from Dialogues with Einstein*. However, Einstein's reputation remained intact. Nevertheless, he was wary of interviewers ever after.

Touring the United States in 1921 to help Chaim Weizmann raise funds for Hebrew University, Einstein went with Weizmann's sophisticated wife, Vera, to give a talk at Boston's Mishkan Tefila Temple, while Elsa remained in their hotel. Afterward they took a cab into the countryside and went for a walk together. Mrs. Weizmann was amused by his flirtatious manner, especially as he confided that he was drawn to women who did physical work and not—perhaps because Mileva had traumatized him—to intellectual women.

Elsa certainly did physical work for Einstein, but she had no significant intellectual or scientific ambitions, saying that it was not necessary for her happiness to understand relativity— or any of Einstein's cerebral work, for that matter.

To his friend Janos Plesch, a wealthy and fashionable physician and not always the most reliable of witnesses, Einstein had a lot in common with a robotic infant and had found in Elsa the perfect wife, who treated him like an absent-minded, unworldly child: "As his mind knows no limits so his body follows no set rules: he sleeps until he is awakened, he stays awake until he is told to go to bed; he will go hungry until he is given something to eat; and then he eats until he is stopped. I can remember his consuming between five and ten pounds of strawberries at a sitting on more than one occasion. . . . As Einstein never seems to feel the ordinary impulses to eat, etc., he has to be looked after like a child. He was very lucky in his second wife."

Einstein had scorned women for not being self-reliant, but he was hardly in a position to talk. He never learned to drive a car and sometimes depended on the kindness of comparative strangers to get him around. He didn't know how to handle money. Elsa would dole him out a small amount of pocket money when he went out alone, knowing that if he had a lot, he was likely to hand it over to the first beggar he met. As for feeding himself, his cooking talent was more or less limited to heating soup and boiling eggs.

Konrad Wachsman, the architect who designed the Einsteins' summer house in Caputh, observed that Einstein acted on women the way "a magnet acts on iron filings," and among those he magnetized were Betty Neumann, Toni Mendel, Estella Katzenellenbogen, and Margarete Lenbach.

When Ilse Einstein married Rudolf Kayser in 1923, the recently divorced Betty Neumann became Einstein's secretary, and almost immediately he fell passionately in love with her. His biographer Abraham Pais first mentioned Neumann's

Playing the violin, accompanied by his second wife, Elsa, on the piano, at the Imperial Hotel, Tokyo, 1922.

existence, without identifying her, in his 1982 book *Subtle Is the Lord*, when he wrote that Einstein's letters in the early 1920s indicated "that for several years he had a strong attachment to a younger woman." He ended their attachment in January of 1924, when he wrote to her, using the vocabulary of a poet, "that he had to seek in the stars what was denied to him on earth." Pais believed that Newmann was probably the great love of Einstein's life and that he had been attracted to her much more deeply and passionately than had been the case in his early romantic days with Mileva.

In their 1993 biography of Einstein, Roger Highfield and Paul Carter identified this woman probably as Betty Neumann, the niece of a close friend of Einstein's, Dr. Hans Muhsam. Indirect evidence comes through letters from Elsa showing that Einstein fell out badly with Muhsam, who had previously visited him almost daily and had been one of his closest confidants.

Albrecht Folsing positively identified her in the German edition of his *Albert Einstein* published that same year, revealing that Einstein had fallen "violently" in love with Betty Neumann. By one account, in order to save her marriage, Elsa had allowed them to meet twice a week so Albert wouldn't "sneak around." Folsing viewed Einstein's "in the stars" renunciation letter cynically, comparing it to a similar letter he had sent to Marie Winteler when breaking up with her, as well as a comment he made at a meeting in 1918 to celebrate Max Planck's Nobel Prize. Then Einstein had said that the chance for a scientist to escape into a world of universal laws is a way "to find the peace and security he cannot find in the narrow whirlpool of personal experience." And he had certainly been losing himself in his work: in December 1923, a month before he broke up with Betty Neumann, he presented a paper to the Prussian Academy, "Possibilities of Solving the Quantum Problem." Still, Folsing does not doubt that Einstein was in love with Neumann.

Soon after he heard that she had been divorced for a second time, Einstein wrote to her to say that she must be breathing a sigh of relief because she had jumped into the second marriage "like a frog into water." He urged her to trust the advice of her uncle Hans and aunt Minna, who loved her. He said he was happy when he heard she was in his neighborhood and told her he missed her lovely smile, but he realized that he mustn't run after her. His only hope was that he would run into her accidentally. Fate was cruel, he wrote, even to someone like him whom many envied, and advised her to laugh at him, "the old donkey," and to find someone ten years younger who loved her as much as he did. He ended the letter with, "I embrace and kiss you."

In the fall of 1925, he was seen with Toni Mendel, a very wealthy and attractive widow about his age—in her mid-forties. She had a large riverside villa and a chauffeur-driven car. Einstein spent days and nights at her home, apparently with Elsa's reluctant assent. He even moored his boat near her villa.

The Einsteins' live-in housemaid, Herta Waldow, reported that "the Herr Professor was fond of looking at pretty women. He had a weakness for pretty women."

Toni Mendel tried to placate Elsa with gifts of chocolates when she was about to take Einstein out for the evening. It didn't always work, judging from one occasion when the housemaid heard a loud argument between Elsa and Einstein, just as Toni Mendel was about to arrive to take him to the theater, and Elsa refused to give him pocket money for incidental expenses. Researchers are unlikely to come across any of the letters between Einstein and Toni Mendel because, again according to the housemaid, at his request they were all destroyed. This was not true of his letters to Betty Neumann.

Another wealthy and attractive woman, Estella Katzenellenbogen, the owner of a chain of florist shops, also frequently turned up with her chauffeur-driven limousine to

*In 1927, Einstein walks in a Berlin street with his
stepdaughter, Margot, and her husband, Dimitri
Marianoff, an early Einstein biographer.*

take Einstein out for a night on the town or a drive in the
country while Elsa waited at home.

When Einstein was in Caputh, a third woman, a pretty
young blond, Margarete Lenbach, visited Einstein every
week, often bringing home-baked pastries, which he particularly enjoyed. The housemaid noted that "when Lenbach
came [Elsa] would go to Berlin to do some shopping errands
or other business. She always went off into the city early in
the morning and came back late in the evening. She left the
field clear, so to speak."

The maid once overheard a lively discussion between Elsa
and her daughters when Einstein was out of the house, which
left Elsa in tears. They told her she must put up with the relationship between him and the young Austrian woman
(Margarete Lenbach) or seek a separation. Elsa decided to put

up with it, although she still flew into jealous rages and would refuse to speak to him for several days. Einstein's stepson-in-law Marianoff and his wife, Elsa's daughter Margot, once witnessed an argument between the two when Einstein, Marianoff recalled, "was aroused and shouting like a lion, and let me tell you, when Albert's voice was raised in anger, one heard it in every corner of the house."

Einstein would invariably call Elsa's behavior childish and go to stay with sympathetic men friends, such as Janos Plesch or Max Planck. The situation was exacerbated when the Einsteins went out together in public, when he would be surrounded by gushing women eager for his attention and often more.

Marianoff recalled that a brief conversation with Elsa as chaperone was not enough for many of these women: "Some managed with stratagems of war generals to meet him; others did so openly. One woman on being presented to him, turned to Elsa, frankly, and said: 'May I speak to Professor Einstein for a few minutes?'—a quite open declaration that she wished to see him alone. Elsa tactfully replied, 'Of course you may.' . . . Both of them understood the motive behind the request. Her tact and delicate instinct were masterly in handling an instance such as this, but some were unavoidable, and many times were accompanied by an atmosphere of distaste.

"Many women tried to come into his life. Some wrote letters recalling to him a brief transitory meeting; others brought flowers and left them with a note and their addresses. We, of the household, understood these to be only the worthless [results] of fame. They reminded me of the stragglers of a romantic period, who followed the leader of a brilliant and dazzling army."

But it was not only fame. He was an outstandingly attractive man in his heyday. A contemporary, Charles Nordmann, raved about him when they met in Paris in 1922, when

Einstein was forty-three: "The strongest impression is of stunning youthfulness, very romantic and at certain moments irresistibly reminiscent of the young Beethoven who, already marked by life, had once been handsomer. And then suddenly laughter erupts and one is faced with a student."

Marianoff believed that Einstein made no attempt to hide his affairs from Elsa. In fact, he seemed compelled to tell her about them. For instance, while the two men were aboard Einstein's boat at Caputh, they discussed "a delicate matter" apparently involving one of Einstein's women friends, and which, Marianoff wrote, "had been bothering Elsa to the extent of involving her health. . . . I said to him: 'Don't ever discuss this again with Elsa, Albert. It troubles her.' Einstein nodded his head energetically in acquiescence. On our return to the house, we had no sooner stepped across the threshold of the door when, exactly like a small boy who had something on his mind that must be told to mother, he blurted out . . . the whole story that only a minute before he had decided to be silent about. I was amazed and speechless." Later, when Marianoff told Einstein that he had wounded Elsa by his confession, he said, after a while, "We do things, but we do not know why we do them."

Although he remained married to Elsa on his terms, he described marriage as "an unsuccessful attempt to make something lasting out of an incident," an institution invented by an "unimaginative pig," and "slavery in a cultural garment." Nevertheless, to outside observers, he seemed as carefree and independent as any bachelor. When asked what he thought of Jews marrying non-Jews, which, of course, had been the case with him and Mileva, he replied with a laugh, "It's dangerous, but then all marriages are dangerous."

Einstein's most curious involvement with a woman began with a series of threats from a Russian refugee, Eugenia Dickson, who first announced in a letter that when she arrived from Paris she was going to confront him because of a flippant comment he had made about the Bolsheviks. Then, in a later letter, she accused him of being a czarist agent-provocateur posing as a physicist, and finally, suggested that she had a more private matter to discuss with him. Elsa was dreading her imminent arrival, and Einstein observed that the woman must be hysterical or mentally unbalanced.

One morning Elsa opened her apartment door to face Eugenia Dickson brandishing a large hatpin. After a brief struggle Elsa disarmed her and called the police, who took her away. Einstein had been somewhere out of sight and sound of the whole thing, and after Elsa told him about it, he set off for the police station to press charges against Eugenia. When he went to her cell, she admitted that she'd made a mistake: his nose was much shorter than the czarist agent she had thought he was. Instead, she claimed that he was a former lover who had deserted her after fathering a child, who had since died. She pleaded with him to save her from being locked up in a mental institution, and after agreeing to do what he could, he left to buy her a few things she had requested.

A Russian journalist later told the Einsteins that Eugenia had recently tried to assassinate the Russian ambassador to France with an unloaded revolver, and that a judge had assumed she was a harmless lunatic and set her free. She had also accused a former czarist minister of fathering her child and then of killing it for political reasons.

Not long after that incident, Einstein was in Davos, Switzerland, to give a lecture, when he seriously strained his heart while carrying his suitcase through the snow. After he returned to Berlin, Dr. Plesch diagnosed the problem as an enlarged heart and put him on a salt-free diet. He was a bedridden invalid for most of the next four months, but, of course, he never stopped working. As he had lost both Ilse and Betty Neumann as his secretaries, Elsa undertook the task of finding a replacement. Obviously she did not have another Betty Neumann in mind.

As honorary president of the Jewish Orphanage Organization, Elsa mentioned her search for a secretary to the organization's executive secretary, Rosa Dukas, and she recommended her sister, Helen, who had just lost her job with a publisher. Helen, a tall, slim, and intelligent young woman, was terrified at the thought of working for the great Albert Einstein, especially as she had left school at fifteen and knew nothing about physics. "You have gone mad," Helen told her sister, when she advised Helen to apply for the job. "I can never do something like that." But she was persuaded to see Elsa, who greeted her with tea and cookies and told her at least to give it a try. She was then introduced to her prospective employer, who was in bed reading. He smiled, held out his hand, and said, "Here lies an old corpse." She was immediately at ease and accepted the job. She worked for Einstein as his secretary for the next twenty-seven years.

Einstein introduced her to a friend as "my faithful helper. Without her nobody would know that I am still alive, because she writes all my letters for me." She was also among the

With his secretary Helen Dukas and his dog Chico.

fiercest protectors of his mythic reputation, telling Einstein biographer Ronald Clark that a book by Peter Michelmore—confirmed as accurate by Hans Albert and exposing some aspects of her employer's private affairs—was complete nonsense. She also gave it a one-word review: "Dung!" In her role as Einstein's secretary, Helen saw a side of him that few were privy to: she played table tennis with him on board the ship taking them to the United States in 1930; watched an old woman break through a police cordon, press Einstein's hands, and say, "Now I can die in peace"; and saw Einstein in tears as the deaf and blind Helen Keller moved her fingers over his skull and face.

The long-suffering Elsa was surprisingly frank in revealing what she thought of her husband after ten years of marriage: "One must not dissect him, otherwise one discovers 'deficits,'" she wrote to friends. "Any genius has those, or does one really think he is without fault in every respect? By no means, nature doesn't work that way. Where it is over-brimmingly prodigal, there it takes something away in another respect, and that means deficit features. He's got to be viewed as a 'whole,' he cannot be placed in one category or another. Otherwise one experiences disappointments. But the Lord has put into him so much that's beautiful, and I find him wonderful, even though life at his side is enervating and difficult, not only in this but in every respect."

When the Einsteins and Helen Dukas left Germany for good in the spring of 1933, heading for their permanent home in Princeton, New Jersey, they stayed en route at the Belgian seaside village of Le Coq sur Mer. Einstein's attractive friend Margarete Lenbach—the blond who had once brought him home-baked cookies—also happened to be there. It was their last meeting. She died in Vienna in 1938.

In mid-May of 1934, after Albert and Elsa had settled in Princeton, Elsa, in great distress, returned to Europe to be with her daughter Ilse, who was dying of cancer and being cared for by her sister, Margot. Ilse believed that her illness was psychosomatic, according to her brother-in-law, Marianoff, and had refused conventional treatment in favor of psychoanalysis. Einstein chose not to go with Elsa despite her entreaties. Ilse died in August and her ashes were interred in the Netherlands, where her husband, Rudolf Kayser, was living.

Elsa herself had only two more years to live. She returned from Europe heartbroken, and it was not until months later that she resumed a social life.

Late that winter they were dining with American friends, the Eisenharts. After Einstein had repeatedly remarked how well Elsa looked after him, Mrs. Eisenhart asked, "Your wife seems to do absolutely everything for you. Just exactly what do you do for her?" With a twinkle in his eye, he replied, "I give her my understanding."

He gave his wealthy biochemist friend Leon Watters a different story. Sounding like a guttural George Bernard Shaw or Noel Coward, Einstein remarked—obviously with Elsa in mind—that women were like delicate scientific instruments and difficult to handle. Watters didn't need any marital advice, judging by Elsa's appraisal of him: "I think you are the most considerate, loving husband. How gladly would I send Albert to you to be taught."

In December 1935, after the now-divorced Margot had joined the Einsteins, Elsa was hospitalized with heart and kidney problems. She was allowed to return home, trembling uncontrollably, with instructions to remain completely immobile. Still she managed to write with pride to her friend Antonina Vallentin that Einstein "believes his latest work to be the best he has ever done." She described him as being a changed man, deeply upset by her illness and wandering about like a lost soul. "I never thought he loved me so much," she wrote. "And that comforts me."

His colleague, the physicist Leopold Infeld, confirmed that

although Einstein "remained serene and worked constantly, he gave his wife the greatest care and sympathy."

Elsa died on December 20, 1936, during a heavy snowstorm, and according to Einstein's colleague and biographer Banesh Hoffmann, her death left Einstein ashen and shaken. When Hoffmann suggested that Einstein stop working for a while, he replied that now more than ever he needed to work.

Helen Dukas took on additional work as housekeeper, with the help of an Irish woman four days a week. And though Dukas was accepted as part of Einstein's extended family and lived in the same house, she "never lost one iota of respect" for him, "nor a certain shyness."

Elsa had hardly been buried when Einstein received several marriage proposals in the mail. One was from a Jewish widow on Long Island, who wrote that her life would be so much brighter if she could persuade him to marry her. She promised to do everything in her power to make him happy and prosperous and to shield him from trouble and anxiety.

The other, from a widow in Vienna, hoped she was not acting in bad taste in writing to him, but a secret voice that rarely deceived her had told her to devote her life to him. She assured him that vanity was not why she wanted to be his wife, but rather, her deep desire to give him the most beautiful evening of his life. Although she was not a worldly woman with painted fingernails, many had told her that she was beautiful, interesting, and engaging. But, most important of all, she had a pure soul, a sunny disposition, and a feeling heart.

Another widow wanted to marry him because his nose and ears reminded her of her late husband. A widow in Maine, giving her name and address, wrote: "I love you although I know I am not worthy of you."

Dukas filed these letters in a folder Einstein referred to as *die komische Mappe*, which means strange, funny, odd, or pathetic.

"I didn't think he would ever marry again," said Alice

Kahler, the widow of Einstein's friend, historian Erich Kahler. "He was still infatuated with the ladies, but his work was more important than women. Once I bought him a Swiss sweater made of cotton with a blue collar (he was apparently allergic to wool), and he called back, happy as a child, and said: 'Never in my life have I owned anything so beautiful as this sweater. Even my blind cleaning woman admired me when she saw how marvelous I looked in it.'"

Dorothy Commins, the wife of editor Saxe Commins, was Einstein's guest for tea soon after Kahler gave him the cotton sweater. She glanced around his upstairs study at the sagging bookcases and frayed book covers, a photo of Gandhi, and prints of Faraday and Maxwell in picture frames, and a small radio-phonograph. She also glimpsed his sparsely furnished bedroom. After Dukas brought up a tea tray and left them alone, they discussed the movement of the planets, Debussy's music, which he found enigmatic, the flower bulbs soon expected to appear through the snow in the garden outside,

Einstein and his affectionate friend Alice Kahler in Princeton. She thought he should have been a lifelong bachelor.

and especially his new sweater. "Perhaps you could tell me," he asked Commins, because he knew she sewed, "how does one put this together?" And he rolled up a sleeve, saying, "I can't find a stitch. There isn't a machine or hand stitch in this garment." She said, "I guess it's a magic garment," and he laughed.

"He first came to our house for a poetry reading," said Alice Kahler. "And Charles Bell described him as 'the idol of my science-loving youth, with parchment face and a corona of hair, a resigned and sphinxlike wisdom, between Saint Bernard and angel, as if he had lived the whole rise from brute to human, and was himself the record of that trial and achievement.' This was a bit exaggerated. He was the most charming friend you can imagine if he was in the mood. And he was the best audience for his own jokes. And he had such a hearty laugh. For his birthday in 1954, a year before he died, Adele Gödel, the wife of Kurt, the mathematician, sent a wreath with two large ribbons. And Einstein said with his usual hearty laugh, 'This looks as if it were for my funeral!'

"He loved to smoke, but his secretary, Helen Dukas, and his stepdaughter, Margot, were adamant about doctor's orders. When he got tobacco, he sent it with a little note to my husband, and when Einstein came to our home he asked Erich, 'Give me a little of the stuff so I can at least smell it.' His desire was so great, that he would pick up cigarette butts from the street—which was nearly tragic.

"Einstein enjoyed puzzles," Kahler recalled, "and he had amazing ones sent to him from all over the world. During my visit to Saranac Lake [where Einstein was on vacation], I bought him the famous Chinese Cross, one of the most complicated puzzles to be put together, he solved it in three minutes. I wouldn't have been able to do it in a thousand days. When I said so, he offered to show me. And he took it apart and put it together in no time. When his son, Hans Albert, came to visit, Einstein was happy to learn his talent with puzzles had been passed on to him. And he remarked, 'He did it beautifully, exactly as I do.'

"Although he initiated the theory E equals MC^2, he never thought it would be put into practice. After the atom bombs Einstein told my husband, 'I could burn my hands off that I wrote that letter to Roosevelt.'

"Once a man stopped Einstein on the street and asked, 'Will the world be totally destroyed in the next war by nuclear bombs?' And Einstein answered: 'It would be too bad if that happened, because we could no longer listen to Mozart.'"

Asked for her response to the accounts that Einstein was a woman hater, she laughed and said, "Listen dear, he loved women. He was very attractive to them and he was infatuated by the ladies. But he once said to me, 'The whole thing lasts just ten minutes and then it's all over.' [She laughed.] Yes, Einstein loved women and he wrote on my most precious photo of him and myself that he regretted I wouldn't sleep with him. I have it in my sleeping room. I would have been interested in him if I wouldn't have had a husband.

"He was such a young, innocent man when he first married [Mileva]. You cannot imagine how naïve he was."

During the summer of 1937, when Einstein was relaxing at his summer cottage at Peconic, Long Island, a yacht-full of visitors arrived offshore, among them playwright Clifford Odets and his Oscar-winning actress wife, Luise Rainer. Einstein helped them disembark to a rowboat. "When it came to Luise and Odets' turn," reports Odets's biographer, Margaret Brennan-Gibson, "it was evident to Odets, from the fact that he playfully pulled her hair, that Einstein found Luise attractive. She, flustered, capsized the boat and almost drowned the great scientist." Several photographs were taken of the group, and when they were printed, Odets, in a jealous fury, scissored out Einstein's face in one of them. Other photos escaped his fury, including two showing Rainer and Einstein together.

Of all the women in his life, Einstein's sister, Maja, was probably closest to him. She left her home in Italy in 1939 because of Mussolini's anti-Semitic racial laws, to live with her brother in Princeton. Her husband, Paul Winteler, settled in Switzerland, and she hoped to join him there after World War II.

Einstein at Peconic, Long Island, with Oscar-winning movie actress Luise Rainer in 1937. Their flirtatious behavior made her husband, playwright Clifford Odets, furiously jealous.

Those who saw Albert and Maja together were surprised not only by how well they got on, but at their remarkably similar looks, voices, gestures, and facial expressions. "Her manner of speaking and the sound of her voice, as well as the childlike and yet skeptical formulations of every statement, are unusually similar to her brother's mode of expression," wrote his friend and biographer, Philipp Frank. "It is amazing to listen to her; it arouses a sense of uneasiness to find a replica of even the minor traits of genius."

In 1946 Maja suffered a stroke, and that and progressive arteriosclerosis kept her bedridden, nursed by her stepniece, Margot.

To their friend Alice Kahler the relationship between Einstein and his sister "was very, very beautiful. They loved each other very much. Even before she became ill, he read aloud to her every night. On vacation at Saranac Lake, New York, I sat in on these evening sessions. Once he was reading Herodotus, and there was a not-so-interesting passage, and I said, 'Maybe we should skip that part.' Einstein was absolutely appalled. 'How can you say such a thing! We might miss

Einstein's sister, close friend, and confidante, Maja Einstein Winteler, when she was living with him in Princeton.

something important! We are not going to go through this without reading every line.'"

When Maja fell ill, Einstein continued reading to her every evening, pleased to see that, although she spoke with difficulty, she remained her highly intelligent self until she died of pneumonia on June 25, 1951. A month after her cremation, he told a friend that he missed her more than could be imagined.

At Princeton, Einstein was never without female company. Margot and Dukas lived with him, and his friend Johanna Fantova was a frequent guest. She would go sailing with him on nearby Lake Carnegie and speak with him on the phone almost daily. She also cut his hair and read Goethe to him.

A mutual friend, Gillett Griffin, said that Einstein approved of Fantova's recording their conversations, because he knew she was poor and that the recordings might give her financial security. He also gave her a manuscript on unified field theory and wrote poems to her. Their conversations, Griffin said, painted "a vivid picture of a truly brilliant, humble and warm man."

They had first met in Berlin in 1929, when Einstein accepted the suggestion of Fantova's husband, Professor Otto Fanta, that she should arrange and classify Einstein's "unique collection of books" that were "rather chaotically scattered throughout the house."

When she emigrated from Czechoslovakia to the United States ten years later, Einstein advised her to become a librarian, and in the fall of 1944, after having studied at the University of North Carolina, she was hired by the Firestone

Library at Princeton University. In 1952 she became its first curator of maps.

According to Griffin, his poems to her were intended to cheer her up, because Einstein thought she had a dark outlook on life.

One, written when he hadn't seen her for some time, reads

> Exhausted from a silence long,
> This is to show you clear how strong
> The thoughts of you will always sit
> Up in my brain's little attic.

During one conversation, discussing the onslaught of mail he received, he told Fantova that he was "a magnet for all the crazy people in the world," yet he admitted he found it "interesting to try to reconstruct their thinking processes. He expresses sympathy for them and says he often tried to help them. . . . In another letter received in 1953, a woman

With his friend Johanna Fantova, about to sail on Lake Carnegie, Princeton.

laments that she is poor and unable to leave an inheritance to her children. She asks Einstein for seven autographs, presumably for their prospective monetary value. The woman is probably stretching the truth, he tells Fantova. [Or she may have been an unscrupulous autograph hunter.] But, perhaps admiring her hubris, he will fulfill her request."

One woman Einstein admired and respected without reservation was Marian Anderson, the African American contralto. He first heard her sing at a Carnegie Hall concert in the 1930s and went backstage to congratulate her. Later, when told she was to sing in Princeton but had been refused a room at the local hotel, he invited her to stay at his home, and she accepted. Anderson was his houseguest again in January 1955. Then, bedridden with anemia, he got up and went downstairs to greet her. After her singing engagement, as she was about to leave his house, he again made a slow and painful descent to say goodbye. "This, though I did not know it," she wrote, "was really goodbye."

When Einstein last spoke with Fantova on April 12, 1955, six days before he died, he was worried that he had not yet completed a speech in support of Israel, and he enthusiastically discussed the importance of the new Salk polio vaccine, pleased to know that Salk was a Jew.

One afternoon Einstein collapsed in his bathroom, and Dukas phoned for help. Three doctors came to his aid. Although seriously ill, he refused to be taken to the hospital. They gave him morphine to ease his pain, and Dukas rested in his study next to his bedroom, feeding him ice cubes and mineral water throughout the night to prevent dehydration. Only when told that he was being a burden to Dukas did he agree to go to the hospital, where he died several days later.

His heartbroken friend Alice Kahler wrote to a relative: "The world has lost its best man, and we have lost our best friend."

Einstein left twenty thousand dollars, his house at 112

Mercer Street, and his furniture and household goods to Margot. To Helen Dukas he left twenty thousand dollars and all his clothing and personal effects, except for his violin, which went to his surviving grandson, Bernhard Caesar Einstein. He left fifteen thousand dollars to his son Eduard, and ten thousand dollars to Hans Albert.

In a conversation with Dr. Thomas Bucky, who knew Einstein well and was the son of one of Einstein's best friends, Dr. Gustav Bucky, I reminded him of his comment that Einstein went for ugly women.

> Bucky: Yes. [He laughed.] Well, not ugly. Women I found unattractive.
>
> Dr. B.: Did Dukas adore Einstein?
>
> Bucky: Everybody did.
>
> Dr. B.: Did Dukas have any men in her life?
>
> Bucky: No.
>
> Dr. B.: How many women was he romantically involved with after Elsa's death?
>
> Bucky: Two or three who were there for a few weeks or a few months, period.
>
> Dr. B.: What was his attitude? Flirtatious?
>
> Bucky: No. He was not flirtatious with anyone. He was charming to everyone.
>
> Dr. B.: Can you speculate where writers got the idea that he despised women?
>
> Bucky: Out of their minds, to make money.
>
> Dr. B.: Did he treat Elsa more like a housekeeper than a wife?
>
> Bucky: No, he treated her kindly.
>
> Dr. B.: Why do some get the idea that he was cold to her?
>
> Bucky: He was aloof, not cold, to everyone. When Elsa died, Einstein said to my parents, "It's like losing a leg. I can manage without her, and hobble along. But I've lost my leg."
>
> Dr. B.: Roger Highfield and Paul Carter, the writers of *The*

Private Lives of Albert Einstein, say that maybe he died of syphilis, an idea the London *Sunday Times* reviewer found "intriguing."

Bucky: He died of a ruptured aortic aneurysm, which was due to atherosclerosis of the aorta, caused by old age.

Dr. B.: Where would they get syphilis from?

Bucky: Their minds. Wait a minute. Aortic aneurysm of the chest aorta is usually syphilitic. Aorta of the abdominal aorta is never or rarely syphilitic. So somebody advising the writers made a mistake about the aorta. "Aha! Aortic aneurysm! That's syphilis!" That's how they made the mistake. It's pure nonsense. This is confusion from someone who doesn't know what he's talking about. Above the diaphragm is the chest: that's where the third stage of syphilis, the syphilitic aortic aneurysms, occur. But below—no. You can look it up in any medical book.

Albert Einstein should never have married, especially as he considered it an unnatural, even barbaric institution. But, of course, he couldn't help falling in love.

The ideal existence for Einstein, as his Princeton friend Alice Kahler once suggested, would have been never to have married, but instead, to have had a housekeeper and secretary like Helen Dukas, and a series of undemanding mistresses who never interfered with his work. Come to think of it, that's exactly what he had for the last, comparatively serene, twenty years of his life. No wonder he always seemed to be smiling.

3 | Was Einstein a Terrible Father? And What Kind of Mother Was Mileva?

E instein's first son, Hans Albert, became an internationally recognized engineer, settled in California, and had two happy marriages (his first wife died). His second son, Eduard, spent much of his adult life as a schizophrenic in a Swiss mental institution and blamed his father for ruining his life. Was Einstein responsible? And what role did their mother, Mileva, play in her sons' upbringing? Let's follow the facts.

Hans Albert was born on December 5, 1903, about a year after the presumed death of the Einsteins' daughter, Lieserl. Einstein was then working as an examiner in the Bern Patent Office and, in his spare time, was obsessed with discovering the secrets of the universe while fulfilling his duties as husband and father.

Visitors to his home soon learned Einstein's original theory of simultaneity: how to study and, at the same time, help Mileva care for their son. Arriving at the Einsteins' apartment, and gasping their way through an atmosphere of damp clothes drying near a woodstove and of Albert's stale tobacco smoke, visitors might find him absorbed in a book while rocking the baby's cradle with his feet, or using one hand to read and the other to rock. He even continued his research while taking his son for a regular airing in a baby carriage through the city streets, stopping from time to time to take a notebook from the carriage and record his latest ideas.

Both parents were proud of their intelligent and "impertinent" young son, and Einstein often spent his free time at

The Albert Einsteins with their first son, Hans Albert, in 1904. Hans had fond memories of childhood.

home playing with him, as Mileva happily informed her best friend, Helene Savic.

During a 1966 BBC program on Einstein, Hans Albert recalled his delight as a four-year-old as he watched his father transform a box of matches into a little working cable car, one of the best toys he ever had. "Out of just a little string and matches and so on, he could make the most beautiful things. We played together with my toys, but he was also trying to educate me in a wider sense than the education one gets in school. He often told me that one of the most important things in life was music. Whenever he felt that he had come into a difficult situation in his work, he took refuge in music and that usually resolved all his difficulties. He was also very fond of nature, surroundings that were gentle and colorful and gave one lightness of spirit. He needed this kind of relaxation from his intense work. In those early days we were a happy family, and often took small trips together and sometimes longer ones. And there was nothing to indicate the separation to come."

When his father had made a tremendous discovery, Hans Albert said, he reacted "just like a child. He was so happy he would walk around telling everybody, and all of a sudden would start whistling. But he was always extremely careful about his findings. That means he would never accept anything until he had tested it all the way through in all directions."

Einstein could be a disciplinarian as well as a playmate, spanking Hans Albert when he justified his "little rascal" reputation.

Hans Albert was six when his brother, Eduard, was born on July 28, 1910. Eduard was a delicate baby and was thought to have inherited his mother's tendency to tuberculosis. As he grew older, he suffered from severe headaches and intensely painful earaches that made him scream in agony. Einstein also sensed there was something mentally wrong with Eduard, confiding to a doctor friend, Heinrich Zangger, that he was depressed by his son's condition, feared he would not live to manhood, and wondered if it would be better for him to die young than to live on seriously handicapped. However, a friend of Mileva's described Eduard at age five as being lively and cheerful.

In the summer of 1913 Eduard was too sick to go with his family on a hiking vacation in the Alps, during which they reached as far south as Lake Como. They were accompanied by Marie Curie and her daughters, Irène and Eve, whom Einstein had befriended on a visit to Paris. Eduard had been left at home in the affectionate care of family friends.

The following year the Einsteins' marriage was on the rocks, and Mileva left their Berlin home, taking her two sons with her to live in Switzerland. Einstein wept as he watched his sons leave, but he was consoled by his cousin Elsa Löwenthall, who was at least part of the reason his marriage

Mileva with her sons, Eduard (left) and Hans Albert,
in Zurich, 1914, after she and Einstein had separated.
He remained alone in Berlin.

was on the rocks. By December, Mileva and her sons had settled into a Zurich apartment, furnished thanks to Einstein. He
had stripped his own bachelor apartment of all but the essen-
tials and shipped the rest to Mileva. He began to send her the
agreed financial support every three months without fail, but
she still had to give math and piano lessons to survive.

He missed his sons and wrote them affectionate, encour-
aging letters, pleased that five-year-old Eduard was reading
Shakespeare and ten-year-old Hans Albert was interested in
geometry.

Einstein spent his summer vacation in 1915—during
World War I—on a remote Baltic Island, together with his
cousin Elsa, the divorced mother of two teenage daughters,
Ilse and Margot. But he wasn't neglecting his sons. Soon
after, he went to Zurich to see the boys and to take Hans
Albert hiking and boating in southern Germany.

Late that winter he completed his astonishing work on the
general theory of relativity, showing that gravity was a prop-
erty of space-time and not a force acting from one body on
another. Afterward, too exhausted to contemplate an imme-
diate trip to Switzerland, he promised twelve-year-old Hans

Albert he would be there at Easter because he was eager to discuss his latest work with him. He also urged his son to continue his piano practice so they could make music together, and described a recent strange experience: at a small party, a complete stranger had read his palm and, to his surprise, told him things about himself that were correct. (This naïve response to the extrasensory did not last.)

Einstein had been urging Mileva to let Hans Albert visit him in Berlin more often, assuring her that it would not spoil her good relationship with her son, who was at an age when he could benefit from his father's mentoring in intellectual and aesthetic matters. But Mileva feared that the influence of Elsa and her family on her impressionable son would turn Hans Albert against her, and she resisted the pressure to cooperate.

Einstein himself was under increasing pressure from Elsa to marry her. She complained that people were gossiping about her lifestyle and felt that the rumors were handicapping the marriage prospects of her elder daughter, Ilse. Einstein capitulated reluctantly and wrote to Mileva in February 1916 asking for a divorce. As if to show he was not forgetting his fatherly duties, in the same letter he advised her to give their boys calcium chloride to strengthen their teeth and bones.

The prospect of divorce and of her uncertain future was a terrible shock to Mileva, who was probably still in love with Einstein. She had a physical and mental breakdown and was unable to care for her sons. Einstein proposed taking Hans Albert out of school to homeschool him, but Mileva wouldn't hear of it. He then considered paying for Hans Albert to live with his aunt Maja (Einstein's sister), but that didn't work out, either. Instead, both boys went to live for a while with Mileva's friend Helene Savic, who had moved from Serbia to Lausanne.

Hans Albert's adopted daughter, Evelyn Einstein, believed that his parents' separation, and their eventual divorce when he was twelve, made him bitter and instilled in him a lifelong horror of divorce. "He was expected to act as the man of the house," she explained. "If there was a faucet to fix, a light-bulb to replace, a banister to mend, then he would have to do it. I think he resented it."

When Mileva had partly recovered from her breakdown and her sons were back with her, Einstein tried to reconcile Hans Albert to his new role and praised him for behaving like a man. Einstein recounted his own early struggles, assuring him that it was through suffering and injustice that one developed a strong character and suggesting that he ask his mother about their difficult early days together.

It was a pleasant surprise to Einstein when his next Easter visit to Zurich went smoothly, at least at first, and with Mileva's approval, his sons eagerly joined him for a hiking trip. They were so polite and pleasant that he sent her a note praising her for their splendid upbringing and for not alien-ating them from him. But on his return, when he proposed taking Hans Albert for another trip, she had a change of heart, adamantly and angrily refusing to let him go. Einstein left in a fury, confiding to his friend Michele Besso that he had decided never to see her again, because the mere sight or sound of her would destroy him. He told another friend, Heinrich Zangger, that his decision had been a matter of life or death.

Because visiting his sons often involved angry encounters with Mileva, Einstein wrote to Savic that he had come to the painful decision that it would be better for his sons not to see him anymore and that he would be satisfied if they grew up to be useful and respected men. But he continued to write to Hans Albert, assuring him that he loved him above all else, was always thinking of him, and would always take care of him.

Hans Albert felt confident of his father's affection when they were together, recalling that "while it was there, it was very strong. He needed to be loved himself. But almost the instant you felt the contact, he would push you away. He would not let himself go. He would turn off emotion like a tap."

As for Eduard, Einstein still worried about his sudden changes of mood, his overemotional responses, and his frequent bouts of illness. But he resolved to accept the inevitable, his attitude being that one should look after the sick and take comfort in the healthy.

He never gave up his conviction that Mileva was to blame for Eduard's condition. She, in turn, believed that he was a bad influence on both of their sons, and she tried to discourage his visits.

Einstein changed his mind about not seeing his sons anymore when he heard that Eduard was seriously ill in July 1917, and he took them to the Alpine village of Arosa, where he left Eduard in the Pedolin Sanitarium for Children to convalesce from a lung infection and a persistent high fever. Then he and Hans Albert hiked in the woods and along the shore of Lake Obersee.

In the fall of 1917, while still living in Berlin, Einstein, who had lost fifty-six pounds in two months, collapsed in agonizing pain. What he suspected as cancer was eventually diagnosed as a stomach ulcer. He then moved into the apartment occupied by his cousin Elsa and her two daughters, where she kept him on a strict diet by preparing all his meals. He asked not to be disturbed—his work still came first—so she often left his meals on a tray outside his door. He stayed in bed much of the time—but never stopped working—and finally produced the quadruple formula for gravitational radiation.

In November, seven-year-old Eduard was still at the sanitarium in the Swiss Alps, and Einstein complained to Besso that he couldn't afford it and didn't believe in X-ray treatment—the new medical magic Eduard was getting.

When in the following spring Einstein was no longer

bedridden and Eduard had been transferred to another sanitarium, his father went to see how he was doing. During their conversation, Eduard asked him why he was so famous, and with his customary modesty, he replied, "When a blind beetle crawls over the surface of a globe, he doesn't notice that the track he has covered is curved. I was lucky enough to have spotted it."

In 1919 he assured Mileva that he would give her his anticipated Nobel Prize to help her support herself and their sons. This seems to have been what she needed in order to give him a divorce, and he, somewhat reluctantly, decided to marry Elsa. The ceremony took place in a Berlin registry office in June 1919.

Knowing that neither Mileva nor Hans Albert liked Elsa, Einstein assured Mileva that if she would let Hans Albert visit him in Berlin, Elsa would remain out of sight the entire time and he and his son could have meals together without her—absurd but necessary conditions, he added, only because females were involved.

Though Einstein and his new secretary, Helen Dukas, treated Eduard affectionately when he visited them in Berlin or at the summer home in Caputh—and presumably Elsa became invisible as promised—the occasional, brief meetings with his father weren't enough for the hypersensitive Eduard, who still felt neglected.

Einstein sailed to the United States with Chaim Weizmann in 1921 to help raise funds to

Brothers Eduard and Hans Albert Einstein in Zurich, Switzerland, 1919. Both had conflicted feelings about their father.

establish Hebrew University. On his return, he took his sons for a vacation in the village of Wastrow on the Baltic coast, where he had booked rooms above a local bakery. In a letter to a close friend, Paul Ehrenfest, he described seventeen-year-old Hans Albert as intelligent, sensible, self-reliant, self-assured, yet modest, and eleven-year-old Eduard, who seemed to have largely recovered from his physical and mental problems, as a lively young rogue, unfortunately somewhat more interested in money matters than in philosophy. They had grown, he wrote, into splendid youngsters and were of "one heart and one soul."

In the fall, he took Hans Albert to Florence and Bologna and, while in Italy, gave a lecture in shaky Italian. Eduard was too young to go with them, but on his return Einstein gave him a silver watch he had owned since his student days to make up for it, which Eduard proudly showed to friends and visitors.

Einstein's relationship with Mileva must have improved, because on arriving back in Switzerland he stayed with her for a while. This became a habit on his subsequent visits to Zurich. Elsa didn't like it, not because she suspected him of carrying on with his ex-wife, but because of the inevitable gossip. Einstein simply ignored what others thought, quoting a saying that a pig sees dirt where the pure see purity.

In 1922 he was awarded the Nobel Prize "for his services to Theoretical Physics and especially for his discovery of the laws of the photoelectric effect," and, as promised, he sent the $32,500 prize money to Mileva. She bought three houses with the money, using one as her home—a lovely five-story building on a tree-lined street. She lived there for the rest of her life, in a third-floor apartment overlooking Zurich Polytechnic, where she and Einstein had been students together, and in love.

Einstein continued to make the tiring ten-hour train journey from Berlin to Zurich to see his sons and to advise Mileva on how to handle them. He accepted Hans Albert's plan to be an engineer, though at first he had opposed it. He was impressed with Eduard's passion for learning and his phenomenally good memory (especially compared with his own weak one), but the youngster's strange intensity worried him.

In 1924, when Hans Albert had been studying civil engineering at Zurich Polytechnic for two years, Einstein wrote to tell Besso how proud he was of his sound, strong, unpretentious, dependable son, who came out on top in a recent exam and was also a first-rate sailor. Sailing was one of Einstein's great pleasures. He admitted to Hans Albert that he was now reconciled to his becoming an engineer rather than a physicist because he realized that science was as difficult as searching for a four-leaf clover. Hans Albert later explained to his adopted daughter, Evelyn, why he had rejected physics as a career: when someone else has picked up all the good shells from the beach, you go to another beach.

The following year, Mileva warned Einstein that their twenty-two-year-old son was determined to marry Frida Knecht, who lived in their apartment building. Frida was nine years older than Hans Albert and almost Mileva's double in looks and personality. Einstein had her family investigated and discovered that at one time Frida's mother had received psychiatric treatment. Horrified, he assumed she suffered from a mental illness that she might have passed on to Frida, who in turn would pass it on to her prospective children—his grandchildren. He voiced his complete opposition to Hans Albert's proposed marriage, saying that it would be a crime if they married. He was only slightly reassured when informed that Frida's mother's "psychiatric treatment" had been for thyroid trouble. Then he found another excuse to object: Frida, he was told, was four foot eleven. To him, this made her a dwarf, and he expressed his concern that dwarfism would be passed on to her offspring.

Just as Einstein's mother had failed to change his mind

about his marrying the woman of his choice, so he failed with his son. But he persisted in the attempt, telling Mileva that Hans Albert had fallen into the clutches of an elderly, sly virgin and that they had to rescue him. The problem was, he said, their son's sexual inhibitions, suggesting that a cure for that was for Mileva to introduce him to an attractive and experienced forty-year-old woman of Einstein's acquaintance, who would get Frida out of his system. Whether this tactic was employed remains a mystery. If it was, it didn't work.

Sixteen-year-old Eduard was proving less of a problem at that time. Although his teachers called him dreamy and unfocused and Einstein still felt there was something wrong with him, his frequent letters to his father were anything but unfocused, containing strong opinions on composers and philosophers. Einstein treasured them, though Eduard didn't know it until years later. He was very popular among his school friends, who thought him quick-witted and intelligent. Various classmates described him as a master of the German language and a brilliant writer. Others called him vivacious, imaginative, and often humorous, with a heartwarming laugh. A lecture he gave to his class on the history of astronomy had been enthusiastically applauded. He wrote clever, satirical poems and played the piano with a fervor matching his father's way with the violin. (Although Einstein had called Eduard's playing intense.) Apparently, writes Abraham Pais, none of them were aware of "the dark sides of his psyche which already then were certainly present."

But Einstein was now more preoccupied with Hans Albert's future. Even on the eve of Hans Albert's marriage to Frida Knecht in Dortmund, he urged the would-be bridegroom to call it off, warning him that separation was inevitable and divorce painful. He was, of course, speaking from personal experience. Finally, Einstein said he would be reconciled to his son's plans only if he promised to make it a childless marriage. But Hans Albert refused. Shortly before the ceremony, Einstein predicted that they would inevitably break up eventually, and if they had children it would only complicate matters. He was certainly speaking from the heart. So was Hans Albert, who married Frida on May 7, 1927.

Sigmund Freud and his wife were in Berlin that year, and Einstein and Elsa paid them a visit. Freud called their two-hour conversation very pleasant, although, he quipped, "Einstein understands as much about psychology as I do about physics." Apparently Einstein did not seek Freud's advice about Eduard, whose piano playing—too intense and mechanical as it still seemed to him—he thought was an indication of a serious emotional problem. Strangely, Freud himself also had a mentally troubled son, Oliver, whom he was powerless to help. He was a gifted engineer, said Freud, with "a flawless character, until the neurosis came over him and stripped off all the bloom."

Later in the year, after attending a meeting of the League of Nations Commission in Geneva, Einstein went to Zurich and took Hans Albert on a hiking trip.

In August 1929, again in Zurich, now for the Sixteenth Zionist Congress, he called on Mileva and Eduard, raising a laugh from his son by answering his question "Why are you at a Jewish rather than a scientific conference?" by saying, "Because I am a Jewish saint." Mileva's response was not recorded.

It is possible to get a glimpse into Eduard's state of mind at that time. A classmate published some of his original sayings, which seem like a cri de coeur, as well as a forecast of his future:

"He who stretches out his arms too longingly, will always be repulsed."

"Nothing is worse for man than to meet someone beside whom his existence and all his efforts are worthless."

"The worst destiny is to have no destiny, and also to be the destiny of no one."

That year he graduated second in his class, with the highest possible marks in German and Latin. Hoping to become a Freudian psychoanalyst, Eduard began to study medicine at Zurich University, where he fell in love with an older, probably married, medical student. But she rejected him, which sent him into a deep depression. When Einstein heard of it, he advised Eduard to get a job (though not to quit his studies), and told him that even Schopenhauer had been depressed through being unemployed—adding that life was like a bicycle and that it was possible to keep one's balance only by moving forward. He also pointed out that Eduard's firsthand experience of depression would help him to become an exceptional psychiatrist, able to empathize with his patients. He also suggested that Eduard should find a playmate rather than a conniving female. Another time Einstein warned his son that although being involved with the opposite sex was a necessary delight, preoccupation with women would harm

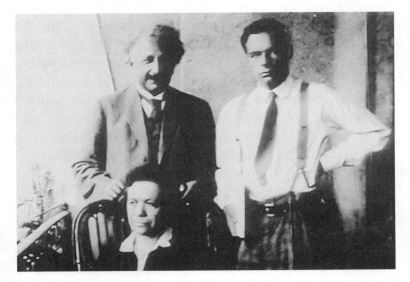

Einstein on one of his last visits to his mentally disturbed son Eduard, and his former wife, Mileva, in the early 1930s.

him. But the distraught twenty-year-old scorned his father's advice. He had lost what he saw as the love of his life.

To Mileva's dismay, Eduard covered the walls of his bedroom with pornographic pictures, read obscene plays, and had such violent fits of rage that she feared for her safety. When he showed no sign of recovering, she had him taken to the nearby Burgholzli psychiatric hospital, where, his brother said, he got electroshock treatment. It must have been only partly successful, because when he was released and resumed his studies at the university, a male nurse was always at his side. During those days a fellow student saw him in the street talking to himself.

Eduard would be institutionalized on and off for the rest of his life, said his sister-in-law (Hans Albert's second wife), Elizabeth Roboz Einstein, a professor of neurochemistry: "In early childhood he was a sort of genius who remembered everything he read. He played the piano beautifully [not according to his father] and spoke English, which he learned in high school, perfectly. He had an unfortunate love affair which caused his breakdown. My husband thought his brother was ruined by electroshock treatment." Mileva devoted the rest of her life to Eduard, "with Einstein paying for his treatment."

Einstein became a grandfather in 1930 when Hans Albert and his wife, Frida, had a son, Bernhard, healthy in body and mind. Einstein had predicted that a tragic fate awaited the child. In fact he became Bernhard's doting grandfather and left him his beloved violin in his will.

Shortly before his visit to Zurich Polytechnic in 1930 to accept an honorary doctoral degree, Einstein received several hate letters from Eduard, claiming that he had put a shadow over his life by deserting him. Einstein went to Mileva's apartment, hoping to reason with his son. Both parents sensed that he had mixed feelings for his father—loving, even adoring him, yet unable to overcome bitter feelings of rejection and personal inadequacy. On Einstein's arrival, Eduard accused him of ruining his life.

Because Eduard had been studying psychiatry and was extremely intelligent, he was in the awful position of knowing that he had serious mental problems for which there was no cure. And nothing he had tried had relieved him of his crippling bouts of depression.

Though Einstein distrusted psychiatry and ridiculed psychoanalysis, he sent Eduard to the best psychoanalysts in Switzerland and, when that failed, to Vienna for treatment—though not to Freud. Eduard disagreed with his father's views: Freud was his hero, and he even had a photo of Freud in his bedroom.

"It's clear that Einstein had a strange feeling about people with mental disorders and weaknesses," says Einstein expert Robert Schulmann. "That's sort of [typical of] his German generation. . . . But it's a complicated situation, where the boys are living with their mother and Einstein feels they are being poisoned against him. So that's one context we have to view him in. He also blamed Mileva's family heritage for Eduard's schizophrenia, arguing that she suffered from the same problems that her sister, Zorka, had. She was completely wacko. Although Mileva wasn't as bad as that, Einstein said that their behavior came from the same source. He says that explicitly. And he said very clearly he thought that Eduard's insanity came from his wife's family. Whether he's right is a different question. It is a fact that he went on record in letters to his friends to say the problem with his life was in some degree Mileva's mental inheritance. And he accused her of having alienated his boys from him after they separated."

Eduard arrived unexpectedly in Italy in the summer of 1932 to visit his aunt Maja for eight days, devoting much of the time to playing Mozart on the baby grand piano, which Einstein had given his sister.

Back home that fall Eduard had a serious mental breakdown and was again admitted to Burgholzli hospital, where he was diagnosed as a schizophrenic and subjected to insulin treatment, which sent him into a coma for two hours at a time, and probably electroshock treatment as well. Such treatment at the time was primitive and terrifying. Patients undergoing it had their bones broken or dislocated, and suffered convulsions and heart attacks. Einstein, it appears, paid for a private suite for Eduard, which included a well-furnished sitting room and a dining room.

One visitor was Maja Schucan, a teenage girl who had met Eduard when Mileva tutored her in algebra at home. She and Eduard had been to dances and parties together, and after finding him unique and fascinating, the young woman fell in love with him. Her love was unrequited, but they remained friends, and Eduard wrote to her from the hospital in December 1932, thanking her for poems she had sent him and apologizing for making her unhappy. "Sometimes my head aches for hours on end like an inflamed tooth," he confided. "You must not think that I am going through this ordeal in order to get wisdom. It would be utterly silly to want to become wise by force. I wish to be nothing more than passably content. Sometimes I feel like the man in Hermann Hesse's beautiful story 'Iris,' who plunged himself too deeply into his own past and never found the way back."

Einstein made a somewhat inept attempt to reconcile Eduard to living a restricted, monklike existence in the sanitarium, by mentioning a friend in California who had entered a similar mental hospital because of depression and praised it as the best place to be for a man doing brain work.

He invited Eduard to visit him in Berlin, because he felt that he was the only one who could help him with his problems. Unfortunately, in the same letter he used a supercilious tone in trying to discourage Eduard's enthusiasm for psychoanalysis. After noting that people who began psychoanalysis never seemed to be able to extricate themselves from it, he suggested that Eduard should teach him about it when they next met, adding that he would try to keep a straight face.

It's puzzling why Einstein, who named curiosity as his driving force, should have scorned psychoanalysis with only a superficial knowledge of it. As Freud had remarked after their only meeting, Einstein knew very little about the subject.

Einstein's flippancy belied his true feelings. His sorrow over his twenty-two-year-old son was eating him up, according to Elsa Einstein, who wrote to her friend Antonina Vallentin that he "has always tried to stay above personal worries, but this has hit him hard. [He] always aspired to be completely invulnerable to everything that touched humanity. Actually, he is much more vulnerable than any other man I know. But this situation is atrocious for him. . . . I no longer see the crazy sense of humor in him."

Einstein's good friend Michele Besso, who at times acted as Eduard's surrogate father, tried to help. Besso himself had feared a nervous breakdown over conflicts with his own mother, but the support of his son, Vero, he wrote, had helped him to avoid it. Now he could once more "rejoice in the sky, leaves on the trees, sun and rain, the sweet look in Anna's [his granddaughter's] eyes, and the happy greeting of my little dog." Which brought him to Eduard's problems and his advice to Einstein. "Eduard has an extraordinary father, a brave mother," he wrote. "He is talented and attractive, although reserved as some young people are. What are you doing . . . about the pain of one who is searching for answers? Help if you can. Take Eduard with you on one of your long journeys. Once you've spent six months with him, you'll end up understanding him and putting up with a lot of things you wouldn't accept from others. Then you'll know what unites you and, unless I'm terribly mistaken, it will lead the way to a flowering of your son's personality."

In his reply over a month later, Einstein informed Besso that he had invited Eduard to join him on his projected trip to Princeton the following year, 1933, adding that he had seen dementia praecox (now called schizophrenia) coming slowly but irresistibly since Eduard's youth. "Outside circumstances and influences only play a small part in such cases, compared to internal secretions, about which nobody can do anything." (What Einstein apparently didn't know is that Eduard's visit would have been impossible. American laws banned foreign mental patients from entering the county.)

With the advent of Hitler and his Nazi thugs, Einstein decided to leave Germany permanently and to settle in America. As a visiting research student at Christ Church, Oxford, he had arranged to lecture there and to meet the noted British physicist Frederick Lindemann before he left for the States. But hearing that Eduard was seriously ill, he postponed the visit in order to see his son, saying that although Lindemann was not a father, he knew he would understand.

This was the last time that father and son saw each other. A photograph of the occasion shows Eduard, at twenty-three, and his father, sitting side by side. Einstein is holding his violin and staring ahead, while Eduard is engrossed in what appears to be a music score.

A month later Einstein assured Mileva that she could always count on his financial and moral support, and he suggested that the best cure for what ailed Eduard would be an occupation of some kind, such as writing a thesis to persuade his skeptical father that Freudian psychoanalysis worked.

In October 1933, Einstein, Elsa, his secretary, Helen Dukas, and his associate Walther Mayer left Europe for the United States. Einstein would never return to Europe.

The following year, Eduard shocked his aunt Maja when he paid a second visit to her in Italy, escorted by his ever-present male nurse. She had become very fond of Eduard, but she hardly recognized the fat, bloated young man who stood on the doorstep. "There also hangs about him a leaden melancholy," she wrote to a friend, "which makes it even sadder when his old sunny smile very seldom flashes like lightning across his face and disappears. Thank God his nurse is here. I could not have managed him on my own. He suffers terribly, poor, poor boy!"

Michele Besso called on Mileva in 1937 and was surprised to find Eduard so overweight and to learn that he hadn't left the apartment in a year. But he was impressed by the brilliant way Eduard discussed psychology—even though he spoke extremely slowly. Afterward, Eduard entertained him by playing Handel and Bach on the piano with what Besso considered great feeling.

Soon after Elsa died in Princeton on December 20, 1936, Einstein invited Hans Albert to be his guest for a three-month visit. He accepted, hoping that his wife and two sons, Bernhard and Klaus, would join him later, with permanent residence in mind. Hans Albert now got on well with his father, the man he had often infuriated as a teenager; he found him a much more benign presence—cordial, friendly, and generous. And when he got an offer to work as a researcher in South Carolina, he sent for his family. Less than a year later, six-year-old Klaus died of diphtheria, and Einstein wrote to Hans Albert and Frida that they were suffering the deepest sorrow that loving parents experience. Unknown to most people at the time, Einstein had also experienced the loss of a child.

Einstein had kept his promise to take care of Mileva and Eduard financially, sending her regular payments and responding whenever she had unexpected expenses. Even so, she had been forced to sell two of the three houses she had bought with the Nobel Prize money. In 1939, when she was again desperate for money, Einstein took over ownership of her apartment building to prevent her from losing it, but he allowed her to retain power of attorney.

During the war, well aware of the Germans' barbaric

treatment of the Jews, Einstein described them as "a badly messed-up people" and hoped that at war's end they would have largely killed one another. A conflicted pacifist, he approved of Hans Albert's joining the war effort by working with the Army Corps of Engineers. Einstein himself worked on various government military projects—but not on the atomic bomb. Although he had persuaded the government to launch the Manhattan Project by warning President Franklin Roosevelt that the Nazis were thought to be working on an atomic weapon, he was not given security clearance to help in the effort.

After the war, in 1947, he learned that while Mileva was on her way to visit Eduard in the mental hospital, she had slipped on the ice and broken her leg. Strangers found her lying unconscious in the street and called for an ambulance. When she had only partly recovered, she resumed her habit of having Eduard stay at home with her until he became dangerously violent. Then she would phone for a van to take him back to the hospital.

At thirty-seven Eduard had become a heavyset, morose chain smoker who heard voices and sometimes behaved irrationally. But at other times, visitors to his windowless basement hospital room encountered a friendly, charming man with an endearing smile and an insatiable hunger for information about the outside world. One of these visitors was Carl Seelig, a wealthy writer living in Zurich, who had a compassionate concern for the mentally ill. Einstein had been impressed by Seelig's intelligence and integrity and was cooperating with him on a biography of Einstein. No biographer had yet mentioned that for some twenty years Eduard had been a mental patient, and Seelig was the first and only one to go directly to the source—Eduard himself—visits that Einstein arranged. He had told Seelig that Eduard's illness, though relatively mild, was serious enough to prevent him from having a career.

Seelig took Eduard to dinner in a Zurich restaurant, where Eduard recalled a visit to his father's Berlin apartment as a boy, when he had eagerly peered at the moon through a telescope and even more eagerly into the apartments across the street. He chain-smoked throughout the evening when not eating, and finished up with a large ice cream sundae. Eduard enjoyed Seelig's company, and after they had been to the theater and for walks together, he came to regard Seelig as his best friend. Seelig was so moved by Eduard's brooding and tormented expression and charmed by his unexpectedly serene smile and truthfulness that he offered to be his guardian. Einstein declined the offer, saying that Eduard already had one.

On May 23, 1948, Eduard was staying with his mother when he began to ransack the apartment looking for something he'd lost. The next day, neighbors found Mileva unconscious on her bed, having suffered a stroke. When she

Einstein's schizophrenic son, Eduard (right), dining with Einstein biographer Carl Selig.

recovered consciousness in a clinic near her home, temporarily paralyzed on her left side, she was frantic about Eduard's welfare. To her astonishment, he had recovered from his previous day's outburst and was holding her hand, trying to comfort and reassure her.

Mileva wanted Hans Albert, now a professor at Berkeley and living with his family in California, to promise to take care of his brother in the future. Einstein offered to pay his fare to Switzerland, but he also warned Hans Albert that seeing his seventy-three-year-old mother in her condition would be an overwhelming shock. He took his father's advice and stayed home.

Mileva died in a hospital soon after, on August 4, 1948. She was alone. Her bedside bell had been taken from her because, it was said, she used it too often without justification.

Einstein had arranged for Dr. Heinrich Meili to represent Eduard as his guardian. Meili placed Eduard in a home for disturbed young men in Uitikon, a Swiss village, run by Pastor Hans Freimuller, who had some knowledge of psychoanalysis. Eduard spent a pleasant year there, although during the first few weeks he did nothing but play the piano so ferociously that the pastor feared he'd break it. When he got over his initial shyness, he entertained the pastor's three young sons with poems and jokes, gave piano recitals for a church youth group, and was accepted as a member of the village community. The pastor's wife even got him a job with a local firm writing addresses on envelopes.

A year later, for some unknown reason, Eduard left the warmhearted home—"a very painful parting" as the pastor recalled—to live with a lawyer's widow in the Zurich suburb of Hongg, when he wasn't in the Burgholzli mental hospital.

Seelig kept Einstein informed about Eduard's life, but in 1952 Helen Dukas intercepted such a disturbing report from him about Eduard's condition that she conferred with Margot Einstein and they agreed to withhold it from

Einstein. After that, Dukas and Einstein's close friend Otto Nathan decided to keep him from any bad news about his son, to keep him from getting upset.

Seelig must have wondered why his letters to Einstein weren't being answered. Presumably, Eduard also told him he wasn't getting any replies from his father. When Seelig finally got a letter through, Einstein replied that he believed that if he entered into his son's consciousness in any form it would only arouse various painful feelings in him. He added that he could not thank Seelig enough for the sympathetic care he had given Eduard, who represented "the virtually only human problem that remains unsolved. The rest have been solved, not by me but by the hand of death."

In Seelig's biography of Einstein, published shortly after Einstein's death in 1955, he neither challenged Einstein's diagnosis of Eduard nor reproached him for what could be regarded as abandoning his son. If Eduard complained to him of his father's behavior, Seelig kept it to himself.

Eduard, in fact, never mentioned any of his family on the several occasions his brother's teenage adpted daughter, Evelyn, spoke with him. While attending a Swiss boarding school in the early 1950s, she visited Eduard from time to time and, like Seelig, found him endearing and fascinating. "We got along great guns," she said. "The two of us clicked very well. He was filled with questions. He was like a sponge. I mean, they kept him isolated from the real world. He asked questions I found strange, like, 'Did they decide to go into electricity on automobiles?'" He then explained to her that the only encyclopedias the staff let him see were from the 1920s.

She was shocked by his living conditions in the Burgholzli psychiatric hospital: "A dark and dreary dump. He had a private hovel, a tenement room with no windows that opened onto a corridor. But he was an institutionalized human being when I met him. He could never have functioned outside. I believe they felt that the less informed he was, the easier it would be to control him. He told me about working in the garden, which he didn't like. But he said it was so important because when the Russians took over Switzerland they were going to kill everyone who didn't work. When I asked, 'Who told you that?' he said the hospital staff did, to get him to work in the garden."

Evelyn knew that Eduard was reputed to hear imaginary voices and to behave violently, but neither happened when she was with him. And after taking him on trips outside the hospital, she was impressed by his conversation, felt he was brilliant, and even wondered if he was truly schizophrenic.

Eduard's nephew (Hans Albert's son) Bernhard, a student at Zurich Polytechnic, went to see Einstein in Princeton in the summer of 1954. "The boy is nicer than his father and grandfather," Einstein told his friend Johanna Fantova afterward. "He will never accomplish any great deeds but he will do all right in life." A few months later Hans Albert, a successful and internationally respected professor of hydraulics at the University of California at Berkeley, arrived and mostly discussed engineering problems with his father.

On his return to California, Hans Albert agreed to let Jerry Tallmer of the *New York Post* interview him about his father, but only after getting Einstein's written consent. He told Tallmer that since leaving school he had never been without a job, and he reluctantly posed by a bust of Einstein in Berkeley university's library, asking the reporter, "Do you know what it is to have your father a statue?" Although he was naturally proud of Einstein's accomplishments, he said he was uncomfortable when strangers stared at him as if he were a freak. And when he saw colleagues whispering together, he suspected them of comparing him intellectually—and unfavorably—with his father. "It tended," he said, "to make a son completely lose his own identity."

Hans Albert's wife, Frida, had to remind Einstein that his son's fiftieth birthday was coming up on December 5, 1954.

Einstein then sent Hans Albert an affectionate greeting, recalling the occasion on which the young Hans Albert had "borrowed" his father's razor to whittle wood—leaving the wood like straw. He expressed his joy in having a son who had inherited much of his own personality, the same restless intellectual curiosity, and the ability to rise above mere existence through years of unselfish dedication to a larger goal. It was a heroic way to

Einstein's son Hans Albert, a professor of engineering in California.

live, he thought, as well as the only way to be unimpeded by circumstances and the unwelcome demands of others. He encouraged his son to maintain his good humor, to be good to people, and to ignore their unkind words and deeds. But it was hard for Hans Albert to forget his father's words and deeds: he was especially disappointed that Einstein needed to be prompted to remember his birthday.

The next year, when told that his father was dying in the local hospital, Hans Albert flew to Princeton and spent a Sunday afternoon at his bedside chatting about scientific topics. He also tried to persuade him to seek a possibly lifesaving operation in a Manhattan hospital, but Einstein refused to leave Princeton. He died in the early hours of the following morning, April 18, 1955.

Three years later, in October 1958, Hans Albert's wife, Frida, died after collapsing at a concert they were attending in Berkeley. The following year he married Elizabeth Roboz, a neurochemist and professor of neurology—a union that, like his first marriage, turned out to be very happy.

For Eduard's fiftieth birthday in 1960, Seelig took him out to dinner. Eduard was overweight, rarely exercised, and smoked cigarettes nonstop. Seelig noticed signs of heart trouble. Eduard told Seelig that he sometimes heard voices. Every few feet as they walked to the restaurant, Eduard had to stop to get his breath. For the first time he declined anything sweet on the menu, and during the meal he broke out in a cold sweat and had to leave the place. Seelig wrote to Otto Nathan about the event and about Eduard's condition, adding that he smiled so sweetly and sadly that it broke his heart.

Four years later Eduard had a stroke, and Hans Albert and his second wife, Elizabeth Roboz Einstein, went to see him. They pushed him around the clinic's garden in a wheelchair, talking to him without getting any response. He died on October 25, 1965.

At first, said Roboz Einstein, "I never figured out why they kept him in a sanitarium, because he never did anything to hurt anyone. He could eat and behave normally, after all. Then, one day, they let him leave the sanitarium alone for a small walk, to see if he really needed to be locked up. He just crossed the street. And then he didn't know where he lived. He couldn't find his way back, although it was just across the street."

Hans Albert was at Woods Hole, Massachusetts, eagerly looking forward to a sailing trip to Martha's Vineyard in the summer of 1973, when he had a fatal heart attack. He once said of his father: "Probably the only project he ever gave up on was me. He tried to give me advice, but he soon discovered that I was too stubborn and that he was just wasting his time."

4 | Whatever Happened to Einstein's Daughter?

O ne tantalizing mystery in Albert Einstein's life involves the fate of his first child, a daughter named Lieserl. How had she remained a secret from the world until thirty-two years after his death, when it was first reported in 1987 in the *New York Times?* The paper's account, under the headline "Einstein Letters Tell of Anguished Love Affair," spilled over onto another page headed "Einstein's Dark Side Emerges in Letters" and reads in part:

> Mileva, an ethnic Serb, was four years older than Einstein and walked with a limp. Over the opposition of his mother, Einstein fell in love with her. Their courtship is familiar to readers of Einstein's early love letters. "So crazy with desire," Einstein wrote in a little poem in 1900. "While thinking of his little Dollie / His pillow catches fire." The next month, he sent Mileva a sketch of his foot so that she could knit socks for him.
>
> Mileva had been a shadowy figure of Einstein's early years, but the letters reveal her to be both lover and intellectual companion. She looked up scientific data for Einstein, suggested proofs, checked his calculations and copied notes and manuscripts. Einstein's letters to her include his first, stumbling attempts at the theories that later made him famous.
>
> In 1902, Mileva gave birth to a baby girl out of wedlock, Lieserl, whose existence was unknown until the

correspondence was discovered. "I love her so much and don't even know her yet!" he wrote in February 1902. The fate of Lieserl is unknown. It is believed that she was given up for adoption.

Sixteen years earlier, in 1971, the Princeton University Press had signed a contract with Albert Einstein's estate to publish his collected papers. But because Otto Nathan and Helen Dukas, trustees of the Einstein estate, were determined to preserve his saintly worldwide reputation—a mixture of Albert Schweitzer, Isaac Newton, and Mahatma Gandhi—at all costs, they delayed publication for decades.

After Nathan and Dukas finally chose Boston University's John Stachel, an expert on Einstein's life and work, to edit the papers, he started work in Princeton in January 1977. Six months later, Nathan tried to fire Stachel and replace him with several editors over whom he would have more control. Nathan took his case to court, lost, and then appealed. The case dragged on until 1980, when Nathan finally lost. Meanwhile, Stachel had shrewdly made copies of the entire Einstein archive, which Helen Dukas had lovingly preserved at the Institute for Advanced Study.

In his strenuous efforts to whitewash Einstein's life, Otto Nathan had antagonized and frustrated several would-be Einstein biographers. Stachel heard that Nathan had even prevented Einstein's son, Hans Albert, from publishing a book based on his own letters to his parents and on their letters to one another. Sometime in the late 1950s, after the deaths of his mother and father, Hans Albert—one of the few people who knew that he had had a sister—wanted to publish his parents' love letters, together with his letters to and from them. But Otto Nathan, dedicated to sustaining Einstein's image as an almost flawless human being, put up a fierce resistance, insisting that Hans Albert hand over all the letters to him so that he could decide what, if anything, could be published. Hans Albert resented Nathan's dictatorial role as censor and held on to the letters. But Nathan in effect checkmated Hans Albert, preventing him from publishing any part of them. When Stachel contacted Hans Albert's widow, Elizabeth, about it, she told him that she had placed the letters under trust with her late husband's grandson, Dr. Thomas Einstein, a physician.

The big discovery came in 1985. Historian Robert Schulmann, from the University of Pennsylvania, had joined the Einstein Project, and at a dinner party in Switzerland, he learned of "beautiful" love letters between the Einsteins. He was told that if he contacted Hans Albert's adopted daughter, Evelyn, living in Berkeley, California, he might be able to locate them.

Schulmann met her there in 1986, when she showed him Frida Einstein's introduction to Hans Albert's manuscript, which Otto Nathan had banned. It included the lines, "The reader is immediately drawn by its enchantment. Even a person familiar with Albert Einstein's personality looks at a world which has been closed to him." Glimpses of that world were contained in paraphrased extracts of Albert and Mileva's love letters. Evelyn agreed to send Schulmann a photocopy of the book's introduction, and as she was working on it, she found copies of the actual letters—which she also mailed to him.

By this time, April 1986, both Otto Nathan and Helen Dukas were dead, and according to Einstein's will, the copyright of his works had gone to Hebrew University. It gave Hans Albert's family permission to publish the book Otto Nathan had banned, although by this time Hans Albert's widow, Elizabeth, had decided not to publish it. Because Dr. Thomas Einstein, Hans Albert's grandson, owned the original letters, the Einstein Project offered him a large amount of money for them. But he handed them over for free.

Of some four hundred letters, fifty-two written just before and soon after the Einsteins' wedding, a few of them tell of a desperately unhappy event in their lives. When they were deeply in love and living in Switzerland before they were married, Mileva became pregnant. She returned alone to her home in Novi Sad, Yugoslavia, to give birth to their daughter. In one letter to Mileva, while she was still in Yugoslavia, Einstein wrote that he already loved the girl they had named Lieserl, although he had not yet seen her and, apparently, never would. He looked forward, he wrote, to the three of them living together. Several months later, Mileva left Lieserl to be cared for by her parents or her friend Helene Savic, and she rejoined Einstein in Switzerland, where they married. If Lieserl had been adopted, it would have been after Mileva's marriage to Albert in 1903. One letter reveals that Lieserl contracted scarlet fever at about eighteen months old. After that there is not one word about her in any of the letters. Because of the silence of Einstein and Mileva, or perhaps because their subsequent letters were censored by some unknown hand, maybe even destroyed, her fate remains a mystery today.

On receiving the letters in 1986, Robert Schulmann made two trips to Yugoslavia and hired a researcher to look at the records in Budapest. Schulmann thought that Lieserl might still be alive, in which case she would be in her eighties. If so, she could create a problem for Hebrew University by disputing the valuable copyright to Einstein's writings now in their hands in accord with his will.

Meanwhile, Abraham Pais, who was a colleague of Einstein's at Princeton's Institute for Advanced Study, a committee member of the Einstein Papers, and the author of what is considered the best scientific biography of him, *Subtle Is the Lord*, anticipated that the news of Einstein's daughter would inevitably be leaked to the press and become sensational fodder for the tabloids. He suggested to the committee that they inform newspapers about the love letters and about Einstein's daughter, even before publication in an official volume of Einstein's correspondence.

This idea was accepted, and a feature headed "Einstein Letters Tell of Anguished Love Affair" told the world for the first time of Lieserl's existence. It appeared in the May 3, 1987, edition of the *New York Times*. At about the same time, the letters were published in the first volume of *The Collected Papers of Albert Einstein*.

The protectors of Einstein's image, his friend and executor Otto Nathan and his loyal secretary Helen Dukas, in their persistent efforts to preserve the popular image of Einstein as a "Jewish saint," had tried but failed to prevent the letters from becoming public.

Meanwhile, members of the Einstein Papers Project had returned from Hungary and Yugoslavia without having tracked down Lieserl or anyone who knew her fate.

After a long and tortuous process involving concessions by the concerned parties, Dr. Elizabeth Roboz Einstein gave the original letters to Hebrew University, where they are today.

In the letters, Einstein expressed his delight at having a daughter. He asked for and received a description of her, but apparently he never saw her. When, after a painful pregnancy and difficult birth, Mileva joined him in Switzerland, she left Lieserl behind. For some reason Mileva returned to her family home in Novi Sad in late August 1903—presumably having heard that Lieserl was very ill. In mid-September she wrote to tell Einstein that she was pregnant again and report Lieserl's condition. He replied that he was glad she would have "a new Lieserl," and was very sorry Lieserl had contracted scarlet fever, because it often left permanent damage. He asked how Lieserl's birth had been registered, and advised Mileva that they must take great care to ensure Lieserl's future life was not compromised.

Some believe that the epidemic in Novi Sad that killed many of the babies in the area also killed Lieserl. But no one knows for certain, because after the account of her illness when she was eighteen months old, not a word about her or her fate can be found in the many letters gathered in a world-wide search by the Einstein Project. Some letters, many by Margot Einstein, will not be available to the public until 2006, and they may provide all the missing details. But Einstein expert Robert Schulmann doubts it.

Einstein's critics imply that he simply abandoned his child and that this was the behavior of a self-centered, cold-hearted individual. His admirers point to the fact that he had just obtained a job at the Patent Office in Bern, Switzerland, after a period of unemployment during which he almost starved, and that to bring an illegitimate child into that puritanical, bureaucratic country would have cost him his job. On the other hand, his critics counter, under Swiss law an illegitimate child becomes legitimate when its parents marry.

"What's more relevant," says Dr. Schulmann, "is that Einstein may have been afraid of losing a provisional civil service position at the Swiss Patent Office. He only got a permanent position there in 1904."

The revelation that Einstein had a daughter who might still be alive aroused intense interest, and Einstein enthusiasts, as well as scientists and biographers, were eager to go to her birthplace to investigate. Unfortunately, war was raging in Serbia (formerly Yugoslavia) in the late 1980s, making it difficult and dangerous to make the attempt. Even so, several determined individuals went, among them Einstein experts John Stachel and Robert Schulmann.

Over several years I discussed the mystery of the missing daughter with Schulmann. He hoped to find that Lieserl was still alive, having long outlived her father, who died in 1955. She might even have been alive as we spoke about her during the 1980s and 1990s, presumably unaware that she was Einstein's daughter. But Schulmann admitted that he had no concrete evidence to suggest that she had survived. He did have a letter confirming that she was still alive at eighteen months, and another that she had contracted scarlet fever.

Schulmann had one more tantalizing piece of evidence that he thought might relate to Lieserl—a photograph of a child four or five years old. He traveled to Yugoslavia (now Serbia) for two weeks in late 1988, hoping to get someone to positively identify her.

On his return to the States on November 15, 1988, he said that he had shown the photo, which he thought might be Lieserl at about four or five years of age, to psychiatrist Milan Popovic, the grandson of Helene Savic—Mileva's best friend. Popovic showed Schulmann an identical photo in his family album. There was nothing written on the back of either photo, but it was clear to Schulmann that both photos came from Mileva, and that the child was of one of her three children. Schulmann finally determined the photo to be of Hans Albert, by matching the outline of the houses behind the child in the picture with a neighborhood in Bern.

Milan Popovic told Schulmann that when he had asked his mother, Helene Savic's oldest daughter, "Was there any correspondence [about Lieserl]?'" she simply replied, "It's so terrible . . . " And didn't finish her thought. When he persisted, "Well, what's it about?'" she ended the conversation with an emphatic, "I won't tell you." And he said that she never did tell him. After Popovic's mother died, he went through all the letters she had left and never found any mentioning Lieserl. He concluded that she had destroyed them.

Schulmann also questioned the officials in charge of civil records in Mileva's hometown, Novi Sad, and in the nearby village of Kac—Mileva's family had homes in both places. But he drew a blank. Lieserl was a mystery to them, too. The best they could give him was vague hearsay. Schulmann then considered hiring a private detective to help in the search but felt he couldn't justify the cost to the various funding agencies. He had ruled out advertising, because it would entail too much expense and effort to winnow out all the phonies.

Remarkably, this wasn't the first time Einstein was suspected of having a daughter he was hiding from the public. In 1935, half a century before the search for Lieserl began, a woman named Grete Markstein turned up in England and persuaded several of Einstein's scientific friends that she was his daughter. She never claimed to be Lieserl, or that Mileva was her mother. In fact, writes Dr. Schulmann, "There is no reason to believe that Markstein knew anything of Lieserl. She put forward her candidacy as a daughter on the reasonable assumption that this would cause a stir and give her some mileage." Also, she may have heard that Einstein had had several extramarital affairs while in Europe—which was true—and she could present herself as the plausible result of one of them.

Einstein was living in Princeton with his second wife, Elsa, when first warned of this by his friend and colleague the mathematician Hermann Weyl, who lived nearby. On November 23, 1935, Weyl had received a disturbing telegram from Professor Frederick Lindemann, a British physicist (who became Winston Churchill's scientific advisor during World War II). The telegram stated that a Grete Markstein, claiming to be Einstein's daughter and having failed to get help from Elsa Einstein, was now trying to find support from high circles—prominent physicists in Oxford. Lindemann, hardly the most reliable judge of women, being a confirmed bachelor and something of a misogynist, took Markstein for a fraud and asked Weyl to discuss it with Einstein personally and then to cable him back immediately.

Apparently Einstein had been in touch with Markstein in the past, when, in response to a begging letter, he had sent her eighty marks. This was not surprising or suspicious: he was known as a soft touch. Elsa was said to have rebuffed her further attempts to get money from him by telling her to get lost and not to contact her or Einstein again. However, Einstein replied to Lindemann's cable, denying any knowledge of Grete Markstein.

A month later, Einstein's physicist friend Max von Laue, who was, like Lindemann, in Oxford, wrote to him: "The matter of your pseudo-daughter has amused me, the only thing that galls me is how credulous the British are. When the lady had heard about our enquiry to you and your response she asked Lindemann by telephone for discretion!!! There is such a thing as naïve impertinence that seems extraordinarily funny."

Some two months after Lindemann's warning cable, Grete Markstein appeared, with a little boy, at the home of Einstein's close friend Dr. Janos Plesch, a physician, who had recently moved to England from Germany. Plesch and Grete spoke together for an hour one afternoon. She convinced him that she was indeed Einstein's daughter and that her son, George, was his grandson. Plesch was especially impressed by the boy, who he thought was intelligent and attractive and even looked like Einstein. From then on, with the assistance of friends, Plesch helped to find Grete a job and to place her son in a good school. Grete continued to see Plesch twice a month throughout the spring and summer, as a patient being treated for tuberculosis.

Ten months after Lindemann's warning cable, Einstein also began to take Grete's claim seriously, perhaps because of Plesch's unflagging belief that the woman was genuine. Plesch also kept the situation alive by sending Einstein clever colored sketches by the boy, as well as his photo, and pointing out how much he resembled Einstein.

Einstein's next move was to ask his secretary, Helen Dukas, to find a detective in Europe to investigate the persuasive young woman. The detective, F. Biel, soon discovered the paper trail: Grete Markstein, he reported, was born in Vienna on August 31, 1894. Her father, Samuel, was born in Hungary and had worked in a bank, and he and her mother had both died in Berlin. An aunt, Melanie Neumann, living in Vienna, described Grete as an actress with a Berlin theater company who left Germany "during the upheavals"—presumably the Nazi takeover. According to a gentleman who knew her personally, said the detective, Grete Markstein had a bad reputation—in what respect was left to Einstein's imagination. Apart from minor errors, his report seemed essentially correct.

Some of the correspondence between Plesch and Einstein on the situation was probably destroyed by Otto Nathan or Helen Dukas, either at Einstein's request or in their effort to sustain his glowing reputation. What they didn't destroy was an exchange of raunchy poems in which Plesch called Einstein a stud and Einstein expressed his amusement at his reputation, at least among his friends, as a Lothario.

To Robert Schulmann the fact that Einstein had hired a private detective to investigate Grete Markstein implied that he thought that she might be Lieserl, and "that though he hadn't been following his daughter's life—Mileva may have been. And it also implied that Einstein believed that Lieserl could still be alive [at thirty-four]."

Grete Markstein died in England of tuberculosis in 1943 during World War II. Four years later, her theatrical friend, Lola Stein, wrote to Einstein, saying that Grete's son, George, owed her thirty-five pounds. She included a copy of the promissory note. Representing herself as a sixty-two-year-old Jewish refugee, alone in the world, and broke, she hoped the esteemed professor would pay the debt of one of his relatives.

Einstein wrote to her at some length saying that he had been able to prove through his detective's report that Grete Markstein was not his daughter, as when she was born, in 1894, he was only thirteen years old (in fact, he was fifteen). He acknowledged that her claim that Grete's son owed her money apparently had more validity than the suggestion that he was Grete's father, but he didn't send her any money.

Lola replied that it was "a special honor to have received such an interesting answer from you. Even though it was a negative result with respect to Markstein—a loss which I must now accept—there exists nothing bad which does not lead to something good." She also asked him to help her to immigrate to the United States. Einstein did not reply.

Grete Markstein's son, George, had a more successful life than his mother. The talented young artist grew up to be the author of several successful spy novels and four British TV series, including *The Prisoner*. He died in 1987.

The search for Lieserl continued apace. If, as seems likely, the Einsteins gave her to the Savic family to watch over or to give to an institution, then, of course, the Savics had to have known what happened to her. Helene Savic, Mileva's great friend and an extremely sensitive woman, would have considered it a terrible thing to abandon a child—as would have the community. But she also would have realized that Mileva had no reasonable alternative. And so she may have kept Lieserl's abandonment a secret, to protect her friend's reputation.

As for Einstein's mother, it seems probable that she at least knew that a baby was on the way. The most persuasive evidence is in a letter (published in volume 1 of the Einstein correspondence). It was from Mileva, who was seven months pregnant with Lieserl at the time, to her friend Helene Savic, and included the sentence: "His [Albert's] parents wrote to my parents and you can imagine what a fuss it caused." Schulmann believed that Albert must have told his mother about Lieserl or that she got it out of him. Hence the angry letter Mileva mentioned to Helene.

Despite the efforts of several investigators, the mystery of Lieserl's fate remained unsolved. On October 16, 1991, I told Schulmann that Einstein's abandoning his daughter, which he had apparently done, seemed so uncharacteristic. He, however, believed that Einstein was much more opportunistic than the popular image of him as the noble sage of Princeton, and that one must be willing to consider, at least, that he was more opportunistic, in the nonderogatory sense of the word. If you do that, Schulmann said, "certain directions he went become easier to understand."

Judging them by their letters and their milieu, I suggested that Einstein's parents would have been horrified if they knew that Albert and Mileva had abandoned their own daughter. Schulmann, on the contrary, thought it more likely that the reaction of Einstein's mother would have been, "'You got the Serbian girl into trouble,' as she predicted in a 1901 letter when she threw herself on the bed and had hysterics. And she would have said, 'Look, now you've got it, and you told me you weren't having an affair with her!' Because of their bourgeois sensibilities the Einsteins would immediately push it on the woman. 'She tempted my son. She's ugly. She's older than he is. She tempted my boy. Get rid of the kid!' And it had nothing to do with anti-Semitism or philo-Semitism. She had, after all, approved of his friendship with the Protestant Marie Winteler."

The Wintelers were a respectable Swiss family, so to speak, while Serbians (such as Mileva) were thought of by some Germans as bandits from the borders of civilization. Einstein's parents might even have regarded Mileva as some regarded gypsies, which of course, would have been unfair. Mileva's father was a civil servant, not, as some writers have called him, a peasant.

Socially, Albert and Mileva were more or less on the same level. And probably Mileva's father had done better than Albert's, because he was a bureaucrat, while Albert's father was an entrepreneur who hadn't done well.

I was unable to reconcile the Einstein who wrote that he already loved his daughter without having seen her and that he looked forward to her joining him, with the man who abandoned her, unless Lieserl had been terribly ill—unable to be moved—or dying.

Schulmann disagreed. He thought that that would be giving too much weight to the words Einstein wrote. He conceded that Einstein may have had good intentions, but those, as everyone knew, were used to pave the roads to hell.

But, I said, Mileva was no pushover and would go on to marry Einstein, live with him for many years, and have two more of his children. So it wasn't, from her point of view, a case of, "You're a monster not to have taken our daughter!" Schulmann conjectured that the marriage was strained already because of Lieserl, and that it was poisoned from the start.

Einstein biographer Peter Michelmore agrees, writing of "a mysterious pre-marital incident which caused a rift between the couple. Friends had noticed a change in Mileva's attitude and thought that the romance might be doomed. . . . Mileva would only say it was 'intensely personal.' . . . She brooded about it and Albert seemed to be in some way responsible. . . . [Mileva] kept it a secret all her life—a vital detail in the story of Albert Einstein that still remains shrouded in mystery."

Einstein biographers Roger Highfield and Paul Carter took a different tack, suggesting that Mileva "had opposed the decision to give away their daughter, and blamed Einstein for pushing her to acquiesce in it. Another possibility is that she agreed to the decision more readily, but was then over-whelmed by feelings of guilt."

What especially puzzled Einstein expert Professor John Stachel was that in January 1903, when Lieserl would have been one year old, Mileva wrote to Helene Savic saying that things were going well, and she didn't even mention Lieserl. Stachel assumed that there were other letters between them that had been destroyed because they mentioned Lieserl.

Einstein and Mileva's elder son, Hans Albert, and his first wife, Frida, had adopted a baby girl, Evelyn, shortly after she was born in 1941. In 1993 the rumor surfaced that Evelyn was actually Albert Einstein's child whom he had foisted on to his son to avoid a scandal. Einstein had been a widower for several years at the time of Evelyn's adoption. As a teenager she had attended a Swiss finishing school, where the director, now dead, and his wife, who was either dead or senile, were the apparent source of a rumor that Evelyn was Albert Einstein's illegitimate daughter adopted by his obliging son.

Schulmann spoke with Evelyn Einstein, who was working at an intriguing and unusual job in California, deprogramming people who had been seduced, or otherwise pressured, into joining cults. Though she told him she believed it possible that she was Albert Einstein's daughter, she at first declined to show Schulmann her adoption papers. So he was naturally somewhat skeptical.

I asked him if she looked like Einstein or had any of his characteristics. Nothing, he said, that bowled him over.

Eventually Evelyn located her adoption papers and telephoned her birth mother in Chicago, hoping they might at least meet. The woman on the other end rebuffed her angrily, saying that she would not be blackmailed. That was the end of their relationship.

When Einstein's brain became available some years after his death, Evelyn agreed to take part in a possible DNA match to settle the question of her paternity. Unfortunately Einstein's DNA was too degraded to be of any use.

Michele Zackheim, author of *Einstein's Daughter: The Search for Lieserl*, spent years in a rigorous and persistent search for Lieserl. One thing that puzzled her was, "How did Grete [Markstein] know that Albert Einstein ever had a daughter? Lieserl was an amazingly well-kept secret. Grete never claimed to be Lieserl by name, only by birthdate [1902]. But how did she know the date of Lieserl's birth? Nobody knew about Lieserl—not Albert's friends [including Besso], not his doctor, maybe not even his second wife."

Schulmann is not convinced: "Zackheim may have been persistent, but I consider the research presented in her book as anything but rigorous. It oozes wishful thinking. There is no reason for Grete to have known of Lieserl to pursue her own fraud. Einstein, of course, had good reason to fear that should his daughter be alive, it might be Grete."

Zackheim continues in her book: "Moreover, how did Grete convince Oxford scholars that she might be Einstein's daughter? And by what means did she continue her association with Plesch *after* the Oxford group had rejected her? If she was a scoundrel, why didn't she take the story to the press, why was there no whiff of extortion?"

Now Zackheim makes several misstatements and flawed suppositions:

- There is no evidence that Grete Markstein knew of Lieserl's existence. Markstein's birthdate, as a detective discovered, was 1894. Being an actress, it's not surprising that she should claim her birthdate as 1897 and even 1902—like Lieserl's.

- There *was* a whiff of extortion. Markstein got eighty marks out of Einstein and support from his friend Dr. Plesch.

- It is not possible to say for certain, as Zackheim does, that none of Albert's friends, including his doctor, knew about Lieserl. How can anyone be sure of what they knew, especially as they are all dead?

- The likely reason Markstein didn't take her story to the press is that an investigation by reporters would have exposed her as a fraud.

- Dr. Plesch may well have continued his association with Markstein after the Oxford scholars had rejected her because he found her friendly and attractive.

Zackheim was an indefatigable researcher in trying to recreate the hidden life of Lieserl, spurred by a biography of Mileva, *In the Shadow of Albert Einstein*, by Gjuric Trbuhovic, a retired Serbian professor of physics who had interviewed Mileva's relatives, friends, her doctor, and her nurse—but not Mileva herself. The book was published in Serbia in 1969, and later in Switzerland. But the author did not solve the mystery.

With good contacts in Serbia, Zackheim decided to take on the challenge, and she made several journeys over five years to the war-torn country, doggedly pursuing every possible lead like a first-rate detective.

One "sophisticated" contact, Milenko Damjanov, told Zackheim, "In my family, it was considered liberal, actually avant-garde, for Mileva and Albert to live together before they were married. My family did not judge them. On the other hand, I know that Mileva's parents had a hard time with the situation. They had never expected her to marry. And, of course, I know about the daughter, Lieserl. You must understand, no one was surprised when Mileva became pregnant—even though it created a bit of a scandal. But her baby . . . was not one-hundred-percent right. Mileva had tried to hide her pregnancy by wearing tight corsets. This cut off some of the oxygen to her unborn daughter. Her baby did not live a long time. This I can assure you. This I know."

Dr. Schulmann's comment about that last quote was that Milenko Damjanov may have been sophisticated, "but truthful? I had a lot of trouble believing Zackheim after she claimed that Serbs do not lie."

At the end of her enthralling book, Zackheim writes: "In Lieserl's story there are seven witnesses who have honorably testified: Dragisa's mother, Ljubica Maric [a first cousin of Mileva], who told me a German-speaking woman came and took Lieserl away; Jovan Ruzik, Mileva's second cousin, who had never spoken of Lieserl until it 'just slipped from my memory into my mouth'; Sofija Galic Golubovic, Mileva's first cousin, who personally knew Lieserl but denied any knowledge of her to Hans Albert, thus preserving her vow of silence; Milenko Damjanov, whose parents were close friends of the Maric family and said that Mileva's baby was not one-hundred-percent right because she had tried to hide her pregnancy by wearing tight corsets; Grete Markstein, who somehow knew about the existence of a daughter."

Again Schulmann is dubious: "How can Grete be an honorable witness if she never met or probably never knew of Lieserl's existence?"

Zackheim continued: "All the witnesses agree that she was the child of Mileva and Albert, that she was born in Yugoslavia, and that Mileva and Albert were not married at the time of her birth. They all agree that she was born in 1902. Most of them agree that Mileva's parents cared for the child while Mileva was living in Bern. They all agree that Lieserl had scarlet fever. Ljubica Maric and Mira Aleckovic remembered that a German-speaking woman came to take her away. Damjanov and [John] Phillips testified to Lieserl's problems. . . . They all agree that she disappeared when she was about two years old."

Schulmann's comment: "Disappeared? If the Serb witnesses are so familiar with Lieserl, how can she simply disappear?"

Zacheim continues: "In addition, Aleckovic, a Serbian children's poet, wrote the following statement . . . on March 29, 1997: 'I remember that my Kovilj Monastery near Novi Sad said the child was then taken by Julka, sister of Milos Maric, and given to a German woman so she could learn to speak German. I heard from my grandmother that the child died in 1903. They called her Lizerel [*sic*].'"

Schulmann is skeptical: "Given to a German woman to learn to speak German at or before the age of one?"

None of the witnesses testified that Lieserl had survived into adulthood.

Michele Zackheim concluded that Lieserl Einstein was born severely mentally handicapped "and Mileva and her family arranged to shelter her at home. Mileva could not bring an abnormal child back to Bern. Albert was on the cusp of his remarkable career."

Schulmann: "Not the case in 1902/1903. Albert first gets real recognition in 1909 at the meeting of the German Natural Scientists and Doctors in Salzburg."

Zackheim continued: "They had no money to care for her, no social system to support them. It was better to leave her hidden in the fold of the Maric family. . . . Besides Lieserl's mental handicap, it was now apparent to him that she was suffering physical problems as well. We know that when Mileva returned to Albert in Bern in September 1903, she was forever changed. She insisted that whatever happened 'was too personal' and kept it a secret all her life."

After more detective work, Zackheim estimated that Lieserl had died of scarlet fever at twenty-one months, on "September 21, 1903, the day of a solar eclipse, the day when the sun disappeared from the sky."

Schulmann: "How in tarnation could she know that she died the day of a solar eclipse? What detective work would have yielded this conclusion? Is there a shred of evidence for this, or is it born only of a florid imagination? My objection to Zackheim's way of working is not the garishness of some of her claims, but that she presents them as if they were irrefutable facts. Her naivete in dealing with 'eyewitnesses' beggars the imagination."

While Zackheim was interviewing psychoanalyst John Phillips in 1996, he recalled a dinner conversation he had had with one of Einstein's Princeton friends, the historian Erich von Kahler, who died in 1970. During that conversation Kahler had said: "Professor Einstein told me that his first child was a Mongoloid idiot." Phillips was certain that Einstein was not referring to his third child, Eduard, who was a schizophrenic, but to Lieserl. "Believe me," Phillips added, "I know the difference between a schizophrenic and a Mongoloid idiot. And so did Einstein."

Schulmann: "This is hearsay evidence, at two removes!!!"

Einstein's behavior would hardly have surprised his friend

physicist Max Born, who said of him: "For all his kindness and sociability, and love of humanity, he was nevertheless totally detached from his environment and the human beings included in it."

One book reviewer on the Internet, Manola Sommerfeld, remarked that the picture displayed on the front cover of Zackheim's book purporting to be perhaps the only existing image of Lieserl is so indistinct that it could "be of a goat, a fence post or a dahlia," adding, "Zackheim speculates whether Einstein and Mileva had sex after their divorce, whether Einstein's syphilis is what caused his children's ailments." The reviewer also felt that "all this speculation becomes slightly sordid after a while."

Schulmann responds: "That Einstein visited prostitutes and had syphilis is a claim that Dr. Plesch made. Plesch is as the Germans would say, '*sehr mit vorsicht zu geniessen*,' 'to be enjoyed with great care.' In historical reconstruction, he was as sloppy as Zackheim. One of his arguments for the diagnosis of syphilis is that it caused his [Einstein's] aneurysm. Now there's proof for you!"

There is no reasonable evidence that Einstein had syphilis. And, to be fair, if anyone passed on a mental weakness to Lieserl and eventually to Eduard, it was more likely to be Mileva, whose sister, Zorka, a psychotic alcoholic, was found dead at fifty-five in 1938, lying on a pile of straw surrounded by her forty-three cats.

A *Publishers Weekly* reviewer considered Zackheim's thesis to be a "withering one-sided portrait, intriguing but inconclusive, based on only a few witnesses' recollections."

The Associated Press reported: "The book is just the latest in a number of revelations about Einstein's personal life that have scholars re-evaluating the image of the wild-haired, iconoclastic inventor of the theory of relativity. Boston University historian Robert Schulmann, director of the Einstein Papers Project, told *Time* that the book's conclusions about the child's fate are 'as good as anything I could come up with, or anyone else. But it's speculation.' Harvard physicist and Einstein historian Gerald Holton was more critical: 'She worked very hard traipsing through all those Serbian cemeteries and came up with nothing.'"

Dr. Lewis Pyenson, research professor at the University of Louisiana at Lafayette, vehemently disagrees with other Einstein experts. He writes: "With grace and conviction, [Zackheim's] book records how Einstein abused his wife and children, and sets it down, in one place, his philandering as well as documenting the systematic suppression of information about Lieserl. . . . Zackheim demonstrates very great merit in focusing our attention on a disjuncture between Einstein's general pronouncements and his personal conduct; she provides clear reasons for inferring a redemptive undertone to Einstein's public morality."

One of the first Einstein biographies—published in 1931— was by his stepson-in-law, Rudolf Kayser, Ilse's husband. Written under the pen name Anton Reiser, with Einstein's reluctant approval, it left out, according to Einstein, "the irrational, the inconsistent, the droll, even the insane." What it also left out was any mention of his first child, Lieserl. It is strange that he should use the word "insane," though there is no mention of Zorka or of his son Eduard's mental problems. However, in a foreword Einstein attested to its accuracy.

It seems that Einstein, the great master at discovering the secrets of the universe, was equally masterful in hiding his personal secrets.

5 | What Was Einstein Like Face to Face?

Anumber of people who knew Einstein personally have shared their impressions over the years, either in interviews or in published writings. Among them are his wives, his stepson-in-law and biographer, his landlady's daughter, his doctor, his students, fellow scientists, colleagues, philosophers, historians of science, journalists, a muckraking novelist, an editor, a photographer, an artist, a woman playwright, an Israeli statesman, an Israeli premier, a Russian commissar, neighbors, friends, and strangers.

Susanne Markwalder, a schoolteacher and the daughter of Einstein's second landlady in Switzerland

Mileva Maric was no match for the thoroughly decent, shy, outspoken, irresistible and impulsive Albert Einstein. [He showed just how impulsive he was] one warm summer day when he heard someone playing a Mozart sonata in a neighboring house and asked who it was. I told him that it must be a piano teacher who lived in the attic. He hurriedly put his violin under his arm and rushed out without collar or tie. "You can't go like that, Herr Einstein," I cried, but either he did not hear or pretended not to hear me. A moment later the garden gate banged and it was not long before we heard a violin accompanying the Mozart sonata. On his return Einstein said with enthusiasm, "That's a really charming little old lady. I shall often go and play with her." We were to meet her a few hours later. It was old Fraulein Wegelin who appeared in a black silk dress and asked shyly the name of the extraordinary young man. We pacified her by saying that he was merely a harmless student. She told us what a shock it had given her when the unknown musician rushed into her room and merely said, "Go on playing."

Hans Tanner, a student of Einstein's who became a physics professor

Our first sight of the new professor [in 1910] was of a scruffy young man [31 years old] whose pants were too short, holding what looked like a visiting card. It turned out be a scrap of paper with the main points of his lecture on it. After the first few sentences he captured our hearts. He encouraged us to interrupt the lecture if anything was not clear and during the breaks he would take one or the other of the students by the arm in the most comradely manner to discuss the subject with him. Weekly, from eight to ten in the evening, we students had to propound a theme and at the end he would say, "Who's coming to the Café Terasse?" The discussions continued there. Once we sat and gossiped until closing time in a café. As we left, Einstein said, "Is anyone coming home with me? This morning I received some work from [Max] Planck to which there must be a mistake." In the apartment he gave us Planck's pamphlet, saying, "See if you can spot the fault while I make some coffee." When we couldn't he pointed it out and said, "We won't write and tell him he'd made a mistake. The result is correct but the proof is faulty. We'll simply write and tell him how the real proof should run. The main thing is the content, not the mathematics. With mathematics you can prove anything."

Adolf Fisch, a student of Einstein's

He spoke in the same way to everybody. The tone with which he talked to the leading officials of the university was the same as that with which he spoke to the grocer or to the scrub-woman in the laboratory.

Hyman Levy, a student of Einstein's, who became a math professor

I was a student at Göttingen from 1912 to 1914 and at that time it was a tremendous center of scientific activity. I remember Einstein coming to Göttingen to lecture on relativity. It was exciting to hear him say that he was going to take change as fundamental, and that his basic concept would be a particular combination of space and time called space-time. The engineering professors who were present were horrified by his approach, because to them reality was the wheels in machinery—really solid entities. And here was a man talking in abstract terms. It was so abstract it became unreal to them. One professor walked out in a rage and as he went I heard him say, "That is absolute nonsense." That really reflected the attitude of most engineers at the time. Others simply thought that here was a clever mathematician talking and after all you can expect anything from a mathematician!

Physicist Frederick Lindemann. While at the 1911 Solvay Conference, Lindemann was Walther Nernst's secretary. He later became Winston Churchill's World War II scientific advisor.

Einstein had already published many masterpieces [but] none had been actually put to the test and his theories were looked on rather as tours de force than as definitive additions to knowledge. But his pre-eminence among the twelve greatest theoretical physicists of the day was clear to any unprejudiced observer. I well remember M. de Broglie [Secretary of the Solvay Conference and elder brother of physicist Louis de Broglie] saying that of all those present [which included Hendrick Lorentz, Ernest Rutherford, Paul Langevin, Marie

Curie, Kamerlingh Onnes, James Jeans, and Jean Perrin] Einstein and Poincaré were in a class by themselves. Einstein was a young man [32 years old], singularly simple, friendly and unpretentious. He was invariably ready to discuss physical questions with a young student, as I then was. And this never changed though the adulation showered on him might well have turned any man's head.

Romain Rolland, a French writer and pacifist, with whom Einstein enjoyed a long conversation at Vevey, Switzerland, during World War I. Afterward, Rolland wrote the following in his diary for September 6, 1915.

Einstein speaks French rather haltingly, interspersing it with German. He is very much alive and fond of laughter. He cannot help giving an amusing twist to the most serious thoughts. Einstein is incredibly outspoken in his opinion about Germany where he lives. Another man might have suffered from a sense of isolation during the terrible last year, but not he. He laughs. He has found it possible, during the war, to write his most important scientific work. I ask him whether he voices his ideas to German friends, and whether he discusses them with them. He says no. He limits himself to putting questions to them, in the Socratic manner, in order to challenge their complacency. People don't like that very much, he adds. [Romain summed him up as] one of the very few men whose spirit had remained free among the general servility.

Ilse Rosenthal-Schneider, who as a student sometimes rode on the tram with Einstein from Berlin University to their respective homes

He would tease me whenever the opportunity offered itself. He knew I loved to read Kant, so he compared Kant's intuition with the Emperor's clothes. Once when we debated for a long time some of Kant's intricate questions and had mentioned the various widely differing interpretations by the

Kantians in their schools of philosophy of which there were about as many as there were universities in German-speaking countries, sometimes several different ones in the same university, Einstein illustrated his views in the following way: "Kant is a sort of highway with lots of milestones. Then all of the little dogs come and each deposits his contribution to the milestone." Pretending to feel indignation, I said: "But what a comparison!" Einstein laughing loudly, remarked: "But your Kant is a milestone after all, and that is there to stay."

American Nobel physicist I. I. Rabi

I attended one of his four lectures at City College in 1921 that were translated by Morris Cohen. There I was about to enter graduate work, and there was the great Einstein. I think he was talking about physics of the day, particularly quantum theory. As a lecturer he was a model of absolute clarity, with a sense of humor. He gave the impression he was very naive on political matters, and very obstinate about scientific ones. I don't think he was at all naive. He was a very sophisticated man, but seemed naive because he cut to the heart of the problem. He would appear naive if one didn't approach those problems in a fundamental way. He certainly was a very great person. Of the great scientists he was certainly the best in this century. His interest was always in profound questions, and his influence will last. He didn't suffer fools gladly, but he didn't reject them.

Felix Ehrenhaft, Chairman of Experimental Physics, University of Vienna. In 1921 Einstein was to give a public lecture in Vienna. When Einstein was told it would be in an immense hall and that he could expect a huge audience of some three thousand, he felt uneasy and asked Ehrenhaft to accompany him to the lecture and to sit near him, which he did.

Einstein came to stay in my home in Vienna with two coats, two pairs of trousers, two white shirts, but only one white collar. When my wife asked him if there was not something that he had left at home he answered "No." However, she found neither slippers nor toilet articles. She supplied everything, including the necessary collars. However, when she met him in the hall in the morning he was barefooted, and she asked him if he didn't need slippers. He answered "No. They are unnecessary ballast." Since his trousers were terribly crumpled, my wife pressed the second pair and put them in order so that he would be neat for the lecture. When he stepped onto the stage she saw to her horror that he was wearing the unpressed pair.

Hedi Born, playwright wife of Nobel physicist Max Born

When I visited him during one of his serious illnesses, he said: "I feel so much part of every living thing that I am not in the least concerned with where the individual begins and ends."

Einstein's doctor, Janos Plesch, who dedicated his book The Physiology and Pathology of the Heart and Blood Vessels *to Einstein*

I couldn't have had a better patient. Einstein was obedient, trusting and grateful. He once explained that he quite realized that "our primitive thought must necessarily be inadequate in the face of such a complicated piece of mechanism as the human body and that the only proper attitude is patience and resignation, supported by good humor and a certain indifference to one's continued existence." He willingly carried out whatever instructions I gave, at the same time watching the phenomena of his sickness and carefully observing the effect of my treatment.

He could see the funny side of situations most people would regard as utterly tragic, and I don't mean utterly tragic for other people, but for himself. I have known him to laugh even when a mishap or misfortune had really moved him.

Life's too short to waste on disagreeable matters is his attitude: there are so many important things to attend to. This may seem to suggest that he has no very deep feelings, but he has.

If you happen to tell him the same joke twice he will not interrupt you, but listen tolerantly and laugh with you again. He greatly appreciates mother-wit and is as delighted as a child with his own witticisms, even when sometimes a biting remark slips from his lips among friends. He certainly is no prude. Though with most thinking men he rejects sheer filth, but if it has real wit it can be as broad as it likes.

Einstein is a man of great good nature. The sight of distress always inspires him with desire to help. He gives away what spare money he has—he never has much—to people in need of assistance.

L. L. Whyte, ex-president of the British Society for the Philosophy of Science

I received a wonderful letter from Einstein saying, "I hear from my friend Emil Ludwig that we both ride the same hobby horse. I always like to talk with people interested in the same things. Please ring me up and come and see me. Don't be put off by Frau Einstein [Elsa]. She's there to protect me."

During the first of my talks with Einstein an amusing incident occurred. I was very nervous and still very shy, and after we had been talking for about twenty minutes, the maid came in with a huge bowl of soup. I thought that this was probably a signal for me to leave. But when the girl left the room, Einstein said to me in a conspiratorial whisper, "That's a trick. If I am bored talking to somebody, when the maid comes in, I don't push the bowl of soup away, and the girl takes whomever I am with away and I am free." Einstein pushed the bowl away, and so I was quite happy and much flattered and more at ease for the rest of the talk. I was deeply distressed to find that somebody of the greatness and world reputation of Einstein had already become a symbol for anti-Semitism, and thought that his very existence in Berlin University was dangerous. I discussed it with some senior figure in Berlin University who told me that it was quite impossible for Einstein then—1928–1929—to fail to be conscious of the fact that he was already perhaps the dominant symbol for anti-Semitism in Germany, so it was really uncomfortable for him to remain there.

Author Fulton Oursler. In the early 1930s Einstein's American friend the novelist Upton Sinclair arranged for Fulton Oursler to interview Einstein while he was in the United States, and they talked for more than an hour. Soon after, Einstein sent him a telegram refusing to give him permission to publish the interview, without explanation. Oursler assumed that in the intervening weeks his ideas about Hitler and the Jews had changed. He published the interview in a book, Behold the Dreamer!, *in 1964, nine years after Einstein's death.*

F.O.: I live in New York City where there are three million Jews. They are tremendously interested about Hitler, his attitude and what is going to happen to the Jews in Germany. You know the feeling in Germany. I would like to be able to tell those people what is likely to happen.

E.: I believe that not very much will happen. It is so in bad times. The feeling about the minority is not so respected. It is so in Africa. You can see it here [in California] with the Filipinos and the Mexicans. In bad times if people are excited and fear danger, then it is easy to agitate this kind of feeling about the minority. Hitler is a very ordinary person, with only a short ability to speak—a very ordinary man. He has only a certain ability to produce emotional forces in the people. He is a leader of the mob. He is an agitator.

F.O.: Would you compare him to Mussolini?

E.: No. Mussolini is more intelligent and he has certain ideas of organization for his people.

F.O.: Could you explain to me what Hitler's objections to the Jews are?

E.: No, I could not say. He is capitalizing on prejudice. It is supposedly racial. But, you know, the Germans are a very mixed people and races do not exist at all. It is ridiculous, but people believe it, and there is a certain racial construction to justify the feeling.

F.O.: Did you know the Kaiser has blamed the bankers for the war [World War I] and for the prejudice against Germany?

E.: No, I have never heard about it. But he has a very weak brain. To be an emperor it is not necessary for a man to have a big brain. He is just a cross on the church.

F.O.: Do you think there is a possibility of a pogrom?

E.: Possibly. They have the police, but if the police are in the hands of national soldiers, as they are now, it could be very dangerous without any change of law.

F.O.: May I use the story of the Russian Cossack and the Jew, which I think illustrates the Hitler point? It is the story of a Jewish man in Russia who had to go to Moscow. He was afraid to travel, so he sat crouched in the corner of a third-class carriage in an effort not to attract any attention. A big Cossack got on the train. "Damn the Jews!" he roared. "The Jews made all the trouble. The Jews made the war." The Cossack turned to the little man and demanded, "Didn't they?" "Yes," said the Jew. "The Jews and the bicycles." "Why the bicycles?" inquired the Cossack. "Why the Jews?" replied the Jewish man.

E.: Yes, of course I know it. It is well known in Germany, but it is impossible to tell it there.

Herbert Dingle, philosopher of science

Einstein and I were both at the Athenaeum of the California Institute of Technology at Pasadena. I had gone there for the 1932–33 session with a Rockefeller Fellowship to study relativity. He was obviously enjoying his stay in Pasadena, and wished to show my wife and me a picture in his bedroom which had excited his admiration. Frau Einstein, however, immediately sprang up in frantic alarm. "Oh no, no, no, you cannot go zere. Ze bed is not made." As though nothing was happening, Einstein gently rose with a smile on his lips, walked calmly towards the door, opened it and waved us in. The still small voice prevailed over the earthquake.

About this time a considerable earthquake actually occurred at Long Beach [near Pasadena]. I was in the office allotted to me and at once hastened back to the Athenaeum to see if all was well. On the way I passed Einstein and Gutenberg, a distinguished seismologist who had come to Pasadena with the hope of experiencing an earthquake. They were standing on the campus closely examining a large sheet of paper. Only later did it transpire that what they had been studying was the plan of a sensitive new seismograph and they had been so absorbed in it that they failed to notice the earthquake.

Einstein impressed all who met him with the gentleness and essential likeability of his character. His intellectual greatness, of course, came across. I never on any occasion saw him in the least degree ruffled, and there was not a trace of conceit or arrogance in his bearing towards anyone with whom I saw him.

Dimitri Marianoff, Einstein's stepson-in-law and biographer

We crossed the Channel to France. He was rejoining Elsa in Belgium, prior to a return to America, and I was returning to work in Paris. On the trip a really terrifying storm arose, the worst I have ever experienced. Everyone was terribly ill, even travelers who had crossed the Channel many times, and who had never known seasickness.

It did not move Albert. He was never prejudiced by how nature looked, whether it was a storm or an ocean gale. The beauty and mystery of it always transferred to him in terms of construction, never destruction. We crossed the English Channel at night. He was the only figure on deck. He stood, as I have often seen him, wrapped in an inflexible calm and an indescribable composure.

The ship was rolling fearfully, with no more weight, seemingly, than a walnut shell. The scene was a pandemonium of the elements enough to strike terror in any heart. I came up on deck twice to look at him. His attitude was a listening one, the roar of the waters, the threat of the height of the waves—he appeared to ignore what frightened human senses were attempting to convey.

A. V. Lunachansky, journalist and Soviet Commissar for Education

There is a dreamy expression in Einstein's near-sighted eyes, as if long ago he had named the greater part of his vision in his inner thoughts and kept it there. Nevertheless, Einstein (at 46) is a jolly fellow in company. He enjoys a good joke and readily breaks into peals of rollicking, childish laughter which momentarily changes his eyes into those of a child. His remarkable simplicity is so charming that one feels like hugging him or squeezing his hand or slapping him on the back—which in no way detracts from one's esteem for him. It is a strange feeling of tender affection for a man of defenseless simplicity mixed with boundless respect.

Count Harry Kessler, writer and man about town. He and Einstein took a train journey with fellow pacifists seeking support for their cause at the International Trades Union Conference in Amsterdam in 1921. Einstein's behavior amused the sophisticated Kessler, because everything delighted him, especially the sleeping car. When Kessler asked him if relativity applied to atoms, he noted Einstein's reply in his diary:

Einstein said that no size comes in to it here. So size, measurement, greatness or smallness, must be an *absolute,* indeed almost the sole absolute that remains, I said. Einstein confirmed that size is the ultimate factor, the absolute that cannot be got away from. He was surprised that I should have hit on this idea, for it is the deepest mystery of physics, the inexplicability and absoluteness of size. Every atom of iron is the same magnitude as every other atom of iron, no matter where in the universe it may be. Nature knows only atoms, whether of iron or hydrogen, of equal size, though human intelligence can *imagine* atoms of varying magnitude.

At a dinner party I gave for the Einsteins, he entered my house looking extremely dignified in a dinner jacket, but justified his "Bohemian" image by wearing heavy boots. He had put on a little weight and had recently lectured before the Franco-Palestine Society. His eyes still sparkled with almost childlike radiance and twinkling mischief. Elsa kept the table amused with tales of her husband's indifference to the medals he had been awarded. She had had to remind him repeatedly to go to the Foreign Ministry to pick up two gold medals awarded by the British Royal Society and Royal Astronomical Society. When they met afterwards to go to the movies and she asked him what the medals looked like, he had no idea. He hadn't even bothered to open the packages.

German physicist and Nobelist Werner Heisenberg. During the Fifth Solvay Conference in 1927, Heisenberg witnessed a discussion between Einstein and Bohr about quantum theory and Heisenberg's equally controversial Uncertainty Principle, an encounter that John Wheeler described as "the strangest debate in the history of the understanding of the world."

Einstein's friend Paul Ehrenfest said, "Einstein, I am ashamed of you. You are arguing about the new quantum theory just as your opponents argue about relativity." But even this friendly admonition went unheard. Once again it was driven home to me how terribly difficult it is to give up an attitude on which one's entire scientific approach and career has been based. Einstein was not prepared to let us do what, to him, amounted to pulling the ground from under his feet.

American artist Samuel Johnson Woolf

Woolf persuaded Einstein to let him paint his portrait. During the sittings, Woolf took notes: "He has a perpetual quizzical expression. Often smiles in a quiet, embarrassed way. Has a bashful, malleable quality, almost childlike, accentuated by his wife's attitude to him. A sweet, motherly woman, she treats Einstein like a doting parent with a precocious child. Talking, he appears to be thinking of other things, gazing, he does not appear to be seeing the object at which he looks. These peculiarities are so marked as to appear almost abnormal." Einstein approved the portrait and asked Woolf for a photo of it.

Later, when Woolf returned with the photo Einstein studied it then hurried into the library from which moments later Woolf heard pounds as if he was wrecking the place.

"Come with me," Elsa said to Woolf, urgently. "I know what he's doing."

When they entered the library, Einstein was manhandling an immense framed painting of himself on the wall. As became clear to Woolf later, his approved portrait had reminded Einstein of how much he loathed this other one. "I've often told you to take this down," he complained to Elsa. "Now I'm going to do it. And if I see it around I'll put a knife through it!" It was too much for him to manage alone, so Woolf helped to remove it from the wall. After that, Einstein resumed his calm, friendly manner and saw the visitor out.

Otto Frisch, nuclear physicist

I was introduced to him while I was carrying a pack of books under each arm. Einstein stood and patiently held out his hand until I had reorganized myself. The quality that dominated his personality was a very great and genuine modesty. When anybody contradicted him he thought it over and if he found he was wrong he was delighted, because he felt that he had escaped from error and that now he knew better than before. There was an occasion when somebody accused him of saying something different from what he had said a few weeks previously, and Einstein replied, "Of what concern is it to the dear Lord what I said three weeks ago?" It was just his way of saying that it did not matter. It was wrong, and now he knew better.

Novelist and muckraking socialist Upton Sinclair

[Sinclair forgot to warn his wife, Mary Craig, of their expected visitor, so she was surprised when her sister, Dolly, said,] "There's an odd-looking old man walking up and down the street and staring. He keeps looking at the house as if he wants to come in." Dolly went out and asked him what he wanted and came back to report, "He says he's Professor Einstein."

Such was the beginning of as lovely a friendship as anyone could have in this world. I report him as the kindest, gentlest, sweetest of men. He had a keen wit and a delightful sense of humor and his tongue could be sharp—but only for the evils of the world.

Mary Craig Sinclair, wife of novelist Upton Sinclair

From first to last the discoverer of relativity never refused a single request that we made of him. If it was a labor struggle, he would write a telegram of sympathy for the strikers, and Upton would give it to the press. If it was a meeting on behalf of free speech, he would sit on the platform, and make a few remarks when requested. If it was a demonstration of Jan Roman Ostoja's psychic powers, he would attend and manifest deep interest. [In fact, he was a skeptic.]

Physician and friend Thomas Bucky

When my father was a physician in Berlin, Einstein's step-daughters, Margot and Ilse, were among his patients. In 1932, when I was thirteen, my parents and brother, Peter, and I were invited to visit the Einsteins in their summer home at Caputh, a few miles outside Berlin. I was very nervous and excited and at first, when I met him, disappointed, because although he was very polite, I sensed a feeling of reserve on his part. I was surprised when he started a conversation with me and seemed to be interested in my opinions. I kept thinking: here I am talking with a genius, the greatest man of our time.

Yo-yos, those little tops that spin up and down on a string, were all the rage at the time, and Einstein had one. He broke the ice by playing with it. I told him that it was off balance and showed him a few tricks with it, explaining that it needed a loop at the end of the string for him to be able to do tricks like free-wheeling, etc. He really seemed interested in the device. By this time I felt at ease and realized that what

A whiz on a bicycle or sailing on a boat, Einstein never drove a car. Thomas Bucky is at the wheel of a Model A Ford in New York City, with his mother, Frida, and Einstein's sister, Maja, in the front and Einstein and Gustav Bucky in the rumble seat.

I took to be reserve was simply his extreme shyness. But even so he was a man who said what he thought.

After dinner, for example, when my mother congratulated Mrs. Einstein on the meal, she replied, "Oh, it was nothing. I didn't go to any extra trouble. We eat like this every night." And Einstein said, "What! We eat like THIS—EVERY night?" obviously showing that they didn't. I think Mrs. Einstein blushed when he said that. You see, he was honest. She wasn't—quite. She was social.

Einstein became absolutely my second father, and I didn't hesitate to discuss politics with him and express my opinions, and was never afraid to challenge him in debate, for he welcomed even the perhaps half-baked opinions of a teenager. He was very tolerant but he despised yes-men, sniffed them out and avoided them. Einstein was a humanist, socialist, and a democrat. He saw no big bugaboo in socialism if it was not totalitarian. He was completely antitotalitarian, no matter whether it was Russian, German, or South American. He approved of a combination of capitalism and socialism. And he hated all dictatorships of the right or left.

Einstein, followed by his friend and occasional chauffeur Thomas Bucky, in the 1930s.

I never saw him lose his temper, never saw him angry, or bitter, or vain, or jealous, worried, impatient, or personally ambitious. He seemed immune to such feelings. But he had a shy attitude toward everybody. Yet he was always laughing, and he often laughed at himself. There was nothing stuffy about him. Still, he was aloof, always shy, hesitant. Einstein had a shell around him that it was not easy to penetrate.

Frida Bucky, Thomas Bucky's mother

A kind of wall of air separated Einstein from his closest friends, and even from his family—a wall behind which, in his flights of fancy, he had created a world of his own. People sometimes glanced at Einstein as if something mystical had touched them—and they smiled at him. And when Einstein caught this smile, he happily returned it. He loved the simple, uncomplicated person who, not recognizing him, felt his humanity.

Anonymous

During the Einsteins' house-hunting in the 1930s, they were shown a house in Princeton. The porcelain in the bathroom was all lavender. Albert Einstein clasped his hands in ecstasy and exclaimed, "This bathroom is sympathetic to me! This bathroom is sympathetic to me!" Another house was selected.

Leon Watters, a close friend

When I first met Einstein in Pasadena I had mentioned a somewhat rare book which I had acquired titled "Memorabilia Mathematica," and which contained interesting anecdotes concerning famous mathematicians and physicists. Einstein had expressed a desire to see it. Accordingly, on Sunday afternoon, March 13, 1934, I motored over to his home at No. 2, Library Place, in Princeton. Arriving there I asked my chauffeur, Martin Flattery, to go to the door, ring the bell and ask if I might see the professor. He came back to the car and reported that a lady had told him that the Einsteins were not at home. I wrote a short note and asked the chauffeur to leave it at the house with the book I had brought. While thus engaged I discerned someone looking through the curtained window and motioning to Martin. He went to the door again and came running back with a broad grin on his face, saying I was to come in.

As I crossed the threshold Mrs. Einstein grasped my hand warmly and was most abject in apologizing, explaining that she had to resort to subterfuge to shield themselves from incessant annoyance by visitors. After a short chat she called out, "Albert," and in a moment Einstein came down the stairs. He had on a worn grey sweater, a pair of baggy trousers and slippers, holding a pipe in his hand, and greeted me warmly.

He set me at once at ease. I then told him about the Hebrew Technical Institute which guided young Jewish boys into other channels than the usual needle trades. He listened attentively, expressed an interest in such work and invited me to stay for further discussion. He told me of the innumerable demands being made upon him to appear at functions of every type, to accept which would leave him no time for his own work or his leisure and which he had to uniformly decline. Before I was about to reconcile myself to a refusal of my request, he added, "Not for a cause like yours. I will gladly come." On leaving at about six-thirty I had the feeling that I had made the beginning of a lasting friendship.

Hiram Haydn, editor of the American Scholar*: When Haydn was in Princeton with Christian Gauss, the dean of Princeton University, a street encounter with Einstein was an epiphany that left him speechless.*

There was light coming out of his face—that light grew there, as hairs do on the faces of men. It seemed to me that this was not a man in the ordinary sense, that the face belonged to another, different species. And then he smiled at me. This act constituted the most religious experience of my life. At the tea [for Einstein] that followed I sat alone in a corner, shaken by the meeting. When Christian had driven me back to the inn, he detained me briefly with his hand on my arm. "Such moments," he said, "tear a rent in ordinary perceptions, cut a hole in the fabric of things, through which we see new visions of reality."

Eugene Wigner, winner of the Nobel Prize in Physics and Einstein's Princeton neighbor

I knew Einstein from 1920 on. I first saw him in the Physics Colloquia in Berlin on a Thursday afternoon. Einstein sat in the first row with other notables like Nernst and von Laue. If something was unclear, he asked questions, tried to explain the physics. Later I attended a seminar on statistical mechanics by Einstein. There were 25 to 30 participants. Einstein gave people topics to review, keeping himself in the background. He would speak up when he realized that the rest of the audience did not understand. He was marvelous at explaining things—he could demonstrate mathematics with his hands. He was very modest, just one of the audience. Since the subject was not relativity, he could be more of an equal to the others, for it was not his ideas that were being discussed. The way he behaved was very charming, and that was even more unusual in Germany at that time. Since he was the director of the Max Planck Institute [called Kaiser Wilhelm Institute at that time, KWI for short], he had no obligation to give such a seminar. All of us were in Einstein's shadow. Just knowing him well helped you to find a job in physics. Most great men are respected, but Einstein also inspired real affection. He had a great many lovable traits.

I worked at the KWI for physical chemistry right next door, and for a long time did not even know that Einstein was the director since he was entirely on an equal basis. Concepts seemed to occur to him, fully realized. Their flaws and implications he saw immediately. He worked to polish his work, but playfully, with a clear idea of what he would find in the end. I could not think quite at Einstein's level, but then no one could.

Einstein's modesty was being tested in 1921 by his great and growing fame. He had already recast the very foundations of modern physics. He was awarded the Nobel prize that year for finding the photoelectric effect; and yet we knew that [it], inspiring as it was, was not his masterwork.

At Princeton his relation to his colleagues and students was much less close. Part of the reason is that he was not at home in English, and that is really needed for a nice conversation. Listening to a speech in English was hard for him. He always said "E quadrat" instead of "E squared." Now that's just as good—but it isn't English. Einstein knew that and it made him a bit uneasy with English speakers. Another reason was that he was preoccupied with his great concern for the political situation. A third reason was that his interest was to modify General Relativity to make a common basis for all of physics, or all of science. His colleagues at the Institute for Advanced Study, on the other hand, were mathematicians, and they had the large influence. The interest of most physicists was application of quantum mechanics, to incorporate chemistry into physics or to apply quantum mechanics to the theory of atoms and molecules, to the properties of metals, and to the principles of chemistry.

Einstein wanted basic knowledge. Eisenhart was interested in the basis of General Relativity, but in the rigorous mathematics, and was averse to speculations about unification with electromagnetism. So Einstein's contacts were confined to a small circle of collaborators and a few friends who could speak German.

Einstein certainly loved children and perhaps my favorite memory of him involves my own children. Around 1950, my wife took some pages of my physics work to Einstein's home one day. He asked her about our small children and she had to admit that they had the chicken pox. Local health regulations had forced her to leave them in the car. Einstein said, "Oh, I have had chicken pox already. Seeing them for a moment surely won't hurt me." And he proceeded to walk down to the car and have a long talk with my children, which they can still recall. I doubt that Einstein even knew what chicken pox was. But he knew what children were.

At Princeton I got to know Einstein quite well and we were, I believe, both open and sincere in our discussions. He did not talk about his personal life, about family and so on.

I doubt that Einstein regretted his flaws as a father or husband. It was enough for him to think about physics and about great human problems. While most men were thinking, "Now, where is my wife? And what shall we have for dinner tonight?" Einstein was wondering, "Oh, why are there Nazis in this beautiful world?" We talked about physics, and what was perhaps even more important than this, about the political situation. That we discussed very much. He was preoccupied with Hitler's plans to subjugate Jews and conquer the world. Perhaps he was less anxious about it than I was, but he was concerned in his own profound way.

We often took walks together and discussed things privately, in German. Alexander Sachs spoke about Einstein's "great shyness and humility," and he called him "a really saintly scientist." I don't know what saintly means, but he surely was very friendly, very humane, very understanding of human problems, and a very nice and kind person. He wanted to be equal to others. He didn't want to be somewhere floating in the air.

He liked jokes and we discussed such questions as, "If we don't look at the moon, does it exist?" Einstein believed very much in objective reality, and his answer would be, "Yes, the moon does exist whether we look at it or not."

The news about nuclear fission had been brought to Princeton by Niels Bohr. We heard also that the Germans forbade the exportation of uranium from Czechoslovakia. This alarmed us, as every physicist who knew about the fission process knew that there is a danger that a bomb based on a nuclear chain reaction can be created [with uranium]. In Chicago we received a cable from Fritz Houtermans, an Austrian who was in Switzerland in connection with the German work on uranium fission: And the cable read "Hurry up! We are on the track!" He was fundamentally opposed to Hitler and felt that all freedom would be endangered if Hitler's men succeeded to make the atomic bomb before the United States could. He tried to say we should hurry up and get it before they did.

Leo Szilard and I were good friends and we were worried that if the Germans got hold of the uranium deposits in the Belgian Congo they could use it to make an atomic bomb. I did not take that as seriously as Szilard did, because in 1939 the Germans had enough uranium from Czechoslovakia to make the atomic bomb.

We wondered how we could warn the Belgian government to prevent the Germans from getting it. We knew Einstein was a friend of the queen mother of the Belgians, and thought that a warning letter from Einstein to her might help. I knew Einstein was not in Princeton in July 1939, but in a summer resort on Long Island. I had never been there before. All we knew was that Einstein was staying in a cabin owned by a Dr. Moore at Peconic, Long Island. I drove Szilard in my car to Peconic and when we arrived there we asked several people how to get to Dr. Moore's cabin. And none of them knew. So after half an hour we decided to give up and return to Princeton. Then we saw a boy of about fifteen, and instead of asking for Dr. Moore's cabin, Szilard asked, "Where does Einstein stay?" The boy knew that and we went to the address and found him.

We arrived on a summer afternoon in July 1939 and there he was dressed in an old shirt and unpressed pants. He didn't express any surprise at seeing us. He was a very friendly person. We sat inside the house and, speaking in German, told Einstein about the process which was discovered in Germany [by Otto Hahn and Lise Meitner] as well as the possibility of using it to set off an explosion.

I don't think, as has been reported, that Einstein said, "That never occurred to me," because he had not known about the process. So that statement is unlikely. He did remark that for the first time in history men would tap energy from a source other than the sun. Most of us scientists realized that a chain reaction is possible, and there is a danger that it will lead to an explosion. I believe I had already spoken with Einstein a few weeks before about a possible nuclear chain reaction, but only lightly. On this July day, we spoke deeply. Einstein was deeply involved in his own work, and unlikely to have been following the latest developments in physics.

The papers he got, like *Nature*, he often left unread, unless there was something of specific interest to him. It is not possible to read all the journals one receives. I received about eighty-three a week.

It is true that Einstein did not foresee that nuclear energy would be released in his time. He believed, however, that it was scientifically possible. He did not know about the discovery of fission, but we told him about it. We explained the fission process and he understood it in fifteen minutes. I was very impressed that he realized the problem of the atomic bomb as a possibility in such a short time. And he became very much aware of the political problem. So Einstein accepted our warning that there is a possibility that the Germans will produce atomic bombs and conquer the earth. Of course, the Germans could have conquered the earth without the nuclear chain reaction. After he had asked us about seven or eight questions, Einstein dictated a letter in German to President Roosevelt [deciding to write to FDR rather than the Belgian queen mother] and I wrote it down and took it to Princeton. He didn't sign it because it was in German and in handwriting. Einstein signed it after I had translated it into English and had it typed. Eventually,

Alexander Sachs took the letter to Roosevelt. I think it was a fair comment of Einstein's when he said: "My participation in the production of the atomic bomb consisted of one single act—I signed a letter to President Roosevelt."

Einstein was not a nuclear physicist and he knew very little about the subject. He did not know about the Manhattan Project and was quite surprised in 1943 when an explosion was produced. Later, Einstein wrote a second letter to Roosevelt suggesting that the atomic bomb not be exploded against the Japanese. The letter arrived on the President's desk two days after [Roosevelt's] death.

I think Szilard and I also discussed that second letter with Einstein. We were at the time both convinced that it was not the right thing to use the bomb. Since then I read a book that says the explosion of the atomic bomb saved a million and a half Japanese lives [by precluding the need for the Allies to invade the Japanese mainland]. And I was surprised, because, you see, what we proposed is to explode it over uninhabited territory to show the effect of it. I know the military objection was, first, they had very few atomic bombs in the arsenal and, second, they were not sure the bomb would explode.

But I was surprised by the comment in the book. And I asked a Japanese friend whether that is so, and he said, "Yes, an explosion over uninhabited territory would have had no effect."

Einstein strongly approved of the creation of Israel. We all agreed that Israel's existence was very good, at least for the Israelis. He had no regrets that he rejected the offer to be Israel's president after the death of Weizmann. He thought he would not be a good president. He didn't want to see fifty people every day. He was not an administrator.

Meyer Weisgal, president of the Weizmann Institute in Israel

He seemed to me a very shy man who did not really belong to our physical world, despite the fact that his genius lay in revealing to us the secrets of this physical world. He would rather probe its mysteries than confront the glare of public adulation. After Dr. Weizmann's death in 1952, Mr. Ben-Gurion, naively, I believe, had a brainwave and asked the Israeli ambassador in Washington to enquire from Einstein whether he would take the presidency. If B. G. had asked me, I would have told him not to waste his time. Einstein was as far removed from the trappings, pomp, and circumstance of a presidential office as I am or you are from an understanding of the theory of relativity.

"The offer from my Israeli brethren moved me deeply," Einstein told a friend later. "But I declined straight away with genuine regret. Although many a rebel has become a bigwig, I couldn't make myself do that." To Ben-Gurion's relief. Awaiting Einstein's response, he had asked his assistant, Yitzak Navon, the future president, "Tell me what to do if he says yes! I've had to offer the post to him because it's impossible not to. But if he accepts we're in for trouble."

Alan Richards, photographer. In 1945 Princeton University assigned Richards to take an official photograph of Albert Einstein.

I climbed the slightly rickety stairs to his study, expecting to find him in a wing collar, and frock coat. With all the dignity of his genius. Instead, he was dressed in baggy slacks and an old sweater, his mustache straggly, his hair looking as if it hadn't been cut or combed in months. I was appalled. I wondered why, since he hadn't done anything about the rest of his face, he had bothered to shave. Once when I brought him a dozen extra prints of a particularly good portrait to give to friends, he had shoved the whole group aside. "I hate my pictures," he said then. "Look at my face. If it weren't for this," he added, clapping his hands over his mustache in mock despair, "I'd look like a woman." On another occasion, when a young couple at whose wedding he had been best man, brought their son—a little boy of 18 months to meet him, the child took one look and burst into a screaming fit. The parents were speechless with embarrassment but Einstein's eyes lighted up. He smiled approvingly, patted the youngster on the top of his head, and crooned, "You're the first person in years who has told me what you really think of me."

Ilya Ehrenburg, a leading Russian writer and a war correspondent who had interviewed Churchill and De Gaulle

I thought I had lost the faculty for feeling surprise: I had flown across the ocean . . . met many famous and a few great men, lived through three wars, the Revolution, fascism, victory, and yet, quite unexpectedly, on 14th May 1946 I was struck dumb, like a child who for the first time witnesses some extraordinary natural phenomenon: I was taken to Princeton and found myself face to face with Einstein. When I met him he was sixty-seven years old; his grey hair, worn very long, gave him something of the look of a nineteenth-century musician or hermit. His features were sharp, clear-cut, and his eyes astonishingly young, by turns sad, alert or concentrated, then suddenly full of mischievous laughter like a boy's. He was young with the youth that years cannot subdue; he himself expressed it in this casual phrase: "I live and feel puzzled, and all the time I try to understand."

On the way from New York to Princeton I felt nervous: what should I, an ignoramus, be able to talk about to a great scientist? I confided my apprehensions to the Jewish writer Brainin who was taking me to Princeton. He replied that Einstein was a simple man and that he had asked to meet me because he was interested in Russia and the threat of a new war. As soon as Einstein began to talk my fears evaporated. Everything amazed me: his appearance, his life story, his wisdom, his spirit of challenge, but above all the fact that I was actually drinking coffee with Einstein while he talked to me.

I remembered Langevin saying in 1934: "Einstein has

upset the whole of natural science. Before him physicists thought that everything was known, but he has proved that there is another way of looking at things. Modern physics begins with him, and not only physics, but all modern science."

Of Americans, Einstein said: "They're like little children, sometimes charming, sometimes unruly. It's bad when children start playing with matches. It's better if they play with bricks. They're very good at forgetting here. During the war the average American's reaction to the word 'Stalingrad' was to take off his wristwatch and send it to a Red Army man. Today you get a very different reaction to that word from many people: show the Russians we've got the atomic bomb. Of course it's a result of the press campaign. I read a hair-raising account of Hiroshima in the *New Yorker* [by John Hershey]. I ordered a hundred copies by telephone and distributed them among my students. One of them thanked me and said, 'What a marvelous bomb!' Of course there are other kinds of people. But all this is very painful."

He went back to the bomb: "You see, the greatest danger lies in trusting logic. You feel certain that 2 and 2 makes 4. I don't. It's a terrible thing that Roosevelt died when he did; he wouldn't have let it happen."

[Ehrenburg knew that Einstein was interested in the Black Book: diaries, letters, and statements by eyewitnesses concerning Nazi crimes against Jews in the occupied territories. Ehrenburg had brought some of the documents with him, which Einstein examined closely.]

Then he said, "I have often said that the potentialities of knowledge are unlimited, as is the knowable. Now I think that vileness and cruelty also has no limits."

[Ehrenburg told Einstein that he was going to the south to see how "Negroes lived."]

"They live in terrible conditions," Einstein said. "It's shameful. The actions of the legislatures in the Southern

States are covered by some of the counts of the Nuremburg indictment."

[Later, when he and Ehrenburg were in the garden being photographed, Einstein recalled how a beautiful young woman, in defending racial discrimination, had asked him what he would say if his son told him he was going to marry a Negro.] "I don't know," Einstein said that he had replied. "I'd probably ask to meet his fiancee. But if my son announced that he wanted to marry you I should certainly lose both sleep and appetite." [As Einstein said this, Ehrenburg wrote,] "his eyes lit up with a challenging gleam."

[Einstein asked if he often saw Stalin. Ehrenburg said that he'd never met him.]

"A pity," Einstein said. "I should like to have known what he was like as a man. A Communist told me that I was behind the times, exaggerating the role of the individual. Of course, I'm not a Marxist but I know well enough that the objective world exists outside the individual's subjective appraisals. And yet the individual plays a most important part. I can picture Lenin to myself far better: I've read about him, met people who'd known him. He commands respect not only as a politician but also as a man of high moral integrity."

[As Ehrenburg was leaving, Einstein said:] "The main thing now is to prevent an atomic catastrophe. It's a good thing that you've come to America. I hope more Russians will come and talk to us. Mankind must prove itself more intelligent than Epimetheus who opened Pandora's box and could not shut it again. Au revoir. Come again."

[Ten days later Ehrenburg heard Einstein speaking over the radio about the need to come to an agreement with the Russians to renounce atomic weapons and to disarm rather than arm.]

In this way, he tried to shut Pandora's box.

Ashley Montagu, anthropologist and social biologist

I was planning a film on both the dangers and the possible advantages of atomic energy for the Federation of American Scientists and phoned my Princeton neighbor, Einstein, for advice.

Helen Dukas answered the phone and when I said it was for a film, she got excited and said, "Oh, Hollywood!" And I said, "No, Pennsylvania." She spoke to Einstein about it and he immediately came to the phone and invited me over to discuss the subject.

My first sight of him was very interesting. I don't know whether he was fond of dancing or not, but I have been all my life. It was very striking. There's a long corridor in the house and he was at the other end when Miss Dukas called him and said I was here. And he seemed to glide towards me in a sort of un-deliberate dance. It was enchanting, as if Einstein were walking on air. It was maybe the way someone else might whistle as they moved. He danced. He seemed somehow to be expressing his love of music as he moved.

He asked me to read the script of the film to him—it took less than fifteen minutes—and he didn't respond until I'd finished. Then he said, "A-one. It's just right." The title was taken from a book published earlier that year, edited by Robert Oppenheimer, *One World or None*. Einstein liked the title.

When I asked how one could get people interested in seeing that nuclear energy isn't misused, he replied, "International law." When I said, "Professor Einstein, international law exists only in textbooks on international law." Einstein exclaimed that that was really an outrageous remark, then took the pipe out of his mouth and thought for several minutes. He finally said, almost mournfully, "You're quite right."

Ernst Straus, Einstein's scientific assistant

Frequently, if I brought up a mathematical argument that seemed to him unduly abstract, he would say, "I am convinced but not convinced," that is to say, he could no longer get out of agreeing that it was correct, but he did not yet feel that he had understood why it was so. For, in order to convince himself that something was so, he had to reduce it to a certain simplicity of concept.

I. F. Stone, newspaperman and political gadfly

I didn't have much personal contact with Einstein until I started *I. F. Stone's Weekly* and he was a charter subscriber. I was so thrilled I wrote to his secretary and said could we please frame the check instead of using it? And she said, "No. Everybody wants to frame his checks and it ruins his bank account. So please cash it." And they will send the check back to me after it had passed through the bank. Which they did. I still have that original check.

He felt I was carrying on the fight he so deeply believed in against fascism and he invited me and my family—my wife, daughter and two sons—to visit him. It was a little like going to tea with God. Not the terrible old God of the Bible, but the little child's father in heaven. Very kind, very wise, and yet himself very much like a child, too.

I know Ashley Montagu said that he was like a good Jewish mother, but I didn't have the same impression, that is being a Jew and having a Jewish mother. Jewish mothers are very overrated. They tend to engulf their children in overprotectiveness. A Yiddisher momma is not at all what's she's cracked up to be. I thought of him as a very benevolent person, benevolent in a saintly sense. He was more than kindly. He was loving. A gentile reading about Jewish mothers might very well have thought, "That's a Jewish mother." On the other hand, Ashley Montagu is an authority on the impalpable—on witchcraft, and might have very good insight. So I don't dispute it. I just don't think that way about it. I don't think there is a large feminine component in men of great talent.

I loved Einstein. Incidentally, his friend, Otto Nathan, has stated that Einstein had asked to see my *Weekly* [*I. F. Stone's Weekly*] on his deathbed.

Christopher Stone, I. F. Stone's son

What struck me was the speaking styles of Einstein and my father. My father spoke more quickly and with a certain energy, like a chess player under a time clock, and was ready to move on as quickly as possible to the next question. Einstein had a much slower pace. Anytime he didn't understand the question, or what underlay it, he wanted to clarify. He took command of the pace of the exchange in a slow, professional style that was superb, making sure that he grasped everything. There was no pretense. You really felt such modesty, and as if there was an envelope around him that seemed so settled. He had such a center.

My own dad was full of movement and potential movement, and in contrast to Einstein, who settled back in a stuffed chair and put his feet up on a hassock. His voice was so marvelously German and his English full of charm.

The menace of the McCarthy witch hunt for communists dominated their conversation and parallels were drawn with the situation in Hitler's Germany. [Or, as I. F. Stone put it: "I don't think Einstein let that vulgar, hysterical fart Joseph McCarthy upset him. Although he must have seen McCarthy's political adventurism as a foretaste of what had happened in Germany."]

George Wald, winner of the Nobel Prize in Medicine

Soon after the end of World War II, I was going from Harvard to a meeting in Princeton. I had a gap of a little time in the course of the meeting and hoped to see Einstein then.

Harvard biologist and Nobelist George Wald
spent "precious" time with Einstein, with
whom he discussed the mysterious universe.

Philipp Frank, a philosopher of physics at Harvard, knew Einstein well and he wrote me an introductory letter to him.

I very much looked forward to meeting Einstein. It wasn't just curiosity. You see, there was a generation of physicists in the first half of this century. Their like doesn't exist now. I don't know why. I don't think it's because the protoplasm of physicists has changed since then. They were in constant correspondence, conversation, contacts of every kind. They climbed mountains together and cooked their meals over an open fire together. There was a continuous rubbing on one another. In the course of that each of them became something more than he would otherwise have been. And they felt they had the universe by the short hairs.

Of that generation I knew only Einstein and Bohr.

On that visit to Einstein, I asked him at a certain point in the conversation would he please explain to me his friendly controversy with Niels Bohr involving the real meaning of the Uncertainty Principle? [Werner Heisenberg's Uncertainty Principle states that it is impossible to determine simultaneously the exact position and velocity of a subatomic particle. His principle does not apply to larger material—from a grain of sand to a planet.]

And Einstein, in a nice elementary way, went ahead and did just that. He never accepted the Uncertainty Principle as an ultimate expression of reality, saying at one point, "Never is a long time." And that it might be possible to get inside, technically, the limits set by the Uncertainty Principle.

It's interesting that the progress of science overtook what he was saying. For instance, he said to me at one point, "We've never seen the other face of the moon, but I'm sure it has another face."

He was a very easy person to converse with and rather jolly. He'd say something and then lean back and laugh. Being with him was a great and relaxing pleasure. He was a lovely person and any time with him was precious. Although he wasn't talking down to me, he was being very gentle with me.

He then pointed out: How can one be sure, if one closes one's eyes, that the chair one has seen a moment before, on opening one's eyes, one sees the same chair? And, though one believes that it must be there all the time, this can't be demonstrated.

Another time he said to me, "Science has become a Tower of Babel. All my life I have avoided this Tower of Babel." Soon after I was interviewed on TV and mentioned the Tower of Babel. One of my colleagues here at Harvard said, "I heard you were on TV last night. What was the funny thing you said about some kind of tower?" Einstein, and I'm one too, was a Bible reader. I don't think he read it religiously. Certainly I do not, but it's very much at the base of our culture. And one can save a lot of time and space by referring to the Tower of Babel, or any of those bits of Biblical mythology provided you are talking to people who are familiar with those myths, like Balam's ass speaking.

He meant that we are living in the midst of an information explosion. It began seriously after World War II. C. P. Snow helped it out in his book *The Two Cultures*, when he reproached the Western world for not producing scientists and engineers on the same scale that the Soviet Union did. After Sputnik the West began to produce scientists and other technical people at an enormously increased rate. It's had some unfortunate consequences and we're paying a heavy price for that. One finds very few, and I think this is what Einstein was referring to, broadly based scientists who can think with a wide view outside their own specialty.

I met Einstein again in 1952 when I was giving the Vanuxem Lectures at Princeton, to which he came.

Before the first lecture we were walking up and down the street in front of the lecture hall. Suddenly he turned and asked me, why did I think all the natural amino acids were left-handed, as they are. I had my head on that lecture I was about to begin in a few minutes and just mumbled something.

Then he said, "For many years I wondered why the electron came out negative. Negative, positive. Those are perfectly symmetrical concepts in physics. [The electron, discovered by J. J. Thomson in 1897, is a fundamental particle of electricity and matter, and electrons exist in all atoms as planetary particles revolving around the nuclei. The electron always carries a negative charge.]

"So why is the electron negative?" he said. "I thought about this for a long time. Finally, all I could think was—it won in the fight!"

And I promptly said, "That's exactly what I think about those left-handed amino acids. They won in the fight!"

The fight he was talking about was the conflict between matter and antimatter, between the negative electrons and the positive electrons, which had already been discovered and which on contact mutually annihilated each other.

When an electron comes into contact with a positron there

is mutual annihilation. The masses of both are annihilated and turned into radiation, according to Einstein's famous formula $E = mc^2$, in which E is the energy of the radiation, m the mass that has been annihilated, and c^2 this tremendous number: c is the speed of light, three times ten to the tenth centimeters per second. So, annihilating even a tiny bit of mass yields a lot of radiation.

As Einstein said in our conversation, positive and negative are perfectly symmetrical concepts in physics. So it is expected that exactly equal amounts of particles and antiparticles entered into the Big Bang. If they then mutually annihilated, we would have been left with a universe containing only radiation, no matter. How come we have a universe of matter?

So there are two possible solutions.

One is that some of the astronomical bodies we see at really great distances might be made of antimatter. Everything close by seems to be matter, and no antimatter.

But we can't be sure that astronomical bodies at great distance from us are made of antimatter rather than matter—because they would look to us exactly the same. All our information concerning them comes to us through radiation and radiation doesn't care. Radiation consists of photons which, as they say, are their own antiparticles. So that's one thought, that perhaps there are places in the universe which are made of antimatter, and other places like our own part of the universe which are made of matter.

The latest thought is that in the Big Bang that started our universe, what came into being were exactly equal amounts of matter and antimatter, or particles and their antiparticles. In that fireball of the Big Bang packed to an almost unimaginable degree, these were in contact and there must have been an enormous firestorm of mutual annihilation. And it's this radiation, the residue of the firestorm—discovered by Penzias and Wilson—that came out of the annihilation at the time of the Big Bang. It's by far the most radiation that exists in our universe. And, in fact, there are roughly one billion times as many photons of that radiation as there are protons and neutrons—the messy particles of our universe.

The present nicest thought is that what got into the Big Bang involved a tiny error of symmetry. And that to every billion particles of antimatter there were one billion and one particles of matter. When all the mutual annihilation was complete, one billionth remained. And that constitutes all the matter in our universe: all the galaxies, stars, planets, and all the life.

It's a strange and wonderful thought and it would have been a result of Einstein's "fight."

Einstein and Niels Bohr were without question the greatest persons I have ever met. There was a little the feeling, in the case of both of them, of meeting an Old Testament prophet. They were at once the greatest and the most *childlike* persons I have ever met. They both had accomplished that wonderful thing of becoming wiser and more learned children as they grew older.

One aspect of that was there were no fences around them, no boundaries beyond which they wouldn't go. They were interested in everything interesting. I thought sometimes of a man walking a puppy. The man walks a straight line, but the puppy's into everything. And they both went like the puppy. Both had a large capacity for enjoyment.

They were the leading spirits in the reworking of what physics makes of the universe, and beyond that changed ordinary people's attitudes towards reality to a fantastic degree. I would say, if anything, Einstein had more effect on lay attitudes; relativity in some sense really got to them in a way that quantum mechanics could not. All of us live with space and time and gravity. The world of elementary particles and atomic structure remains hidden.

In another conversation I had with him at Princeton, Einstein was very sadly saying that his great hope—which he worked on for many years—was to achieve a Unified Field Theory, and clearly he was not going to succeed, and someone else would have to do that.

Linus Pauling, winner of the Nobel Prize in Chemistry and the Nobel Peace Prize

Every time I came to Princeton, which was two or three times a year, perhaps 1948 was the first time, he invited my wife and me to come and talk with him. Each time, a dozen or so times, we spoke for about an hour in the study of his home at Mercer Street. The room had books in disorder on the shelves. The room itself was something like my own study. [He chuckled.] Sort of a mess. His room looked out over the garden at the back of the house.

Our conversations were pretty much concerned with world affairs—some talk about other people. My wife especially has emphasized that Einstein had a very good sense of humor. It was very well developed. He would break out into boisterous laughter telling a joke, or commenting on somebody. My wife and I were quite impressed with him.

The only minor eccentricity I observed was his habit of

Nobelist Linus Pauling and his wife, Ava Helen, enjoyed several memorable meetings with Einstein. They relished his sense of humor.

curling the hair on the back of his head with his finger while he was thinking. He would reach back and twist curls of hair around his finger.

I had the feeling that I was speaking with one of the greatest minds of our time, not because of the nature of the conversation or the presence of the man, but because I knew what he had done. I knew he was very smart from our talks together. And we got along extremely well. He was always friendly and relaxed.

I had accepted the invitation to be a member of the board of trustees of the Emergency Committee of Atomic Scientists. Einstein was also a member of the committee. He seemed to be interested in talking with me and my wife, more than with the other members of the board. Why? He expressed to me once the feeling that he and I thought about world problems in more nearly the same way than he and the other board members. And I would judge that his feelings about the Universe were essentially the same as mine.

He is quoted as having referred to God as "subtle but not malicious." That was his way of saying that Nature can be complicated—subtle—but not wicked in introducing aspects of Nature such as nonreproducibility, which would cause trouble for the scientist trying to understand Nature. And in his "God doesn't throw dice, " comment he was expressing the same thing. By God he meant Nature, and the dice comment, of course, referred to his dissatisfaction with quantum mechanics, where one makes predictions on a statistical basis only. He just couldn't accept that an event happens—such as emission of an alpha particle—by a random act, without anything in the past that would require that particular radium atom to emit the alpha particle.

Einstein has been criticized in that he rejected ideas in physics that essentially all other physicists had accepted—because they were displeasing to him. But this didn't interfere with his making important contributions.

With many older scientists, there's a failure to understand new ideas and then a rejection of them just because of lack of understanding. In Einstein's case, he understood, and in fact discussed the problems in as natural a way as anyone else. Yet he was still able to say that some parts of theoretical physics would be given up in time because of what he considered to be flaws.

Much of his physics was emotional or aesthetic, you could say. He believed that it would be possible to simplify the basic theories, and this is what he strove to do: to formulate the principles in mathematical terms that were aesthetically satisfactory to him, because of their simplicity and symmetry.

During our meeting on November 11, 1954, we probably spoke in English. Einstein had a good knowledge of English but he had a pronounced German accent. He first said: "I think I have made one mistake in my life to have signed that letter [to FDR]." Einstein didn't write the letter, of course. He just signed it. He may have edited it a bit. Then he went on to say: "But perhaps I may be excused because we were all afraid that the Germans would be getting the atomic bomb." He didn't say that he wouldn't have signed it had he known the Germans were not far advanced in their production of an atomic bomb.

Einstein was for perhaps a somewhat limited world government. My own feeling is that an all-powerful world government would be pretty dangerous, no matter who was in charge of it.

Einstein said to me something like: "Now that a single atomic bomb can destroy an entire city and kill a million people, war has become so irrational that we have to replace it by a better system for settling disputes between nations."

I think it's pure nonsense to call him a dupe of the Communists as some of his critics did. [Among them FBI chief J. Edgar Hoover—and which explains the FBI's huge Einstein file.] I have been accused of the same thing. I think he knew perfectly well who he was working for and against.

I remember Senator [Thomas] Hennings of Missouri at a hearing he held when I was present, saying to an assistant secretary of state: "Instead of Dr. Pauling following the Communist line, it seems to me that the Communists follow Dr. Pauling's line." I think that applies to Einstein, too.

On more than one occasion when Einstein came to the front doorway to say goodbye to us, people driving by in automobiles would stop in the street to look. He probably joked about it to us.

It's said that Einstein was interested in things rather than in people, that he didn't feel close even to members of his own family. But he didn't give the impression of being cold or remote. He always seemed, to me, warm and friendly.

Robert Oppenheimer, nuclear physicist

Einstein was one of the friendliest of men but he was also, in an important sense, alone. Many great men are lonely, yet I had the impression that although he was a deep and loyal friend, the stronger human affections played a not very deep or very central part in his life. I remember walking home with him on his seventy-first birthday. He said, "You know, when it's once been given to a man to do something sensible, afterward life is a little strange." His simplicity, his lack of clutter and his lack of cant, had a lot to do with his preservation throughout of a certain pure, rather Spinoza-like philosophical monism. There was always with him a wonderful purity at once childlike and profoundly stubborn.

John Kemeny, who eventually became Dartmouth's first Jewish president. A Hungarian refugee from the Nazis in World War II, Kemeny was having trouble with his thesis while studying to be a physicist at Princeton.

My thesis on mathematical logic was of no conceivable

interest to Einstein and about which he knew absolutely nothing. But a mutual friend, Paul Oppenheim, recommended that I talk it over with Einstein, who was looking for an assistant.

I had to describe to him what type theory was, what set theory was, what the problem was, and what I did with it. It must have taken me half an hour and I was feeling intensely guilty taking up his time. But he insisted on my doing this. He interrupted me with a number of questions to understand fully what I had done. And then my favorite line I'll never forget. He said: "That's very interesting. Now let me tell you what I'm working on," in exactly the same voice as if somehow the two of us were of equal importance.

I'm sure he interviewed other candidates, and then he offered me the job. Since I hadn't finished my thesis, he said, "Go home, finish it, and then come back." It took me a little over a month to finish it.

As a 22-year-old Hungarian refugee, John Kemeny became Einstein's assistant in 1948. Later, Kemeny was the first Jew to become president of Dartmouth College.

I regarded him with awe when I first met him. To anybody who worked in math or science Einstein was the greatest hero you idolized. But he was wonderful at putting people at their ease. There was something about his personal style, so understated and so warm. He would always talk to a professional as if he were an equal.

It was his last year on unified field theory. He had narrowed it down to one of three possibilities. Though similar, they had important differences. And the year was spent in trying to decide which of the three versions to publish. He did choose one at the end, and unified field theory was published a year after.

His secretary, Helen Dukas, clearly was an enormously important part of his life. She was technically his housekeeper, but she was a great deal more. She arranged his private life for him completely and guarded him from the outside world. She guarded his health, helped with his correspondence, and looked after him in every possible way. And, of course, she became quite knowledgeable about his work. She could certainly discuss relevant subjects as well as any intelligent layperson.

I remember a very interesting visitor to his office. A physicist, a student of Niels Bohr, was trying to convince Einstein that he was completely wrong about quantum mechanics, the hot subject of the day. The style of the two people was absolutely fascinating. First of all, Einstein remained firm but totally calm throughout the entire discussion. And the other man became more and more vehement. Einstein kept explaining patiently the things about quantum mechanics that bothered him. For example, that it implies action at a distance. And the more excited the other became, the more his arguments began, "Yes, but Bohr said so and so." While Einstein avoided saying anything about Bohr and talked substance, the other man continually quoted higher authority, which was Bohr. Einstein clearly got the better of the argument.

Several times during the year he said that he was absolutely convinced that there would be a unified field theory. He believed that the laws of the universe cannot be fragmented into relativity on the one side and quantum mechanics on the other. On that he was absolutely firm. He was not stubborn on whether *he* had found the right theory. But what he said was, "If there is a theory along the kind of lines I used to develop the general relativity theory, then I believe I have found the right one." Or maybe he said, "I'm sure I found the right one."

On the other hand, I've heard him say repeatedly that it may turn out that just as general relativity required an entirely new kind of mathematics, it's possible that the correct unified field theory would require mathematics Einstein did not even know. In which case, he said, "I will just never find it. Somebody else will have to find it." He may be right, but nobody yet knows whether the unified field theory is correct or incorrect.

He was extremely shy, not person to person, but in a group. Miss Dukas told me he was once mobbed in Atlantic City by an adoring group, which he found a frightening experience, and since then he shied away from being in large groups. Clearly one of his problems was that anybody could recognize him. He felt very comfortable in Princeton, and I've seen him in modest-sized groups being charming and relaxed. But crowds bothered him.

He was the *nicest* person I ever met. There was a childlike quality about him, but he was certainly not childish. He was only unexpected in the workings of his brain. I am not modest about my own brain; I have only met two human beings in my life whose brains were clearly in order of magnitude better than mine. One was Einstein. The other was Von Neumann, the mathematician, also a fabulous person.

Victor Weisskopf, physicist. Founder of The Bulletin for Atomic Scientists, *Weisskopf celebrated his retirement at MIT by playing the piano in a Beethoven trio and conducting an orchestra in a Brandenburg concerto. He also made music with Einstein.*

His violin playing was not as good as his physics. He was a real amateur. My piano playing was better than his fiddle.

Isidor Rabi, winner of the Nobel Prize in Physics

Whoever said Einstein wasted the last forty years of his life was ignorant or an Einstein hater. There are such. The world's full of them. He died at the age of seventy-six. Forty years brings you back to 1936, a few years after he came to the Institute for Advanced Study at Princeton. All I can say is, whoever criticized him has awfully high standards.

I knew Einstein and I think I understood his character. This man should be treated with great respect.

He once remarked to me in a discussion concerning the newly discovered meson: "We already know that the electron is quantized in charge and mass. Should not this be enough empirical information for a theory of matter?" It was a goal of this grandeur that drove him in his search for a unified field theory. Like a mystic who has had a divine illumination, Einstein in his search for the ideal could be satisfied with nothing less than a theory which would encompass all phenomena—atomic and cosmic.

Einstein was a unique personality. He was not attracted by fame or fortune, nor swayed by the opinions of the majority. He knew his talent and guarded it jealously against outside interference.

He was the prince of physics, and the imprint of his mighty strides will give direction to his beloved science for generations to come. Of the great scientists he was certainly the best of the century.

Abraham Pais, Einstein's colleague and biographer

He wasn't like the truly very great men I've met. He was a man in whom the child was still very much alive. He was not juvenile, ever, in his behavior, but something like the playful lust of the child somehow lived in him forever.

He often surprised me by showing a great perception of the real world. He might live his own style of life, but his eyes were very clear in his head. He knew quite well what the world was about. Not only the political and social world, but in his comment on an individual.

He would have laughed had he known that the FBI kept a file on him. [Apparently, he did know.]

David Ben-Gurion, Israeli premier: In 1951 Ben-Gurion visited Einstein in his Princeton home, and they sat together in the garden discussing universal truth.

Einstein's biographer and colleague Abraham Pais.

Einstein is a scientist who needs no laboratory, no equipment, no tools of any kind. He just sits in an empty room with a pencil and piece of paper, and his brain, thinking. He agreed [with me] even with his great formula about energy and mass, that there must be something behind the energy.

Martin Buber, philosopher: Einstein had known Buber for forty years. He told his son Hans Albert that each meeting with the philosopher was a great joy.

When I had once pressed Einstein hard to reveal his religious belief, he had replied: "What we physicists strive for is just to draw His lines after Him." [In my latest visit] we were delighted to discover that we both liked Ellery Queen mystery stories.

Arthur Komar, Princeton student

I remember Einstein coming to Palmer Physical Laboratory and giving a talk containing two striking comments. First: "The laws of physics should be simple." Someone in the audience asked, "But what if they are not simple?" Einstein replied, "Then I would not be interested in them."

Then Einstein was asked why he rejected quantum mechanics, and he said that he could not accept the concept of a priori probability. Which spurred someone else in the audience to say, "But you were the one who introduced a priori probability, in the A and B coefficients."

"Yes," he said, "and I have regretted it ever since. But when one is doing physics, one should not let one's left hand know what one's right hand is doing."

At the end of the lecture he sat down, leaned back, sighed, and said, "This is my last examination."

John Wheeler, physicist and Princeton neighbor

Einstein used to walk past my house on his way home from the Institute every day, and from time to time my chil-

Physicist John Wheeler (right), with Einstein and Japanese physicist H. Yakawa, in Princeton, New Jersey, in 1954. Wheeler's cat often strayed to Einstein's home.

dren's cat would follow him home. Soon afterwards there would be a telephone call from his home telling us not to worry—that our cat was there. Then my children would go to pick it up.

The debate between Einstein and Bohr, to my mind, is the greatest debate in intellectual history that I know about. In thirty years I never heard of a debate between two greater men over a longer period of time on a deeper issue with deeper consequences for understanding of this strange world of ours.

I. Bernard Cohen, Harvard historian of science and an expert on Isaac Newton: Einstein's last interview.

I arrived at Einstein's front door at exactly 10 A.M. on April 3, 1955, a cold spring morning. His secretary, Miss Dukas, took me to the second floor and said, "The visitor has arrived." Einstein emerged from his study, eyes shining as if he had been laughing or crying. He wore an open blue shirt, gray flannel pants, and leather slippers. He greeted me with a smile and went somewhere to get his pipe, then led the way back to his study. Dominating the whole room was a very large window looking out on a pleasant green view. The free spaces on the walls were occupied by portraits of the founders of electromagnetic theory, Faraday and Maxwell. After sitting in front of a little table, Einstein tucked a rug around his feet, and nodded for me to take a chair facing him.

He had a very beautiful and extraordinary face. It was contemplatively tragic, deeply lined, and yet had sparkling eyes that gave him a quality of agelessness.

I had a head full of questions but was so overcome with emotion that I couldn't say a word. After a while, Einstein came to the rescue, as if answering a question: "There are so many unsolved problems in physics," he said, "so much that we don't know and our theories are far from adequate." I mentioned something about the theory of photons and Einstein replied laughing, "Not a theory." He had very definite ideas as to what constituted a theory, and the theory of photons failed, because it did not give a complete account of optical phenomena.

He himself said we would have had special relativity theory, even if he hadn't lived. And he thought that the person most likely to have done it was Paul Langevin. But the implication was that no one except Einstein would have done the general theory.

He told me most emphatically that he thought the worst person to document any ideas about how discoveries are made is the discoverer. And that many people had asked him how he had come to think of this or that, but he had always found himself a very poor source of information about the genesis of his own ideas. He thought that the historian is likely to have better insight into the thought processes of a scientist than the scientist himself.

And [he mentioned] that, when what was thought to be an international committee was set up to investigate the claims [of priority for differential calculus], Newton anonymously directed the committee's activities. Einstein made a famous comparison apropos that controversy: that if Newton and Leibniz hadn't lived, we would still have had differential calculus. But if Beethoven hadn't lived, we wouldn't have had the Eroica Symphony.

Einstein also recalled with pleasure his visits to Mach, and said that Mach, Newton, Lorentz, Planck, and Maxwell were the scientists he most admired. In fact, they were the only ones Einstein ever accepted as his true precursors.

He spoke softly but clearly. He had a remarkable command of English, although he spoke with a marked German accent. And the contrast between the soft speech and ringing laughter was enormous. He enjoyed making jokes, and every time he made a point he liked, he would burst into booming laughter that would just echo from wall to wall. I had been prepared from having seen pictures to know what he would look like and what he would wear and I had heard the study described, but I was totally unprepared for this roaring, booming, friendly, all-enveloping laughter.

I tried to explain to Einstein how Newton believed that there had been a primitive Christianity that has somehow been corrupted and that some primitive original message was found in the Scriptures hidden behind some later corruptions. He therefore took certain important words and tried to find out their meaning in different usages. I thought Einstein would be interested to know how a scientifically minded man would treat such questions. On the contrary, Einstein said that he thought that this was a weakness in Newton and went on to explain why. It seemed to him that, if Newton found that his ideas were at variance with orthodox ideas, he ought to have rejected orthodox views. For instance, if Newton could not agree with the accepted interpretations of the

Scriptures, why did he believe the Scriptures were true all the same? I tried to explain that a man's mind is imprisoned by his culture and the environment that molds him, but I did not get very far, and it did not seem to me that I ought to press the point.

[Einstein was impressed when Cohen told him that Newton did not want his vast quantity of theological writings to be published, because, he said, it indicated that Newton realized that his theological conclusions were flawed and that he did not want to publish anything that did not meet his high standards.]

Then he said with great passion that, if Newton did not want to publish his own writings, he hoped no one else would. Obviously he was concerned with the problem of privacy because he had been so hounded by reporters and people who wanted every detail of his life all the time. On the other hand, he felt that it was permissible to publish the correspondence of great men because, if you wrote a letter and

Einstein entertained Quaker work campers at his home in the summer of 1954.

sent it, you clearly intended that it should be read. But even there he added a warning that some letters are personal and should be withheld.

He also discussed Velikovsky's shabby treatment by certain scientists. I think he misunderstood their position and thought they were trying to suppress Velikovsky's book, and Einstein was very strongly opposed to suppressing anyone's book, whether it was sense or nonsense. Shapley and others didn't want to suppress Velikovsky's book; they just didn't want it to appear under the guise of a sound textbook published by Macmillan, the leading scientific textbook publisher.

Einstein once said to Velikovsky: "Why can't you have a sense of humor about this criticism? Why are you so worked up about it?"

I feared I was tiring Einstein and got up to leave several times, but he pressed me to stay, saying, "There is still more to talk about."

When I finally began to descend the stairs, I was horrified to note that we'd been talking for almost two hours, and I turned to thank Einstein for the conversation, missed a step and almost fell.

Einstein chuckled and said, "You must be careful here. The geometry is complicated. You see, negotiating the stairs is not really a physical problem but a problem in applied geometry."

I was almost out of the door when Einstein called from his study, "Wait. Wait. I must show you my birthday present."

He returned, and he showed me what looked like a curtain rod with a cup on top and a ball attached to it by a piece of string. It was a gift from his neighbor Eric Rogers, the physics teacher whose children Einstein helped with their homework.

His eyes gleamed with delight as he demonstrated how the odd contraption illustrated the equivalence principle. He pressed the rod against the ceiling, then brought it down to the floor, and the ball popped into the cup.

Despite his age and the appearance of age, as shown by his

white hair and in his eyes, which were watering while we talked, I had the feeling of someone really filled with life and exuberance.

Philippe Halsman, photographer

Einstein's intervention on my behalf in 1940 resulted in my coming to this country and probably saved my life. My wife and I visited him often in Princeton. We came in contact with a human being full of empathy and warmth, always ready to oppose injustice, to fight for an underdog, or to help a victim. A man of rare selflessness and touching modesty.

I remember the heroic stoicism of his last months. He continued his work to the end, trying by sheer force of concentration to forget his tormenting pain. But I also remember his sense of humor, and his deep laughter still rings in my ears. Once he told us how on a bus ride an elderly lady was constantly staring at him. Finally she said, "I am sure that somewhere I must have seen your picture published. Will you, please, tell me who you are?" Prof. Einstein chuckled when he told us, "I said I was a photographer's model."

Abba Eban, Israeli statesman

One day in April 1955 our information officer in the consulate in New York, Reuven Dafni, called me to say that Einstein had written to express deep consternation at Israel's plight. I made my way to Mercer Street, in Princeton, with Dafni. Einstein opened the door to us himself. He was dressed in a rumpled beige sweater and equally disheveled slacks. This time he was without a tie as well as socks. He came straight to the issue. He said that the radio and television networks were always asking him for interviews, which he always refused. He now thought that if he had some "publicity interest" he might as well use it. Did I think that the media would be interested to record a talk by him to the

Einstein, Abba Eban (left), Moshe Sharrett (right), and an unknown man, at a New York dinner in honor of Chaim Weizmann, 1950.

American people and the world? I exchanged glances with Dafni, as if to say that this was the newspaperman's dream.

Einstein took out a pen, dipped it in an old-fashioned inkwell and began to scratch some sentences on a writing block. We soon decided that he needed more time and arranged for Dafni and me to come back and help him with the formulation of the text another day. Einstein courteously asked if we would like some coffee. Assuming that he would get a housekeeper or maid to produce the beverage, I politely accepted.

To my horror Einstein trotted into the kitchen from which we soon heard the clatter of cups and pots, with an occasional piece of crockery falling to earth, as if to honor the gravity theory of our host's great predecessor, Newton.

That night I spoke by telephone [to his wife] and added with calculated nonchalance, "Oh yes, I forgot. Einstein made coffee for me today." I was celebrating a splendid moment in my career of marital conversation.

When Dafni and I were to meet him [again] we were told that the professor had been taken to the hospital with an affliction of the aorta. A few days later he died. Among his papers were found the hand-written pages that he had prepared for the opening of his address.

His unspoken text began: "What I am trying to do is simply to serve truth and justice with my modest strength. You may think that the conflict between Israel and Egypt is a small and unimportant problem. 'We have more important concerns,' you might say. That is not the case. When it comes to truth and justice there is no difference between the small and great problems. Whosoever fails to take small matters seriously in a spirit of truth cannot be trusted in greater affairs."

Bertrand Russell, philosopher and social activist

I got to know him fairly well when we were both at Princeton in the early forties. He arranged to have a little meeting at his house once a week at which there would be some one or two eminent physicists and myself. We used to argue about moot points in the philosophy of physics in an attempt, sometimes vain, to reach fundamental agreement. We did not talk much about international politics, chiefly because in such matters we all thought alike. There was, however, one exceptional occasion. I remarked at a meeting that, when Germany had been defeated, the victors would lend money to the German government and would forget the German crimes. Einstein indignantly repudiated the suggestion, but subsequent experience proved that on this occasion he was mistaken. Einstein was not only a scientist but a great man. He stood for peace in a world drifting towards war. He remained sane in a mad world, and liberal in a world of fanatics. Of all the public figures I have known, Einstein was the one who commanded the most wholehearted admiration.

Dorothy Commins, Princeton friend and neighbor

During the summer heat wave of 1953, my husband, Saxe, had a heart attack and was rushed to the hospital. Although it was a hot, humid day, Einstein walked to the hospital—he didn't have a car and didn't want one—and I think the asphalt must have melted under his shoes. When he walked into the intensive care unit and Saxe saw him, he said, "My God, Professor Einstein, how could you come on a day like this?" And Einstein said, "Where there is love there is no question." I shall never forget that. And that tells you how close they were. They understood each other completely. He also sent Saxe a bouquet of flowers and a message: "Well, it needed the devil to get you to rest a bit. Heartfelt wishes."

Dr. Clair Gilbert, an Einstein family friend. When Helen Dukas went on vacation, Clair's mother, the sculptress Gina Plunguian, volunteered to replace her.

My mother would show him letters addressed to him from children and crackpots and Indian mystics and he would say, "How delightful!" and scribble answers on the bottom of the pages. He talked to her about the trivial and the cosmic, and she made notes. She was there every week when she was doing his bust, and when Robert Oppenheimer, the head of the Institute, or others came to see him, she'd say, "Don't mind me," and sit in the corner, and take notes of their conversations at lunch, and of Einstein's phone conversations. It was a diary of daily life in the household in a combination shorthand, German, and English.

Helen Dukas absolutely idolized Einstein, and he prospered greatly under her rule. Dukas was occasionally very stern and barked at people, but he felt comfortable with her. He knew she was protecting him. He had a sly sense of humor, and in his younger days he must have been hell on wheels. But when we knew him, he was relaxed and secure.

Dukas did a wonderful job of being the housekeeper and screening out the world for him. He was a kind of kindly grandfather guy that we knew in the later years. That was one of the faces of Einstein, but not the only one. I've always thought there was a hellcat underneath.

Gillett Griffin, art historian at Princeton's Firestone Library

In 1954, when I was a curator of graphic arts at Princeton University, the head librarian, Mr. Dix, and I were invited to dinner at the apartment of our colleague Johanna Fantova, to celebrate her friend Albert Einstein's seventy-fifth birthday. Fantova was a very moody woman, and she hadn't invited Helen Dukas, which I thought was mean. I believe she was jealous of Dukas. Maybe she thought Einstein had had an affair with her.

Einstein brought a large book of Daumier cartoons with him, which he knew I would enjoy. Einstein was always afraid, I think, of stuffy, self-important people and political types. He didn't know what Mr. Dix was going to be like, but he was anything but any of those things. The two of them smoked pipes after dinner—Einstein's was dry on doctor's orders—and Mr. Dix said, "Dr. Einstein, what do you think is going to happen to this country?" Because at that time brothers were turning against brothers. People had had their lives ruined—it was just horrible [the McCarthy era].

And Einstein took the pipe from his mouth and his eyes twinkled as he said, "Well, I came to this country because I believed Americans had a national sense of humor and I think in time they'll laugh him out." And within ten days or so all sorts of people were laughing at McCarthy. And I think he did die of people laughing at him, really.

Soon after I was invited over to the Einsteins' for Sunday dinner, Dukas had received wheelbarrow-loads of cards for Einstein's birthday. One was from a woman in the Midwest who wrote that she understood he was interested in music and one of these days he'd be hearing themes from hell.

After dinner, Einstein said he had work to do and excused himself. I offered to help him with the dishes and he said, "Ach, in Europe only women do the dishes!" But he did wash the dishes and I dried. When he spoke, he had a thick accent and occasionally would break into German, then apologize for not speaking in English. Then he excused himself and went upstairs to his study. As I was about to leave, Helen Dukas asked me, "Did Dr. Einstein show you his bird?" And I said no, and she called up to him and he came down and took from a drawer this wind-up toy, a bird with suction cups for feet, and he put it on a mirror and it climbed to the top and then fell off. And here I was standing with my jaw down to my clavicle, and Einstein was watching me intently the whole time. He asked, "Did you like it?" And I said, " Yes, yes, I loved it."

Next morning I got calls from the three ladies, Margot, Dukas, and Fantova, all saying, more or less, "You're part of the family now." Apparently the toy was a sort of test.

Margot Einstein was a good sculptor. I have a cast of her hands. She also did a piece of sculpture using Japanese paper and wildflower petals from her garden and she made one for Madame Pandit Nehru and one for me. I had lent her a tenth-century classical Indian sculpture because I thought it would inspire her. She'd had it for a year and a half and she called up and said, "I think you should pick up your sculpture." And I said, "Let me bring you something else to replace it," and she said, "No, no, no," and told me that Einstein was very ill.

Anyway, I went there on a Sunday morning in 1955, and Einstein called down and said, "Would you like to come up and talk with me?" Knowing he was very ill and not wanting to sap his energy, I said, "I really can't stay." Now I realize he really did want to talk with me. And he was gone within a week or so.

Fantova was very reserved about her association with Einstein. And she was very uptight and paranoid about something she was going to write. It started out with such earthshaking revelations as: "Trenton is ten miles to the south of Princeton." That kind of thing. Einstein said she was the only one person he'd ever met who couldn't be understood in any language. She was a Czech and one evening she was out to dinner in Ohio and two men had been seated near her. When they got up to go, one said "I'll grab the check." And she was afraid they were going to kidnap her.

Einstein left her the only manuscript of one of his theories that did not go to Israel [Hebrew University]—that is, Unified Field Theory, and then he wrote her nearly forty little poems and letters. She trusted me, and my parents had just died and left me some money. So I bought from her all of the letters that Einstein sent to her and all the poems. Then I got the best two manuscript appraisers in the country—both women—to give independent appraisals and they came up with about the same thing—something like $25,000.

Fantova put a thirty-five-year moratorium on them. They were not to be looked at for thirty-five years—that's now come to an end.

I thought the Unified Field Theory manuscript should be bought by Princeton Library for the Rare Books room, because he spent much of his life here. And my boss, the chief of Rare Books, Howard Rice, was interested in Albert Schweitzer, and thought of Albert Einstein as a funny little poppycock surrounded by little old ladies. Thought he was just nothing. So he refused to buy it.

I went to the head librarian, Mr. Dix, and said, "This is shocking. Einstein lived here much of his life and this was his home and this is the only theory he produced in America." And he said, "Well, you know, Mr. Rice is the chief of Rare Books, and we shouldn't go over his head."

I could have afforded it—an $8,000 appraisal price, can you imagine?—but anyway, it went to another university library, I believe.

I went to Einstein's home several times after his death. He'd been given presents from all over the world, but very little was of any monetary value. A lot stayed in the house and is still there. The Institute for Advanced Study owns the house and a physicist lives there.

The three ladies—Margot, Dukas and Fantova—scattered his ashes [in a river] between Trenton and Princeton.

When he was living, his house was painted yellow with white trim and blue shutters. Immediately after he died, the two ladies, Margot and Dukas, had it painted white. They just wanted a positive statement that things had changed.

I have the cushion he used when he sailed on Lake Carnegie and his pipe and a portrait. I was also left some of the little games he used to play with and a sketch he made of himself.

Albert Einstein and I had the same taste in music, Bach, Mozart, and Vivaldi, and he knew I wasn't trying to cash in on his fame. I once gave him a present of a Bach Cantata number seventy, and when I next saw him he seemed remote. I understood later that he thought I was trying to convert him to Christianity. I didn't realize what was in the text—perhaps a little extra for Christ. But he soon realized it was a misunderstanding.

In a way I think he would love to have been a peasant, talking over the back fence with neighbors and taking care of flowers.

I thought Einstein was absolutely wonderful and it was a remarkable privilege to know him.

6 | Einstein's Food for Thought: Was He a Gourmet or a Gourmand?

Because Einstein had never tasted caviar, as a treat for his twenty-fourth birthday in 1903 his friends Conrad Habicht and Maurice Solovine schemed to surprise him with it. They were holding a meeting of the Olympia Academy (their study group) that same night. While the three of them discussed Galileo, Solovine made the switch, replacing the usual simple snack of sausages with caviar. Then he and Habicht watched furtively as Albert ate the lot, talking all the time and without so much as a murmur of appreciation. He had been completely absorbed in the subject—Galileo's inertia principle. When they laughed and explained why, Einstein sat for a moment in stunned silence, then said apologetically that delicacies were wasted on him.

Some days later they again dipped into their meager savings for caviar. This time they repeatedly chanted, "Now we are eating caviar!" to Beethoven's Symphony in F. Einstein admitted it was delicious but added, "You have to be an epicure like Solovine to make such a fuss about it."

They concluded that good food was wasted on him. Clearly Einstein was no gourmet.

In another instance, left to his own devices in a Berlin apartment during World War I, and estranged from his wife, Mileva, who had moved to Switzerland with their two sons, the twenty-six-year-old Einstein decided to put into practice a unique method for streamlining his cooking arrangements.

To spend as little time as possible away from his work, he

Conrad Habicht (left), Maurice Solovine, and Einstein, the "Olympia Academy" of Bern, 1902. They gave Einstein his first taste of caviar but—his mind in the stars—he didn't notice.

often skipped meals and worked far into the night. And when he felt the irresistible urge for food, he would prepare it as quickly and simply as possible.

One day, his future stepdaughter, Margot, caught him at it. To her horror, she watched him boiling an egg—not in water, but in a saucepan of soup, meaning to eat both. He cheerfully admitted that he hadn't even bothered to wash the egg's shell before popping it in the soup. Could this explain his frequent bouts of indigestion?

On another occasion, after moving to Princeton, Einstein prepared lunch for himself and three girls. Even though Helen Dukas, his secretary and housekeeper-bodyguard, usually protected him from unwanted interruptions, children sometimes got through her defenses, especially if Einstein happened to open the door and liked the children. One neighbor's eight-year-old daughter frequently called on him for help with her math homework, and he never disappointed her. One day, having a problem with arithmetic, she called on him. Sometime later, the girl's sister and her friend, fourteen-year-old Jane Swing, arrived to pick her up. Einstein again answered the front door. Jane Swing later recalled the event: "Things downstairs were all neat and tidy, but then Einstein took us upstairs to his study. I guess he practically lived there—with a view of the backyard. And he invited us into this terribly messy room. There was a long table littered with papers and books. More books were stacked on the stairs. I became an artist, so now I have a very untidy room, too. But then I was just plain flabbergasted. I had never seen anything like that before. As for Einstein, he looked like the room: a very untidy gentleman, hair going in every direction. He did have a tie on, but that was around on the wrong side of his face. He had a huge shock of grey hair and food all down the front of him. He reminded me of an untidy Mark Twain.

"He was highly unusual, like nothing I'd ever met before, with a very high voice, almost like a woman's. And he asked if we'd like to have lunch and we said, 'Certainly.' So he moved a whole bunch of papers from the table, and moved things off stools for us to sit on, opened four cans of beans with a can opener and heated them on a Sterno stove, one by one, stuck a spoon in each can. And that was our lunch. He didn't give us anything to drink.

"During lunch he was discussing mostly things with my friend's sister, about arithmetic. My friend's younger sister went there practically every day. He loved the little girl and I think most of our conversation with Einstein was about her and her math problem."

Albert Einstein was certainly also not a judge of fine wines, or of anything alcoholic. When he was in the United States and Prohibition was a subject of great moment, a newsreel cameraman asked him what he thought of the drinking law. "I don't drink," he replied. "So I couldn't care less."

Probably Einstein's favorite meal was soup, sausage, and ice cream. And his favorite drink was coffee.

Clearly, Einstein was neither gourmet nor gourmand.

His friend and Princeton neighbor Dorothy Commins confirmed that food was not a priority with him. She recalled how "Einstein was planning to write an article in English. He called up my husband, Saxe, and asked, 'Saxe, can you help me? My syntax is all wrong.' So Saxe went over and got it all straightened out. My husband, then the editor in chief at Random House, would take the train home to Princeton from New York and get off near Einstein's house with literature Einstein wanted to read. At the time Bertrand Russell was writing, and he wanted that, and a short visit would turn into a long one. They'd walk each other home, like schoolboys. Finally, Helen Dukas would call me, 'Is Professor Einstein there?' I'd say, 'Yes, he is." She'd say, 'Send him home. He needs his dinner and it's getting cold.' And Saxe would say, 'You must go back, because dinner's waiting for you.'

"And then Einstein would say, Oh, that doesn't interest me. Let's go on walking and talking."

7 | Did Einstein Believe in God?

At seventy-six Albert Einstein faced his death head-on, telling friends who came to visit him in the Princeton Hospital not to look so upset, that everyone had to die someday. He had started to write a tribute for Israel's Independence day that began: "What I seek to accomplish is simply to serve with my feeble capacity truth and justice at the risk of pleasing no one." He had also been working on equations with a pad and pencil, even while in great pain, encouraged by the thought that he was close to succeeding with his unified field theory.

Just after midnight on April 18, 1955, a nurse heard him mutter something in German, but unfortunately she didn't understand the language.

At about 1:30 in the morning, he took two deep breaths and died. According to his wishes, there was no funeral service or grave. He was cremated, then, watched by a few close friends and relatives, his ashes were strewn in the Delaware River.

The Einstein family attorney, David J. Levy, announced in the *New York Times* on May 15, 1955: "I am requested and authorized to say that the ashes have now been privately, finally and irrevocably disposed of in conformity with the wishes of Professor Einstein [and] the ultimate fact is that no physical traces are left anywhere."

In fact, somebody had taken his brain, to study, and someone else had taken his eyes, as a keepsake.

Had Einstein's last muttered words been a question to God? Einstein had often spoken of God as if he were a friendly colleague who had all the answers to the mysteries of the universe. And as if they communicated telepathically through mathematical equations. But Einstein needed to frame the right question before he got a reply. It was like a game with very high stakes.

His entire adult life was a sustained effort to understand not the conventional view of God, but his own version of God. And this, he thought, could be achieved by solving the mysteries of the universe. For years the still puzzling aspects of light, time, space, energy, and gravity were Einstein's enthralling preoccupations, which he endlessly discussed with colleagues and friends, especially Michele Besso.

His stepson-in-law, Rudolf Kayser (pen name Anton Reiser), described this search to solve the mysteries of the universe: "Conceptions which had dimly engaged him in his student days were now taking definite form. Einstein saw that his efforts began to endanger the supposedly impregnable foundations of science. As a man possessed, he was carried away by these most difficult problems of theoretical physics. . . . If he felt that he was nearing a solution to his problem, he would tell his friend [Michele Besso]—his eyes glowing—that the success of his efforts was at hand. But the next day he would merely inform him that all his experiments of the past were wrong. Through many long years of hope and disappointment, Albert carried on his experiments till he reached the solution. When, unknown to him, he almost held the key, with which he was to open the closed door, he despaired, and said to his friend, 'I'm going to give it up.'" Of course, he didn't.

In 1905 the twenty-six-year-old Einstein, then an examiner in a Swiss patent office, felt he was close to the answers after, as he said, "years of anxious searching in the dark," with intense longing, periods of despair and exhaustion, and at times "living in a state of confusion and psychic tension, and visited by all sorts of nervous conflicts."

Then he suddenly woke one morning, greatly agitated, as if a storm had broken loose in his mind. And with it came the astonishing answers.

Later that same morning, when he arrived at work, he "whispered feverishly [to Besso] that now he was on the right track. He had made the revolutionary discovery that the absolute character of simultaneity was a mere prejudice, and that the velocity of light was independent of the motion of coordinate systems." Einstein expert Stanley Goldberg said that Einstein's waking thought on that momentous morning was that simultaneity was closely involved with time and space. It took him five weeks to get it down on paper as a treatise titled "Towards the Electrodynamics of Moving Bodies."

Yet some of it defied common sense, especially the fact that nothing could change the speed of light. If, for example, as

Michele Besso, Einstein's friend and colleague at the Swiss Patent Office.

he explained, he was traveling in a train toward or away from the source of light, according to his theory, the light would appear to him, and to an observer on the ground, to be moving at exactly the same 186,000 miles a second. His own speed or position in the universe, or that of the outside observer, made absolutely no difference. Nor did the movement of the light source. This is how all freely moving observers, no matter where they were and whatever their speed, would experience the constant speed of light.

If he, Einstein, was in a train traveling at 50 mph and threw a ball moving at 20 mph in the same direction, from the viewpoint of someone standing alongside the tracks, the ball would be moving at 70 mph.

In explaining the speed of light, Einstein imagined himself on the same train that had accelerated to half the speed of light, 93,000 miles a second. But instead of throwing a ball he switched on a flashlight and pointed it ahead. The light from the flashlight as seen by him and the outside observer would still be traveling at 186,000 miles a second, the train's speed and the position of the observers being inconsequential.

How could that be possible? Because, he reasoned, the light's speed was exactly the same for him aboard the moving train and for the observer on the ground and under any other circumstances.

But time and space were another matter. He speculated that if he traveled aboard a spacecraft as it approached the speed of light, although everything on board would appear normal to him, time measured by Einstein's watch would move more slowly than the earthbound observer's watch. It would take him just a few seconds, for example, to tie his shoelaces. Yet, if an observer on Earth could see him, he would appear to be taking hours. Returning to Earth, after traveling in space at near light speed, he would have aged two years, while everything else on Earth would have aged two hundred years! He also concluded that although he could travel forward through time, he couldn't go back in time. So according to Einstein's special theory of relativity, as it became known, one could move through time only in one direction, a reality ignored by writers of science fiction.

In an interview with Einstein in 1920, Alexander Moszkowski brought up astronomer Camille Flammarion's science fiction story "Lumen" in which the hero moves faster than light, achieves time reversal, and sees the Battle of Waterloo before it starts, watching cannonballs fly back into cannon barrels and dead soldiers come back to life and resume fighting. "Simply impossible," Einstein said.

"Of course, we can imagine events which contradict our daily experiences without taking them seriously. Relativity shows that nothing can exceed the speed of light. Assuming that Lumen [the hero] is human, with a body and sense organs, at the speed of light his body's mass would become infinitely great." Einstein had concluded at twenty-six that his youthful thought of riding on a light beam had been an impossible dream, and that as mass increases with speed, in an attempt to get aboard the light beam his body's mass—like Lumen's—would have become infinite. Had he been "an oversized quantum," Dr. Robert Schulmann suggests, he would have turned "into pure energy, but certainly nothing at the mesoscopic level could even approach this [speed of light] limit."

Equally astonishing and even more momentous on that fateful morning was the clue, now in his hands, to the simple equation involving the speed of light: $E = mc^2$. The potential energy in anything equals its mass times the speed of light squared. This aspect of the special theory of relativity meant, explained Einstein's colleague and biographer Banesh Hoffmann, that "every clod of earth, every feather, every speck of dust is a prodigious reservoir of untapped energy." Another great—and awesome—secret of the universe explained.

But it seemed too good to be true. Einstein wasn't absolutely sure he was right, telling a friend, Conrad Habicht, that relativity required the mass to be a direct measure of the energy contained in bodies. And, because light transfers mass, in the case of radium it should result in a remarkable decrease in its mass. Einstein found the idea amusing and enticing, but he still wondered if the "Almighty is laughing at it and leading me up the garden path."

Banesh Hoffman. Einstein told him that ideas came from God.

Instead, the Almighty metaphorically patted him on the back for having discovered the incredible fact that all energy has mass, and sometime later, that mass and energy are interchangeable.

In Cambridge, England, in 1932, John Cockroft and E. T. S. Walton experimentally demonstrated the conversion of mass into energy by splitting an atom The following year, the Curies' daughter and son-in-law, Irène and Frédéric Joliot-Curie, took a photo in Paris showing the conversion of energy into mass.

Einstein's new ideas now replaced the old assumptions that saw mass as never changing and having nothing to do with energy, and saw time as flowing in the same way for everyone.

Banesh Hoffmann confirmed Einstein's modus operandi, in which he put questions to God. Once when they were working on a problem together, Einstein said to him, "'Can we get another idea that will solve this problem? Ideas come from God.' Now he didn't believe in a personal God or anything like that. This was his metaphorical way of speaking.

You cannot command the idea to come, it will come when it is good and ready. He put it in those terms, 'Ideas come from God.'"

Although Einstein didn't always attribute his discoveries to a supernatural source, when interviewed by Robert Shankland, a Case Institute of Technology physics professor, in 1950, he was more cautious, saying that in physics the solution often comes by indirect means.

Throughout his adult life, in his conversations and writings, Einstein constantly used God's name to explain the universe. Yet he didn't believe in the popular concept of God as the Supreme Being. This confused people almost as much as his theories did. He didn't believe in angels, either, or devils, ghosts, hell, or heaven, nor in the theory that one's fate is written in the stars, nor that prayers can move mountains. All ancient superstitions, he would say, echoing his father.

According to Jamie Sayen, another Einstein biographer, "He believed it was a fatal mistake of the ethical religions, in an effort to educate and indoctrinate their followers, to have tied their moral and ethical precepts to epics and myths which, although beautiful from a poetic point of view, are not essential to the truth of the moral teachings." And that by dogmatically insisting on the validity of the creation myth, for instance, which science had repudiated, creationists and others who took the Bible literally had both undermined the truth of the moral codes and weakened all aspects of religion.

Einstein saw the Bible as an intriguing, partly beautiful, and partly wicked monument to past times, written by human beings. Humans were known to be fallible, so there was no reason to believe every word of it, except that it was in the interest of the privileged classes to keep alive what they called "eternal truths," and what Einstein called "superstitions," and which he thought should have vanished long ago.

He conceded that although religious movements often started as moral exemplars, they had degenerated into big businesses bent on accumulating and preserving political and financial power, which used superstition, fear, and "divinely sanctioned" dogma to control the credulous masses.

As he once said, if the existing religions were "freed of their myths, they would be basically alike, because the moral attitudes of a people supported by religion must always aim at 'preserving and promoting the sanity and vitality of the community.'" And, in fact, the Bible's ethical teachings had a strong effect on his own moral values.

So what did he mean when he said he wanted to know God's thoughts? That God didn't play dice? That maybe "the good Lord" was laughing at him after leading him up the garden path? That God was subtle but not malicious? In all these statements he used God as his metaphor for an as yet unknown force. His "religion," as he explained, took "the form of rapturous amazement at the harmony of natural law, [instead of the expected chaotic world] which reveals an intelligence of such superiority that, compared with it, all the thinking and acting of human beings is an utterly insignificant reflection." He sometimes defined this as "cosmic religion."

Whenever he said or wrote "God," he never meant a supernatural being who reigned in heaven, took an interest in the fate of mankind, and answered prayers.

When pressed, Einstein attributed intuition, imagination, and inspiration for his discoveries, stressing the special importance of imagination.

Born in Germany in 1879, he was brought up in a nonreligious household where his father was proud of not observing any religious strictures and maintained that religion was based on ancient superstitions. However, German law required all children to be given religious instruction. As Einstein's schoolfellows were overwhelmingly Catholic and there was no rabbi around, he was taught at home the basic values of Judaism by a distant relative. It caught on. He became a fervent Orthodox Jew, refusing to eat pork, vainly trying to persuade his parents to follow suit, and singing songs of praise to God, which he had composed as he walked to school.

This religious fervor lasted until he was twelve, when he read several scientific books and concluded that the Bible was full of lies and he had been duped. He became, after his boyhood conversion from religious faith to science and for the rest of his life, a born-again skeptic with regard to the conventional view of God.

"It is quite clear," he wrote long after, "that the religious paradise of youth, which I lost, was a first attempt to free myself from the chains of the 'merely personal,' from an existence which is dominated by wishes, hopes, primitive feelings."

Yet he still often spoke of God and was regarded by friends and himself as essentially religious. For example, at eighteen, he wrote to a friend, Rosa Winteler, "Strenuous labor and the contemplation of God's nature are the angels which, reconciling, fortifying, and yet mercilessly severe, will guide me though the tumult of life."

What he meant was that working hard and trying to discover the secrets of the universe, demanding as it may be, would help him through tough times.

When struggling with his quantum theory in 1909, specifically the paradox that light might be both wave and particle—suggesting the idea of complementarity fifteen years before Niels Bohr brought it up—Einstein asked a leading physicist, Arnold Sommerfield, "Can the energy quanta on the one hand and Huygens's principle on the other be combined? Appearances are against it, but the Almighty—it seems—managed the trick."

During World War I, when his country, Germany, was fighting England, a Swiss colleague, Edgar Meyer, wrote to him that "God should punish the English." "Why?" Einstein asked in reply. "I have no close connection to either one or the other. I see only with deep regret that God punishes so many of His children for their numerous stupidities, for which only He Himself can be held responsible. In my opinion, only His nonexistence could excuse Him."

Yet he continued to refer to a metaphorical God in describing his reservations about quantum theory, writing to his physicist friend Max Born, in 1916: "An inner voice tells me that this will not be the true Jacob. The theory accomplishes a lot, but it scarcely brings us closer to the secret of the Old One."

Three years later, after the war, the forty-year-old Einstein showed a student, Ilse Rosenthal-Schneider, a telegram he had just received saying that Sir Arthur Eddington had confirmed one aspect of his theory of general relativity—that the sun caused light to bend. What would you have done, she asked, if he hadn't confirmed it? Again Einstein spoke metaphorically, replying that he would have pitied "the dear Lord" because the theory was correct.

During his first visit to the United States in 1921, after he had given four lectures at Princeton University on his relativity theory and received an honorary degree, someone asked him what he thought of the experiments being conducted by physicist Dayton C. Miller at the Case School of Applied Science. Miller had boasted that his experiments on Mount Wilson to confirm the Michelson-Morley experiment [that the earth moved through the ether] would give relativity a knockout blow. Princeton mathematician Oswald Veblen overheard Einstein reply: "*Raffiniert ist der Herr Gott aber boshaft ist Er nicht.*" (Subtle is the Lord, but He is not malicious.) Veblen wrote down the remark, and later asked Einstein if he could have the phrase engraved on the mantelpiece of the new faculty lounge of the Princeton Mathematics and Physics Departments. Einstein said that he had meant to say, "*Die Natur verbirgt ihr Geheimnis durch die Erhabenheir ihres Wesens, aber nicht durch List.*" (Nature hides its secrets through the sublimity of its being, but not through cunning.) Also rendered as: "God is slick, but he ain't mean." And

Einstein in 1921, when he first visited the United States to raise funds for Hebrew University. During that year at a Princeton reception he said: "Subtle is the Lord, but He is not malicious."

"God is subtle but he is not bloody-minded." But the more formal statement Veblen overheard can be seen today, carved in stone in Fine Hall's common room.

Einstein's view of his metaphorical God's creation meant that he could never accept Werner Heisenberg's Uncertainty, or Indeterminacy, Principle, which held that it was impossible to determine, at the same time, a particle's precise position and velocity, suggesting that the subatomic world resembled a crapshoot in which no one could predict the outcome. Or as Wolfgang Pauli described it: "One can view the world with the p eye and one can view it with the q eye, but if one tries to open both eyes together, one gets confused."

Einstein's friend and future biographer Philipp Frank was surprised that he resisted "the new fashion" in physics, reminding him that he himself had invented quantum theory in 1905. "A good joke should not be repeated," Einstein replied. "I shall never believe that God plays dice with the world."

In his long-running argument with Niels Bohr over some aspects of quantum mechanics and Heisenberg's Uncertainty Principle, which implied that the subatomic world, at least, was unpredictable, Einstein insisted that God was not a gambler, saying that "God does not play dice with the cosmos," and that quantum theory represented "a blind man's bluff with the idea of reality."

Responding to someone who spoke favorably of astrology during a Berlin dinner party in 1927, Einstein scornfully rejected the pseudoscience as disproved by "the Copernican system," which, he asserted, "conclusively made a clean sweep of the anthropocentric view which thought of the entire firmament as revolving around the earth and humanity. That was probably the severest shock man's interpretation of the cosmos every received. It reduced the world to a mere province, so to speak, instead of its being the capital and center." When, despite this declaration, another guest asked

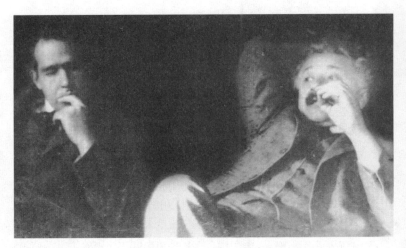

Two of the century's greatest minds, Niels Bohr and Einstein, in Paul Ehrenfest's home. During their discussion on their theories of the Universe, Niels Bohr told Einstein to stop telling God what to do.

Einstein if he was deeply religious, he replied: "Yes, you can call it that. Try and penetrate with our limited means the secrets of nature and you will find that, behind all the discernible concatenations, there remains something subtle, intangible and inexplicable. Veneration for this force beyond anything that we can comprehend is my religion. To that extent I am, in point of fact, religious."

Interviewed by George Sylvester Viereck for the *Saturday Evening Post*, Einstein had a chance to explain himself in more detail. He didn't believe in immortality, and one life, he said, was enough for him. He continued, "I realize that every individual is the product of the conjunction of two individuals. I don't see where and at what moment the new being is endowed with a soul." He couldn't say if he believed in the God of Spinoza "with a simple yes or no. I'm not an atheist and I don't think I can call myself a pantheist. [Pantheists believe that God is not a personality but that all the laws and manifestations of the universe are God. Put another way:

God is everything and everything is God.] Though Einstein admitted that he was "fascinated by Spinoza's pantheism . . . the first philosopher to deal with the soul and body as one, not two separate things."

When asked how he would explain his own view of God, Einstein replied: "We are in the position of a little child entering a huge library filled with books in many different languages. The child knows someone must have written the books. It does not know how. It does not understand the language in which they are written. The child dimly suspects a mysterious order in the arrangement of the books but doesn't know what it is. That, it seems to me, is the attitude of even the most intelligent human being toward God."

Viereck was curious to know if Einstein had been at all influenced by Christianity. Einstein said, "As a child I received instruction both in the Bible [New and Old Testaments] and the Talmud. I am a Jew, but I am enthralled by the luminous figure of the Nazarene."

He had read Emil Ludwig's recent biography of Jesus Christ and thought it "shallow. Jesus is too colossal for the pen of phrasemongers, however artful. No man can dispose of Christianity with a *bon mot*." He accepted the historical existence of Jesus "unquestionably," adding, "No one can read the Gospels without feeling the actual presence of Jesus. His personality pulsates in every word. No myth is filled with such life."

Yet in a conversation with a friend, W. I. Hermann, Einstein said: "It is quite possible that we can do greater things than Jesus, for what is written in the Bible about him is poetically embellished."

In 1929 Einstein wrote that physicists not only sought to know how Nature works, "but also to reach as far as possible the perhaps utopian and seemingly arrogant aim of knowing why Nature *is thus and not otherwise*. Here lies the highest satisfaction of a scientific person. [One feels], so to speak, that God himself could not have arranged these connections in any other way than that which factually exists, any more than it would be in His power to make the number 4 into a prime number. This is the promethean element of the scientific experience. . . . Here has always been for me the particular magic of scientific considerations, that is, as it were, the religious basis of scientific effort."

That same year, interviewed by a *Daily Chronicle* reporter, Einstein explained his general theory of relativity as reducing "to one formula all laws which govern space, time and gravitation, and thus it corresponded to the demand for simplification of our physical concepts. The purpose of my work is to further the simplification, and particularly to reduce to one formula the explanation of the field of gravity and of the field of electromagnetism. For this reason I call it a contribution to 'a unified field theory.' . . . Now, but only now, we know that the force which moved electrons in their ellipses about the nuclei of atoms is the same force which moved our earth in its annual course about the sun, and is the same force which brings to us the rays of light and heat which make life possible on this planet."

Disappointed that Einstein had omitted God from the equation, Boston's Cardinal O'Connell attacked general relativity as a cloak "for the ghastly apparition of atheism," and "befogged speculation, producing universal doubt about God and His creation." Anxious to defend Einstein, New York rabbi Herbert Goldstein cabled him: "Do you believe in God?" Einstein replied that he believed "in Spinoza's God who reveals Himself in the orderly harmony of what exists, not in a God who concerns Himself with fates and actions of human beings." This delighted the rabbi, who tried to educate the cardinal, by explaining: "Spinoza, who is called the God-intoxicated man, and who saw God manifest in all nature, certainly could not be called an atheist. Furthermore, Einstein points to a unity. Einstein's theory if carried out to its logical conclusion would bring to mankind a scientific formula for monotheism. He does away with the thought of dualism or pluralism. There can be no room for any aspect of polytheism."

Einstein's first sentence in a front-page article, "Religion and Science," in the *New York Times Magazine* for November 9, 1930, could have been written by Freud: "Everything that men do or think concerns the satisfaction of the needs they feel or the escape from pain." In it, he speculated that religion began among primitive peoples from fear, developed into a religion based on morality and might in time become a "cosmic" religion "which recognized neither dogmas nor God made in man's image."

Rabbi Dr. Nathan Krass of Temple Emanuel on Sixty-fourth Street and Fifth Avenue stated that although some sectarians would disapprove of Einstein's religious outlook, "it must and will be approved by the Jews." The flamboyant Catholic evangelist Bishop Fulton Sheen was not among the sectarians who approved. Addressing twelve hundred members of the Catholic Teachers Association, he accused the magazine of degrading itself by publishing "the sheerest kind of stupidity and nonsense" and asked whether anyone would be willing to "lay down his life for the Milky Way." He also suggested that the letter "s" should be deleted from Einstein's proclaimed "cosmic" religion. Which doubtless made Einstein, a *Times* reader, laugh.

He was always shocking some group or other. He shocked a Christian group when he refused to speak at their peace rally with a cutting remark. "If I had been able to address your congress, I would have said that in the course of history the priests have been responsible for much strife and war among human beings. They have a lot to atone for."

Soon after, Einstein paid a rare visit to a synagogue because, according to biographer Jeremy Bernstein, "the more Einstein became aware of German anti-Semitism the closer a bond he felt to his fellow Jews. There is no more moving photograph of Einstein anywhere than one taken in a Berlin synagogue in 1930. Here he sits, skeptic and free-thinker . . . his unruly hair flowing from beneath the traditional black yarmulke—holding his violin, prepared to play in a concert [to raise money for fellow Jews]. In the background one can make out the congregation and can only imagine, with grief, what was to be their fate."

That April, when thirteen-year-old violinist Yehudi Menuhin made his debut, the audience was so excited that the manager called the police to restore order. Before they arrived, Einstein hurried to Menuhin's dressing room, crossing the stage to get there, and, hugging the youngster, exclaimed, "Now I know there is a God in heaven! "

Though Einstein resorted to the same theological metaphor for almost every sublime event, on one occasion he seemed to waver. It happened in 1930, during a conversation with actress Elisabeth Bergner, when she asked if he believed in God. He implied that he was struggling with the answer: "One may not ask that of someone who with growing amazement attempts to explore and understand the authoritative order in the universe." "Why not?" she persisted. "Because," he said, "he would probably break down when faced with such a question."

Einstein gave a detailed account of his credo in a remarkable speech to the German League of Human Rights in Berlin in 1932. Then he said: "Every one of us appears here [on Earth] involuntarily and uninvited for a short stay, without knowing the whys and wherefores. . . . Although I am a typical loner in daily life, my consciousness of belonging to the invisible community of those who strive for truth, beauty, and justice has preserved me from feeling isolated. The most beautiful and deepest experience a man can have is the sense of the mysterious. It is the underlying principle of religion as well as all serious endeavor in art and science. He who has never had this experience seems to me, if not dead at least blind. To sense that behind anything that can be experienced there is something that our mind cannot grasp and whose beauty and sublimity reaches us only indirectly and as a feeble reflection, that is religiousness. In this sense I am religious. To me it suffices to wonder at these secrets and to attempt humbly to grasp with my mind a mere image of the lofty structure of all that is there."

Though he did not believe in the supernatural, his novelist friend Upton Sinclair persuaded Einstein to try to make contact with the other world at a séance in California. Einstein was as skeptical as a person could be, once saying that even if he saw a ghost he wouldn't believe it. The trance medium, Roman Ostoja, a self-proclaimed Polish count, had a glowing reputation, but with Einstein in the circle he could only gasp and grunt incoherently. The séance was a bust, and a counterinfluence in the room was blamed for it—a nonbeliever. It isn't hard to guess who that was.

Einstein attributed the interest in spiritualism and the belief in ghosts to weak, confused people. After all, he wrote, "since our inner experiences consist of reproductions, and combinations of sensory impressions, the concept of a soul without a body seems to me to be empty and devoid of meaning."

Later, having left Germany permanently and settled in Princeton, Einstein's second wife, Elsa, was conversing with a neighbor, Carolyn Blackwood, a Presbyterian minister's wife. Elsa said that she and Albert believed in the creative force, but not in a personal God who took an interest in people on Earth, that he read the Old and New Testaments regularly, for the literary value and stories, not for the specifically religious message. The Einsteins had lost their Bible in moving to the United States from Berlin, and when Carolyn gave Elsa her Luther's translation, she hugged it to her heart and said, "I wish I had more faith."

When Carolyn mentioned that she and her husband hoped to meet Zionists during their imminent journey to Palestine, Elsa said, "My darling, I did not know you were Jews." And Carolyn replied, "We are not. We are Christians and Presbyterians on top of that." Elsa was dumbfounded that anyone other than Jews would associate with, even seek out, the Jewish community in Palestine. So Carolyn explained that there were close bonds between the Jewish heritage and the Christian faith. "And besides," she said, "Jesus was a Jew." Elsa, amazed, replied, "No Christian has ever said that to me in my life!" and hugged Carolyn affectionately.

Einstein spelled out his religious views again in 1936, when a young girl wrote to ask him if most scientists prayed and, if so, what for. He replied that a scientist is unlikely to believe that prayers can influence events—as naïve religious people do. But serious scientific study makes a scientist conclude that "the Laws of Nature manifest a spirit which is vastly superior to Man, and before which, with our modest strength, must humbly bow."

He characterized those who clung to a belief in life after death as feeble, frightened, egotistical individuals.

After visiting a local art gallery, where a stranger had insisted on shaking his hand, Caroline Blackwood asked Einstein, "Does it ever get monotonous being the greatest living scientist?" "I'm not great," he replied. "Anyone could have done what I did. Besides, what I have is a gift." "A gift from God?" asked the minister's wife. "I express it differently," he said. "I believe down here"—he put his hand on his heart—"what I cannot explain up here"—he put his hand on his head. "But I believe it all. I believe it all." Blackwood's son, James, said: "What I think Einstein meant by that is that he had a religious dimension to his thinking. He read both of the Testaments regularly, and his early training was in both."

Einstein speculated that the genesis of the various religions arose from fear by primitive people—of hunger, wild animals, pain, sickness, and death. They may have imagined that powerful beings not unlike themselves could protect them from such terrors when offered gifts or sacrifices.

In the spring of 1937, a few months after the death of Einstein's second wife, Elsa, his friend, author Max Eastman, a disillusioned Communist, called on him at Princeton. They sat chatting in armchairs on the small sunny lawn in the back of the house. Eastman mentioned how Einstein had often been quoted as not believing in an anthropomorphic God, yet considered himself religious, and that the scientists' striving toward rational knowledge of the universe was "religion in the highest sense." But "I don't think you are really religious," Eastman said. "And it's a mistake for you to use the term. For the sake of clear thinking the word religion ought to be used only to mean a faith that something in the external world is sympathetic to man's interests."

Einstein conceded that was true of religion in its origin and early development, the primitive religion of fear, and the social and moral religion which grew out of it. In both of those phases, he agreed that religion assumed that a force or forces in the external world were sympathetic to man's interests. But he thought that "there is a higher religion which is free from fear and has nothing to do with morality. This higher religion is an attitude of humility toward universal being."

Eastman gathered from their conversation that Einstein regarded human aims and wishes as insignificant compared to the grandeur of a rationally ordered universe. And that Einstein believed that this religious feeling sustained such scientists as Newton and Kepler, as well as himself "in their arduous efforts to understand the universe."

Speaking at the Princeton Theological Seminary in May 1939, Einstein said: "Scientific method can teach us nothing else beyond how facts are related to, and conditioned by each other. The aspiration toward such objective knowledge belongs to the highest of which man is capable. . . . Yet it is equally clear that knowledge of what is does not open the door directly to what *should be*. One can have the clearest and most complete knowledge of what *is* and yet not be able to deduce from that what should be the goal of human aspirations. . . . The ultimate *goal* itself and the longing to reach it must come from another source. . . . Here we face, therefore, the limits of purely rational conception of our existence. . . . It is the mythical, or rather the symbolic, content of the religious traditions which is likely to come into conflict with science. This occurs whenever this religious stock of ideas contains dogmatically fixed statements on subjects which belong to the domain of science. Thus, it is of vital importance for the preservation of true religion that such conflicts be avoided when they arise from subjects which, in fact, are not really essential for the pursuance of the religious aims."

The theologian Thomas Torrance believes that the Christian church's opposition to Hitler and the Holocaust drew Einstein into closer relations with his Jewish friends Max and Hedi Born, who had become Quakers, and with the Ross Stevensons and the Andrew Blackwoods of Princeton Theological Seminary. This seems credible, based on a letter Einstein sent to an American Episcopal bishop saying that as a lover of freedom, he had expected the universities and the great newspaper editors to be among its defenders, but, to his despair, it only took a few weeks for the Nazis to silence them. "Only the church stood squarely across the path of Hitler's campaign for suppressing the truth," he wrote. "I never had any special interest in the church before, but now I feel a great affection and admiration because the church alone has had the courage and persistence to stand for intellectual truth and moral freedom. I am forced to confess that what I once despised I now praise unreservedly."

A Princeton friend of theologian Torrance told him that during World War II when Einstein heard that a group of Christians were at a prayer meeting nearby to make intercessions for Jews in Germany, Einstein went there with his violin and asked if he could join in. They welcomed him warmly, and as they prayed, he gave them music. He was not "praying" for the Jews, which as a scientist he thought could have no effect, but thanking those who were concerned enough to pray to *their* God to help Jews.

As Torrance points out, "In relation to petitionary prayer, Einstein not infrequently reacted against 'the fact that men appeal to the Divine Being in prayers and plead for the fulfillment of their wishes,' for that implied to him a selfish 'anthropomorphic' idea of God which he rejected."

Ensign Guy Raner, serving in the Pacific during World War II, wrote to Einstein that he had met a Jesuit priest who claimed to have converted Einstein from atheism. Was it true? Einstein replied that he had never talked to a Jesuit priest and was "astonished by the audacity to tell lies about me. From the viewpoint of a Jesuit priest I am, of course, and have always been an atheist," because, he said, he had repeatedly expressed his disbelief in a personal God. "It is always misleading to use anthropomorphic concepts in dealing with things outside the human sphere—childish analogies." But he was not an atheist, because he did "not share the crusading spirit of the professional atheist whose fervor is mostly due to a painful act of liberation from the fetters of religious indoctrination received in youth. I prefer an attitude of humility corresponding to the weakness of our intellectual understanding of nature and of our being. We have to admire in humility the beautiful harmony of the structure of this world—as far as we can grasp it. And that is all."

Though seriously ill in 1948 with an aneurysm, which eventually killed him, he managed to finish an article for the *Library of Living Philosophers*, satisfied to have defended "the good Lord against the suggestion that he continually rolls dice."

In his last few years, apart from his unified field theory, hoping to connect gravity and electricity, what really interested him, he said, was "whether God could have made the world differently; in other words, whether the demand for logical simplicity leaves any freedom at all."

In 1950, some American scientists decided it was time to come up with a new definition of God that would be acceptable to fellow scientists. A reporter asked Einstein about it, and he said that it was ridiculous. When the reporter suggested there was a public yearning for science to provide the spiritual help organized religion seemed unable to give, he replied: "Speaking of the spirit that informs modern scientific investigation, I think that all the finer speculations in the realm of science spring from a deep religious feeling, and that without such feeling they would not be fruitful. I also believe that this kind of religiousness which makes itself felt today in scientific investigation is the only creative religious activity of our time. . . . But the content of scientific theory itself offers no moral foundation for the personal conduct of life."

Einstein did not disagree when the reporter brought up the historical fact that Catholic and Protestant churches had invariably been bitterly opposed to science, but there was no antagonism toward science in the Jewish religion. And Einstein explained why: "The Jewish religion is, more than anything else, a way of sublimating everyday existence, and it entails no narrow discipline in doctrinal matters affecting one's personal views of life. As a matter of fact it demands no act of faith—in the popular sense of the term—on the part of its members. For that reason there has never been a conflict between our religious outlook and the world outlook of science." Which might explain why so many great scientists are Jewish.

Although scornful of rigid rituals sanctioned by religion, especially if they seemed irrational in modern times, according to his colleague and biographer Abraham Pais, Einstein never lost his admiration for the fundamental ends and aspirations of the Judeo-Christian tradition and did not doubt the significance of what he called those "super-personal objects and goals which neither require nor are capable of rational foundation. [It was] in this independent spirit as a 'typical loner,' as he spoke of himself, without religious commitment, but with deep religious awe, that he cultivated and retained throughout his life—unabated wonder at the immensity, unity, rational harmony, and mathematical beauty of the universe."

Einstein's former student Maurice Solovine must have read some of these recent statements, because he wrote to him in alarm on March 30, 1952, afraid that he had "got religion," and was a "victim of clergy." Einstein denied it, but also stressed that he did not agree with the positivists and professional atheists who were happy to think that they had not only made the world "god free," but "wonder free." He said that he had never lost his sense of wonder.

A woman in San Francisco was also anxious for Einstein to clarify his views. She had received a rigid orthodox education but now was tending toward atheism or agnosticism. She had believed that Einstein, too, was a freethinker but had been surprised in reading Lincoln Barnett's book *The Universe and Dr. Einstein* that Einstein believed that a Divine Mind is God of the Universe. It would mean a lot to her, she wrote, if he would clarify his views.

Einstein denied he was a freethinker in the usual sense, because he thought freethinkers of that ilk were simply motivated by the wish to oppose naïve superstition. He was, he said, deeply conscious of the inadequacy of the human mind to fully understand the harmony of the Universe, "which we try to formulate as laws of nature." It was this consciousness and humility he missed in the freethinking mentality.

According to Banesh Hoffman, "C. P. Snow called Einstein almost a saint, and Einstein himself referred to himself as the Jewish saint, rather self mockingly. I would say Einstein was saintlike, because he had a sort of purity to him and a modesty. I have met various Nobel prize winners and not *one* of them has been anything like Einstein. He was an incredibly natural man of great humility."

When the Israeli leader Ben-Gurion was in the United States in 1951 to raise money for Israel, he called on Einstein at Princeton, eager to discuss cosmic mysteries. Ben-Gurion did not believe in the conventional view of God but wondered what accounted for a thinking being and suggested that a "something infinitely superior to all we know and are capable of conceiving" must have been its creator. Even Einstein, Ben-Gurion later reported, "with his great formula about energy and mass, agreed that there must be something behind the energy. And when I spoke of this to Niels Bohr, he too

Israeli premier David Ben-Gurion with Einstein in 1951, when they discussed the creator of the universe.

agreed, and thought it was probably true of the entire cosmos, that behind it there must be some superior being. This is what Spinoza must have meant. If then, by 'God' is meant such a superior being, which is neither material nor tangible, I say that I believe in God." Pretty much Einstein's view.

In December 1953, he chatted with his longtime friend, Johanna Fantova, a Princeton University librarian, who kept notes of their almost daily phone conversations. He said that he admired the flamboyant Roman Catholic bishop Fulton J. Sheen, who appeared with a flowing robe and a winning smile on his own TV show every week to promote the Christian faith. Even though Sheen had once ridiculed Einstein's religious views, Einstein regarded him as "one of the smartest men in the world today" and recommended his *Religion Without God* in which Sheen defended religion from the inroads of science. (At St. Basil's Church in Los Angeles on Good Friday, 1978, Bishop Sheen said: "The most brilliant ideas come from meeting God face to face." Which sounded like one of Einstein's statements, except, of course, that when Sheen said God he meant the accepted version.)

During their conversation, Einstein also gave Fantova an enthusiastic account of his other recent reading, especially "What Is an Agnostic?" by philosopher, mathematician, pacifist, and fellow socialist Bertrand Russell, reprinted in Leo Rosten's *Religions of America*. Einstein raved about Russell as one of his favorite thinkers, and the best of living writers.

Einstein once said that a person who regards his life and the lives of others as meaningless is not only unhappy but hardly fit for life. Yet, a year before his death, when George Wald visited the seventy-five-year-old scientist in his Princeton office at the Institute for Advanced Study, he said, "People keep writing to me asking, 'What is the meaning of life?' And what am I to tell them?" Wald, his fellow Nobelist, was equally perplexed. That same year Einstein was laughing with his friend Gillett Griffin, an art historian at Princeton's Firestone Library, over a letter he had received from a Catholic priest who wrote that he prayed for him daily through the Virgin Mary, and that Einstein shouldn't mind because Mary was a nice Jewish girl.

Max Jammer, an Israeli physicist and former Einstein colleague at Princeton, believed that Einstein's understanding of physics and religion were profoundly bound together. And Swiss playwright Friedrich Durrenmatt wrote that Einstein used to speak of God so often that he almost regarded him as a disguised theologian.

Theologian Torrance thought that Einstein's references to God could not "be dismissed simply as a *façon de parler*, for God had a deep, if rather elusive, significance for Einstein which was not unimportant for his life and scientific activity. It indicated a deep-seated way of life and thought. 'God' was not a theological mode of thought but rather the expression of a 'lived faith.'"

However, Einstein's God is not the author of the Ten Commandments, did not part the Red Sea, does not reward and punish, did not beget a son through a married woman to take on the sins of the world, is not watching your every move like a never-off-duty detective.

He continued to refer to God as "cosmic intelligence," never as a personal or super-personal being, in agreement with Spinoza that "personal" as applied to humans could not be applied to whatever created the harmony and beauty in the universe. He also agreed with Spinoza, writes Max Jammer, "that he who knows Nature knows God, but not because Nature is God but because the pursuit of science in studying Nature leads to religion."

And this was also in line with the rationalist Maimonides, says Jammer, who argued "on the one hand that 'the highest knowledge of God consists of knowing that we are unable to comprehend Him,' because no positive attributes can be attributed to Him, and on the other hand, that we know of His existence because it can be inferred from His 'ways' or actions as manifested in Nature. Einstein never regarded his rejection of a personal God as a denial of God. [He once] declared that a belief in a personal God seems 'preferable to the lack of any transcendental outlook on life.'

"In spite of his denial of [a personal] God and his rejection of religious customs and rituals, [Einstein] had a high respect for traditional religion. 'The highest principles for our aspirations and judgments,' he said, 'are given us in the Jewish-Christian tradition. It is a very high goal which, with our weak powers, we can reach only very inadequately, but which gives a sure foundation to our aspirations and valuations.'"

In later years, in an argument between Einstein and his physicist friend Niels Bohr about the nature of the universe as he thought it should be, the somewhat exasperated Dane exclaimed : "Stop telling God what to do!" And Einstein told Banesh Hoffmann: "When I am judging a theory, I ask myself whether, if I were God, I would have arranged the world in such a way."

Author Max Jammer suggests that British physicist Stephen Hawking was influenced by Einstein's thinking when Hawking wrote: "It would be perfectly consistent with all we know to say that there was a [Supreme] Being who was responsible for the laws of physics. However, I think it could be misleading to call such a Being 'God,' because this term is normally understood to have personal connotations which are not present in the laws of physics."

Hawking thinks that if we knew the answer to the question "Why is there a universe?" we should know the mind of God, but that providing the answers is beyond the limits of physical science and mathematical equations, just as Einstein said with respect to singularities. "All we have to realize is that the equations may not be continued over such regions."

No organized religion can claim Einstein as one of its own. He once remarked that not believing in a personal God was no philosophy, and a year before his death in 1955 he quipped that he was a member of a somewhat new kind of religion, being a religious nonbeliever.

For Einstein, God remained the big mystery with which he wrestled all his life.

8 | Einstein under Attack: Was He a Plagiarist and Was Mileva His Scientific Partner?

I
rrational attacks on Einstein began before World War I
and still persist. In Germany, Professor Ludwig
Bieberback called Albert Einstein an alien mountebank, and
Professor Wilhelm Muller charged that Einstein's theory of
relativity was a bid for Jewish world rule.

Perhaps his most prestigious critic was physics professor
Philipp Lenard, a 1905 Nobel Prize winner for his work on
cathode rays. He gave vent to such emotional outbursts as:
"The Jew conspicuously lacks understanding of the truth, in
contrast to the Aryan research scientist with his careful and
serious will to truth."

Lenard first called special relativity nonsense and, when
that didn't stick, tried to credit its discovery to a so-called
pure German named F. Hasenohrl, who couldn't speak for
himself, having died in World War I.

Einstein's opponents in the Study Group of German
Natural Philosphers, which Einstein derisively called the Anti-
Relativity League, booked Berlin's Philharmonic Hall for
August 24, 1920, where spokesmen denounced Einstein
before a full house as a publicity hound, a plagiarist, and a
charlatan. Einstein sat in the audience with his physicist friend
Walther Nernst, laughing and applauding at the more outrageous statements, especially a distorted account of relativity,
as if he were watching a play.

It must have touched a nerve because, when he got home,
he wrote an angry article that was published on the front page

of the *Berliner Tageblatt*, saying that they wouldn't have attacked him had he been a German nationalist instead of a Jew with international views, that prominent theoretical physicists throughout the world supported relativity, and that Lenard was the only scientist of international repute to oppose it.

He said that he admired Lenard as "a master of experimental physics," but that he had "so far achieved nothing in theoretical physics, and his objections to the

Einstein's bête noire, Philipp Lenard.

general theory of relativity are of such superficiality that until now I had thought it unnecessary to answer them in detail."

Lenard and Einstein met face to face at a conference the following month, and this exchange took place:

> Lenard: Relativity violates common sense.
> Einstein: What is seen as common sense changes over time.
> Lenard: At best relativity has limited validity.
> Einstein: On the contrary, an essential aspect of relativity is universality.

Max Born then spoke in favor of relativity, and Gustav Mie repeated Lenard's charge that others, not Einstein, had discovered relativity.

Max von Laue, Walther Nernst, and Otto Rubens, all of whom supported Einstein, issued a joint statement for the press: "Apart from Einstein's relativistic researches his work has assured him a permanent place in the history of science." And Max Planck wrote to Einstein calling the attacks on him "scarcely believable filth."

For almost a decade Lenard helped to prevent Einstein

from getting the Nobel Prize in Physics for relativity by telling the Nobel judges that it hadn't been proved and was valueless. When he did get the prize, it was for the photoelectric effect.

Now, his critics have returned with a vengeance, calling Einstein a fraud and a plagiarist who stole other men's work on relativity and falsely claimed it as his own. Yet the record shows that Einstein repeatedly and publicly acknowledged his several sources. In 1919 he wrote to the London *Times* that his special relativity was "simply a systematic extension of the electrodynamics of Clerk Maxwell and Lorentz." And he admitted that Lorentz and Fitzgerald had helped him create his special relativity theory and that Michelson and Morley had helped him with his general relativity theory.

At Caltech in 1931, at a banquet in his honor attended by Albert A. Michelson (America's first Nobel Prize–winning scientist), C. E. St. John, and E. P. Hubble, Einstein said: "Dear Friends, I have come among men who for many years have been true comrades with me in my labors. You, my honored Dr. Michelson, began with the work when I was only a little youngster hardly three feet high. It was you who led the physicists into new paths, and through your marvelous experimental work paved the way for the development of the Theory of Relativity. You uncovered the insidious defect in the ether theory of light, as it then existed, and stimulated the ideas of H. A. Lorentz and George F. Fitzgerald, out of which the Special Theory of Relativity developed. [Physicist Gerald Holton, an editor of the *Einstein Papers*, points out that the following crucial sentence has been left out of many previous accounts of the Einstein speech. This restored sentence shows that Einstein was referring not to special but to general relativity.] These in turn led the way to the General Theory of Relativity, and to the theory of gravitation. Without your work this theory would today be scarcely more than an interesting speculation; it was your verifications which first set the theory on a real basis."

So here is Einstein's public acknowledgment that Lorentz and Fitzgerald were among his sources for the special and general theory of relativity, although the only one he had mentioned in his special relativity paper was his friend and patent office colleague Michele Besso.

Physicist John Stachel, an editor of the *Einstein Papers*, says that Einstein "was quite aware that his way of trying to understand the physical universe had grown out of a long history of previous attempts. He had to criticize these attempts in order to go beyond them."

When the British mathematician and historian Sir Edmund Whittaker attributed relativity mainly to Poincaré and Lorentz, with Einstein playing a minor role, Max Born, Einstein's friend and Whittaker's colleague at Edinburgh University, warned Einstein of this insult, saying that "despite the contrary evidence which Born had submitted [including translations from the German originals of some relevant articles he had prepared for Whittaker]," he had failed to persuade Whittaker to include them in his 1953 book, *Histories of the Theories of Aether and Electricity*.

Einstein replied that he didn't resent it, that if Whittaker convinced others, that was their fault—and, after all, he didn't have to read the book. Soon after, when a celebration in Bern to mark the fiftieth anniversary of his theory was about to take place, he wrote to Born, ever generous, that he hoped that the contributions of Lorentz and Poincaré would be mentioned.

Although, as Einstein biographer Albrecht Folsing remarks, "After nearly half a century this was the first time that Einstein ever mentioned Poincaré in connection with the special relativity theory." For his part, Poincaré had been remarkably reluctant to even mention Einstein and relativity in the same sentence. Some still claim that the

French mathematical genius Henri Poincaré, author of chaos theory, discovered special relativity before Einstein. But the weight of scientific authority still supports Einstein, giving Poincaré the credit for the equations, and Einstein the credit for the audacious step of creating the theory.

As Ian Stewart, professor of mathematics at England's Warwick University sees it: "Einstein said, 'This is not just an interesting mathematical gadget, this is not just a way of thinking about certain problems in mathematical physics, this is reality, this is how it works, things really do get shorter and move faster.' And he really put his reputation on the line by saying this because it is no longer just a little intellectual game. This is trying to tell people that reality is totally different from what they expect. Einstein was courageous enough to risk his reputation." "This does not preclude the fact," adds Michel Paty, director of research at the National Center for Scientific Research, "that Poincaré made a large contribution to works in the field."

Einstein himself said that if he hadn't discovered special relativity, his bet was on Paul Langevin to have done it.

And Gerald Holton concludes: "That Einstein's work in 1905 was independent of Poincaré's investigations on electromagnetism (based on his belief in the ether) and has now been repeatedly and adequately established."

Note that none of the following ever publicly accused Einstein of stealing their material without acknowledgement: Mach, Lorentz, Michelson, Morley, Fitzgerald, or even Poincaré. And all—with the exception of Poincaré—applauded him.

A London *Times* editorial writer of May 25, 1931, having no British dog in the race, might be accepted as an unbiased commentator. He wrote that "the genius of Einstein consists in taking up the un-interpreted experiments and scattered suggestions of his predecessors. And welding them into a comprehensive scheme that wins universal admiration by its simplicity and beauty." The same newspaper had once called relativity an affront to common sense.

An amusing aspect of Einstein's special and general theory of relativity—the latter to include all of physics, especially gravitation—is that Hermann Minkowski, the Zurich Polytechnic math professor who had called Einstein a lazy dog, developed Einstein's special theory after the fact as a mathematical concept and introduced the idea of a four-dimensional world.

In 1955, just two weeks before his death, Einstein told I. Bernard Cohen, a Harvard historian of science, and the last person to interview him, "It has always hurt me that Galileo did not acknowledge the work of Kepler." As if he himself had a clear conscience about crediting his own sources, even with regard to David Hilbert.

In the summer of 1915, David Hilbert, considered the world's leading mathematician since the death of Poincaré in 1909, and Felix Klein, also an outstanding mathematician, invited Einstein to Göttingen, where he gave six two-hour lectures on his general relativity theory and stayed at Hilbert's home. Einstein believed both Klein and Hilbert had been convinced of the theory's validity. He called Hilbert a great man and was absolutely delighted with him. But a few months later he wrote to his friend Zangger that Hilbert was trying to steal his ideas.

Six days before Einstein submitted his general relativity equations in Berlin on November 25, 1915, Hilbert sent his virtually identical equations to the Royal Society of Sciences in Göttingen. For that same month Einstein had been corresponding almost exclusively with Hilbert on the subject, during which he sent Hilbert his publications, and Hilbert sent Einstein the draft of his treatise. Einstein biographer Folsing asks, "Could Einstein, casting his eye over Hilbert's paper, have discovered the term which was still lacking in his own equations?" Possibly but not likely, Folsing concludes, adding that Einstein's "approach was . . . quite different from Hilbert's, and Einstein's achievements can, therefore, surely be regarded as authentic." And, eventually, "Hilbert, like all his other colleagues, acknowledged Einstein as the sole creator of relativity theory."

But a new wave of critics, anti-Semites, Neo-Nazis, or searchers for the truth have launched a concerted attack on Einstein—mostly on the Internet, calling Einstein a liar and a plagiarist, and naming new claimants to relativity's authorship including Ludwig Gustav Lange, Joseph Larmor, Paul Drude, and Olinto De Pretto.

In 1997 an international research group at the Max Planck Institute for the History of Science—including John Stachel, director of the Center for Einstein Studies at Boston University, and science historians Jurgen Renn and Leo Corry—studied the evidence for and against, and refuted the charge that five days before Einstein published his theory of general relativity Hilbert beat him to it. In fact, they concluded that Hilbert, who died in 1943, had plagiarized Einstein.

Meanwhile a growing number of Einstein's critics have charged that his first wife, Mileva Maric, has been deprived of her rightful place as a partner in his work. Some even claim that she was the sole author of the special theory of relativity.

Physicist Evan Harris Walker speculates that Einstein or his agents destroyed letters from Mileva that would prove she had cooperated fully in his scientific work and actually wrote his doctoral thesis, and that he took credit for the turning points of relativity theory, which were her ideas, and gave her his Nobel Prize money not only to get a divorce and support their sons but to buy her silence about her part in the theory.

Other critics suggest that those letters in which she demonstrates irrefutably that she was Einstein's scientific partner, or at least did the math for him, have been destroyed or suppressed. They quote his letter to her referring to "our work" as proof that she was his scientific partner. Einstein's advocates say these are the wishful-thinking words of a man in love attempting to persuade his beloved that they are a team.

Even their son Hans Albert recalled Einstein at work on his theories during his childhood, but he never mentioned his mother taking an important part. Nor did she, according to Gerald Holton. And although Albert's letters to Mileva often mention his new ideas in physics, in all of her letters to him or to her close friend, now in the Einstein archives, she does not express even a tentative original idea.

The introduction to volume one of *The Collected Papers of Albert Einstein* concedes that Mileva's significant role was a "possibility [but] the available evidence suggests that [her] role was that of a sounding board for Einstein's ideas, a role also played by his friends Michele Besso and Conrad Habicht."

In a joint response to these promoters of Mileva as a major contributor to Einstein's work, Robert Schulmann, director of the Einstein Papers Project, then at Boston University, and Gerald Holton, wrote: "All serious Einstein scholarship by Abraham Pais, John Stachel, and others, has shown that the scientific collaboration between the couple was light and one-sided. The documentary evidence is that Maric encouraged and aided Einstein in the early years, when their intense passion for each other made their life at the margin of society bearable, when he expressed and shared his groundbreaking ideas freely with her and a few friends, while developing them in isolation from the physics community."

On the other hand, they agree that "she helped him by looking up data and checking calculations. Einstein never acknowledged this help publicly; but neither did Maric claim more in her letters to him or to others. The true collaboration which they had originally planned when they both intended careers as high-school science teachers never did develop. Nor is there a shred of documentary proof of her originality as a scientist. Ironically, making Maric into a victimized genius demeans the tragedy of her life. When excessive claims about her role in physics have to be disproved, the public might take less seriously that she was one of the early pioneers, at great personal sacrifice, in the movement to bring women into science at last."

Einstein's shabby treatment of Mileva also spurred Dr. Lewis Pyenson, a historian of science, to question his reputation as a moral authority. Pyenson writes: "In one of his most widely available popular collections in English, *Out of My Later Years*, Einstein was not shy about instructing ordinary people in moral matters. A text from 1948 has the revealing epigram: 'Moral conduct does not mean merely a stern demand to renounce some of the desired joys of life, but rather a sociable interest in a happier lot for all men.' Eulogizing the French physicist Paul Langevin, known in popular circles in part for his callous rejection of wife and family in favor of an *affaire de coeur* with Marie Curie, Einstein emphasized: 'The moral grandeur of his personality earned him the bitter enmity of many of the more humdrum intellectuals.' Remembering his physicist friend Paul Ehrenfest, Einstein recounted Ehrenfest's affection for his wife while alluding obliquely to a marital separation provoked by Ehrenfest's lover. These are significant choices of expression for someone like Einstein, who championed open and transparent discussion of evidence and who hoped for a 'moral force' to create world government."

However, what is known in popular circles is a fragile source for a historian to rely on. Pyenson fails to mention that Langevin was greatly concerned with the welfare of his children and, in fact, returned to his wife and family. And as Einstein regarded marriage as "barbaric," it's unlikely he would have considered marital infidelity in a brilliant and affectionate friend such as Ehrenfest as a reason not to eulogize him.

But even Einstein's most enthusiastic and informed supporters join his detractors in being unable to explain how a twenty-six-year-old, largely self-taught, physicist working as a third-class patent clerk, who had never even seen another theoretical physicist, and whose previous scientific papers had been unremarkable, turned out four theories in one year, profoundly influencing the course of twentieth-century physics.

The simple answer is that he was a genius and, as such, defies explanation. But Gerald Holton takes a good shot at it in his essay "On Trying to Understand Scientific Genius": "There is his legendary, iron ability to concentrate, often for years on a single basic problem in physics, regardless of contemporary schools and fashions. Similarly, there is his stubborn faithfulness to a clearly established personal identity, characterized by uncompromising rejection of every *Zwang* and external, arbitrary authority in physics as well as in clothing or in the demands of everyday life. But opposite to this glorious obstinacy and solitary intransigence with which to search for the basic permanence and necessity behind nature's phenomena, there is also his ever-ready openness to deal after all with the 'merely personal' from which he so longed to flee—to deal with the barrage of requests for help and personal involvements that appealed to his fundamental humanity and his vulnerability to pity."

9 | Einstein's FBI File and the Soviet Spy He Loved

The Federal Bureau of Investigation kept a secret file on Albert Einstein, starting in 1932 and gathering steam in 1950. It grew to be at least eighteen hundred pages long, far longer than any of his biographies—and full of fiction.

Why did FBI director J. Edgar Hoover spend such a massive amount of time and money on a man whose life—with the exception of personal episodes that had nothing to do with national security—was an open book? Oddly, one episode, only recently revealed, which the FBI completely missed out on, involved his love affair with an attractive Soviet spy who tried to recruit him—about which Hoover and his agents never had a clue.

As his close friends would attest, Einstein was a straight shooter who said what was on his mind in public and in private and made no attempt to hide his political views or activities.

Yet Hoover suspected him of leading a double life when he lived in Berlin, as the leader of a dangerous Communist spy ring and, after he immigrated to the United States, of secretly working on a death ray with which a small band of men could control a nation.

This is first spelled out in a 1942 FBI report from an anonymous tipster self-described as "patriot," who gave the following misinformation: "At a November 1, 1938 meeting of a group, 'The Music Boys,' at the Biltmore Hotel, in New

In 1921, on Einstein's first visit to the United States, with Rabbi Stephen Wise (center) and New York Mayor Fiorello La Guardia.

York City, Rabbi [Stephen] Wise [a nationally prominent Reform rabbi, leader of the U.S. Zionist movement and a civic activist], presided [and] opened the meeting." [Wise said that] "It is necessary to have 500 divisional or district leaders know our plans and give full cooperation on a nation wide basis. The 500 in turn have agents in each of 3,000 communities, both urban and rural. Louis Lipsky (a noted Zionist leader and journalist) was the next speaker. He said— Einstein is experimenting with a ray which will help us to destroy armed opposition—aircraft, tanks and armored cars. He hopes that with it a dozen men could defeat 500. Through it 5% could rule a nation."

Fred Jerome, in *The Einstein File: J. Edgar Hoover's Secret War Against the World's Most Famous Scientist*, confirms that some of Hoover's unnamed sources were Nazi agents on the U.S. payroll. The anonymous "death ray" tipster may well have been one of these Nazi propagandists hired to discredit Einstein, whom the German government considered its Public Enemy Number One.

On April 17, 1938, the year he was supposed to be working on what amounted to a death ray, Einstein had addressed three thousand people at a Passover seder service in New York's Hotel Astor. Then, obviously referring to Nazi Germany, Einstein had said, "Anti-Semitism has always been the cheapest means employed by selfish minorities for deceiving the people. A tyranny based on such deception and maintained by terror must inevitably perish from the poison it generates from within itself."

Nazi sympathizers responded by spreading the false rumor, published in an American magazine, that he was a Communist who had attended a party congress in Russia. He was, in fact, not a Communist and had never been to Russia nor to any Communist Party congress.

While Hoover continued his efforts to nail him as a dangerous Communist by recording his friendships with several well-known left-wingers such as Charlie Chaplin, the African American actor-singer Paul Robeson, and architect Frank Lloyd Wright, he appears to have taken no special interest in his purported experiments with a death ray.

But the "death ray" rumor surfaced again, in the summer of 1950, jazzed up by a rewrite man with science-fiction pretensions. An FBI agent spotted it and reported to Hoover that "according to the 'Arlington Daily,' May 21, 1948, Professor Einstein, and 'ten former Nazi research brain trusters,' held a secret meeting at which they put on asbestos suits and watched a beam of light. This article pointed out that a block of steel was melted as quickly as the light switch in any home could be turned on and that this new and secret weapon could be operated from planes to destroy entire cities. It was further stated that the atomic bomb was 'little boy stuff' compared to this new development."

Instead of first asking the paper's editor to reveal the story's source, Hoover had Colonel C. C. Blakeney of Army Intelligence check it out. Einstein was exonerated. The FBI disclaimer reads: "The Intelligence Division of the Army subsequently advised the Bureau that this information could have no foundation in fact and that no machine could be devised which would be effective outside the range of a few feet." That was true—at least for that time. It is also true that as early as 1917 Einstein had recognized the existence of stimulated emission, but it was not until the 1950s that Charles Townes discovered how to put it to use as a laser beam. However, a laser able to vaporize the hardest and most heat-resistant materials was not constructed until 1960. And Einstein had nothing to do with it.

Anyone who knew Einstein could have told Hoover why the report was false: he would never have worked with Nazis or even former Nazis on anything—except perhaps their extinction. And, although he did have some two dozen inventions to his credit, they were as harmless, for example, as a gyrocompass and a refrigerator.

The entire FBI file on Einstein is an incredible mix of tips and poison-pen fabrications from the disgruntled, the misinformed, the paranoid, and the prejudiced, further adding to the Einstein myth. In their wild eyes he was a fantastic character with evil intent, a man none of his friends, relatives, or colleagues would recognize as remotely like the Einstein they knew. A monster, in fact. Yet the FBI seemed to be falling for it.

Other reports considered serious enough to go into his file describe him as a triple threat. According to them, he was the inventor of a mind-control robot able to read people's minds and control them; the kidnapper of the young son of the famous aviator Charles Lindbergh, who then framed Bruno Hauptmann, who was executed for the crime; and the leading light in an attempt to hijack Hollywood and make it a Communist fiefdom.

The early reports of FBI agents to their boss were full of mistakes that a cub reporter on a local newspaper would have avoided. They didn't even know where Einstein worked. Both pieces of information could have been easily obtained by a call to Princeton's postmaster or a local telephone operator, or by contacting one of his biographers.

As for his being the leader of a Communist spy ring, as previously mentioned, Einstein was never a Communist. He was a Social Democrat who advocated world government and a less militaristic approach to foreign policy. Although he abhorred dictatorships of any kind, he did sympathize with many Communist goals and causes.

Why the FBI was so inept in its investigation of Einstein is partly explained by Richard Alan Schwartz, an assistant professor of English at Florida International University in Miami, who, by using the Freedom of Information Act, first obtained Einstein's FBI file, or as much of it as they were willing to hand over.

"Perhaps most perplexing," Schwartz writes, "is the way in which history is ignored by the FBI. The Depression, the rise of Nazism and World War II might never have happened as far as the FBI was concerned. That someone might have supported communist causes during the 1930s in response to an economic crisis that represented at least a temporary failure of capitalism or to the spread of communism is not even considered. The FBI appears to have thought that a Communist or suspected Communist from the past is necessarily a Communist in the present, and just as necessarily a threat to the American system. More than anything else, the 1,500 pages of the FBI File (some three hundred more were eventually released) reveal how powerful and wide-spread that belief was. In the end, the file is not only a lode of information and innuendo about Albert Einstein; it is also a record of the F.B.I.'s mentality during the early 1950s."

Here is the FBI's biographical sketch of Einstein in which even the headline is wrong. It has him located at Princeton University instead of at the Institute for Advanced Study, a separate entity.

It reads: "Dr. Albert Einstein was born in Ulm-an-der-Donau, Germany, March 14, 1879, the son of Hermann and Pauline (Koch). He was educated in Germany and Switzerland. He holds a great many honorary degrees from universities all over the world. He was married to Mileva Maree [Wrong. Maric.] in 1901, and a second time to Elsa Einstein in 1917. He has one child by his first wife. [Wrong. Two sons and a deceased daughter.] He is connected with many universities in Europe.

"He came to the United States in 1933, [and 1921] and has been located at Princeton University. [Wrong.] He is the author of many books on relativity and other matters. His home address is 112 Mercer Street, Princeton, New Jersey. [At least they got his correct home address.]

"Even in the political free and easy period of 1923 to 1929, the Einstein home was known as a Communist center and clearing house. [Not true.]

"When the German police tried to bridge [*sic*] some of the extreme Communist activities, the Einstein villa at Lanssee [Caputh] was found to be the hiding place of Moscow envoys, etc." [Not true.]

Hoover even believed that Einstein might have a son living in Russia—again, not true.

The file continues: "It is the belief of this office that Professor Einstein is an extreme radical, and that a great deal of material on him can be found in the files of the State Department. This office has knowledge of one incident

*Einstein walking to work at the Institute for
Advanced Study in 1950, where he worked for
over twenty years.*

which was newspaper headlines in 1933 when Einstein and
his family left Berlin for the United States.

"The American Consul General at Berlin, Mr. George
Messersmith, was asked by Mrs. Einstein to visa the passports
of herself, Dr. Einstein, and her daughter [Margot]. She
made this report by telephone. Mr. Messersmith told her
that Dr. Einstein would have to appear personally at the
Consulate and that he would have to swear to an affidavit
that he is not a member of any radical organization.
Mrs. Einstein then wired prominent Jewish women in New
York that Mr. Messersmith was obstructing their coming,

and a press campaign was started in American papers demanding that the President recall Mr. Messersmith. The State Department upheld Mr. Messersmith, and Dr. Einstein signed the declaration."

In fact, it was Messersmith's assistant, Raymond Geist, who questioned Einstein for about forty-five minutes, during which he admitted to joining the War Resisters International which did not require being a member of any political party, and when asked, "Are you a Communist or anarchist?" Einstein responded angrily, "What's this? An inquisition?" He then said that if a visa wasn't granted at noon the next day he'd cancel the trip. He woke in the morning convinced that he would not be going to the United States. But at eleven he got a call from the U.S. consulate to tell him that his visa had been issued.

Jamie Sayen, author of *Einstein in America*, has the most informed view of the scientist's attitude toward Communism and the Soviet Union, having had his manuscript vetted by Otto Nathan, who shared Einstein's political outlook and was among his closest confidants. Sayen maintains that during World War II Einstein's greatest concern was to defeat Hitler, and when the support of the Soviet Union became vital, he rationalized Stalin's repressive policies and was persuaded that Russian Jews were being treated fairly when, in fact, they were being forcibly assimilated. After the war he focused on preventing future wars and, toward that goal, advocated the international control of atomic weapons. He always viewed Soviet actions with these two critical issues in mind. Consequently, he attempted to establish a reasonable dialogue with Soviet intellectuals.

"At first," wrote Sayen, "he viewed the Russian Revolution with sympathy and optimism until the brutal means employed by the regime to limit individual freedom became known." He continues:

After 1945 when the overriding issue for Einstein was the need for an effective world government, he felt it was essential that the United States and the Soviet Union discover a way to cooperate. As a result, in the years 1945–1947 Einstein played down the significance of Stalin's responsibility for the Cold War impasse. And he continued to search for a means of securing Soviet cooperation. . . . When Russians made clear its unwavering opposition to world government, Einstein, although disappointed, blamed Russian xenophobia on the treatment the Soviet Union had received from the Western powers ever since 1917—the support by the West of the Soviet regime's enemies, political and economic boycotts, appeasement in the face of fascist aggression in the thirties, and the ill-fated attempt at Munich to turn Hitler's expansion to the east. By the end of 1947, in response to Russia's refusal to cooperate, he began to advocate that plans for a world government proceed without the Russians. . . . Privately, Einstein was already highly critical of much of what was happening in the Soviet Union, but he refrained from making his criticism public for fear of adding to the prevailing warlike atmosphere. In addition to impatience with Russia's attitude to world government, Einstein discovered on several occasions . . . that fair dealings with Stalin's Russia were next to impossible.

In July 1946 the American ambassador in Moscow, Walter Bedell Smith, sent the State Department a memo, which was forwarded to J. Edgar Hoover, about a rumor in Jewish circles that the Russian scientist Peter Kapitsa had invited Einstein to immigrate to the Soviet Union. Kapitsa was purported to have written to Einstein that they could pursue their scientific research together, "in a land of true democracy, free from selfish taint, unhampered by restrictions imposed by capitalist society." Einstein was assured that whatever funds, laboratories, buildings, equipment, books, and assistants he might need would be immediately and completely placed at his disposal.

Einstein was said to have replied in Hebrew not to Kapitsa but to Stalin himself, saying that before he could consider the offer, he wanted the answers to several questions, such as: Were Jewish scientists not permitted to hold prominent posts? Why were apparently unnecessary obstacles placed in the way of Jewish scientific and research workers? And why were outstanding Jewish professors of medical science, whom he named, not elected to the recently created Medical Academy?

According to the rumors, Molotov had denied the truth of the implications of anti-Semitism, and Einstein was again invited to immigrate to the Soviet Union. Certain important Soviet officials were discharged for anti-Semitism and the medical professors named by Einstein were elected to the Academy.

"The Embassy had been unable to determine whether or not this is true," wrote Bedell Smith, who thought that the rumor was a "significant illustration of the feeling of unease amongst Jews in the Soviet Union that they are discriminated against."

The entire thing sounds unlikely, starting with Einstein writing in Hebrew. And, of course, he never went to the Soviet Union—for any reason.

Einstein did, in fact, write to Stalin, but for humanitarian reasons. Hardly a day went by that someone didn't write, phone, or visit Einstein asking for his help and, despite Helen Dukas's efforts to let him concentrate on his work, he responded to many of them, including Guy von Dardel, a physics student at Cornell. Two years previously, in 1945, von Dardel's half-brother, Raoul Wallenberg, after saving tens of thousands of Jews from being sent to concentration camps, had disappeared. When last seen, Wallenberg had been in the "protective custody" of Russian soldiers. At his half-brother's request, Einstein wrote to the Soviet leader:

Dear Mr. Stalin, as an old Jew I appeal to you to do everything possible to find and send back to his country the Swede Raoul Wallenberg who was one of the very few who during the bad years of Nazi persecution on his own accord and risking his own life, worked to rescue thousands of my unhappy Jewish people.

A month later, says Einstein's FBI file, the Soviet embassy in Washington reported that Stalin had received the letter and that a search had failed to find Wallenberg. His fate is still a mystery.

FBI agents continued to add to his and Dukas's bulging files with mainly inaccurate or ludicrous material, or, as Shakespeare would have put it, a tale told by an idiot.

There is no hint that anyone at the FBI read anything that Einstein had written regarding his philosophy of life, which would have told them that they were after the wrong man. As Fred Jerome points out: "Overall, the FBI's dossier quotes remarkably little of Einstein's own opinions. Except for his 1947 pamphlet, 'Atomic War or Peace,' and a few scattered remarks. It contains virtually none of his published articles, essays or interviews."

Of course, not everything that was printed about him was false, such as the *New York Times* report of February 5, 1937, in which Einstein declared that he felt ashamed that the democratic nations had failed to support the Loyalist Government of Spain.

And, "The records of the Military Intelligence Division of the Army revealed that Einstein was recommended for clearance with the 'limited field of study for which his services were needed.' The Navy gave its assent, but in a letter dated July 26, 1940, General [George Veazey] Strong [of Army Intelligence] stated that the Army could not clear Einstein."

And, "In 1947, Einstein stated that the French Communist Party was the only real party in France with a solid organization and a precise program. In this public statement, which appeared in the French Communist newspaper in Paris, Einstein was critical of the United States military policy and expressed the opinion that international inspection would be insufficient to preserve peace."

Hoover never let go of the fantasy that Einstein had been the kingpin at the center of a Communist spy ring in Berlin in the 1920s and 1930s. To establish this as a fact and to have him deported as a security risk, the FBI teamed up with U.S. Army Intelligence in 1951 and launched an intense four-year investigation. Having failed to catch Einstein red-handed, Hoover focused on Einstein's secretary-housekeeper, Helen Dukas, mistakenly suspecting her of having access to atomic secrets. Her file also grew to hundreds of pages. Yet she was as innocent as Einstein of being a threat to the United States. FBI agents secretly pored over her incoming and outgoing mail, testing it for a hidden codes or messages in invisible ink. They drew a blank.

Meanwhile Einstein was playing with puzzles, writing poetry to his woman friend Johanna Fantova, suffering various debilitating illnesses, helping others in distress, and trying to find a simple equation to cover his Unified Field Theory.

When the meticulous study of Dukas's mail came up with nothing incriminating, the FBI tapped her long-distance phone calls and again came up with nothing.

Finally, two agents from the FBI's Newark, New Jersey, office tried to discover if she had been a spy for the Russians while working for Einstein in Berlin between 1928 and 1933. They interviewed Dukas at her 112 Mercer Street home. She was charming and cooperative and their report to Hoover on March 9, 1955, reads: "During the interview, DUKAS was extremely friendly and appeared quite sincere in her answers. She did not appear to be evasive in any manner, spoke quite freely . . . and the interview was conducted in a discrete [*sic*] and circumspect manner as suggested by the Bureau. The premise for the interview was given to DUKAS as an opportunity for her to assist in developing information concerning activities in Berlin, Germany, during the period 1928 to 1933. At no time did she give any hint or indication that she was aware the investigation concerned her in any way."

The report continues: "It is to be noted that DUKAS claimed that she was the only employee of Dr. Einstein since 1928 and that in itself tends to discredit the allegations by G-2's source, who furnished the information that EINSTEIN'S office had a staff of secretaries and typists and that his senior secretary was the one engaged in contacts with Soviet couriers. . . . The chief or senior secretary referred to in most probability was EINSTEIN'S wife, ELSA EINSTEIN, now deceased, or his oldest stepdaughter, name unknown, also deceased." Her name was Ilse, which, of course, Dukas could have told them.

She did reveal that Einstein was in poor health, having suffered from a severe attack of the flu during the past winter, and that he had developed a case of anemia that had confined him to his home for several months.

The report continues: "It is also noted that the interview has identified EINSTEIN'S children and their current whereabouts, discounting any possibility of children being held behind the Iron Curtain as possible hostages of the Soviets."

During the long, friendly interview, Dukas told the agents that Einstein's elder son, Hans Albert, was a professor at the University of California at Berkeley, and his younger son, Eduard, was "confined in a mental institution in Zurich, Switzerland, since he was twenty-one [1930] and was a hopeless mental case." She said that she had no interest in politics except to have opposed Hitler, and had not known of any Communists in Germany who had attempted to infiltrate Dr. Einstein's office or those of any of his scientific friends. She

Einstein walking home from the Institute for Advanced Study.

stressed that her only interest in life was Einstein—that she followed all his wishes—and never engaged in any outside activity without first asking his permission.

Convinced that she was telling the truth, the agents advised ending the investigation because "of the long lapse of time since Einstein's office was allegedly used by the Soviets, the lack of corroborating information, and the fact that the personnel involved are scattered in many countries and in many cases are deceased. [In fact they had never existed.] Therefore, both the Dukas case and the Einstein case are being closed in the Newark Office, and will not be opened . . . unless advised to the contrary by the Bureau."

So Hoover called off the hunt. The FBI memo to him on May 2, 1955, reads: "A review of this file reflects that there are no logical outstanding leads in this matter and inasmuch as ALBERT EINSTEIN is now deceased, it is not believed that any additional investigation is warranted in the matter. Therefore, this case is closed."

It's sobering to think that in twenty years of investigation—which cost taxpayers a bundle—and with all the resources available to him, the FBI chief never came close to understanding who Albert Einstein was. He should have hired a biographer. And, amazingly, despite their concentrated efforts, his agents were totally oblivious of Einstein's contact with a Soviet spy. They missed his longtime liaison, between 1935 and 1945, with an attractive Soviet spy, Margarita Konenkova, the forty-one-year-old wife of a noted Soviet sculptor, Sergei Konenkov. Apparently, Margot had innocently introduced Margarita to Einstein, then fifty-six. Her task during World War II was to persuade him, Oppenheimer, and other scientists at Princeton to leak secrets of the atomic bomb. In no instance did she succeed in this goal. Einstein, in fact, had none to leak, having been denied security clearance for the Manhattan Project. She did talk Einstein into meeting the Soviet vice-consul Pavel Mikhailov. But nothing came of it. (Einstein was also working with the U.S. Navy, as a $25-a-day consultant, for which he proposed new weapons and critiqued others in the works. But the weapons were all at an embryonic stage, and there is no evidence that he discussed this work with Margarita or Mikhailov.)

According to a close friend, Dr. Thomas Bucky, Einstein never knew that he was under FBI surveillance, but had he known "he would have laughed."

But he did know. According to author Fred Jerome, at a dinner in 1948, hosted by the Bulgarian minister to the United States, Dr. Nissin Mayorah, Einstein told the Polish ambassador to the United States, Winiewicz, "I suppose you must realize by now that the U.S. is no longer a free country, that undoubtedly our conversation is being recorded. This room is wired, and my house is closely watched." Sure enough, Einstein's comments appear in his FBI file.

Abraham Pais implies that the FBI tactics were blatantly obvious, informing fellow Einstein biographer Jamie Sayen that it was "common knowledge" among physicists that they were "under surveillance."

Margarita's cover, which obviously fooled the FBI, was extremely effective, because she was the wife of a sculptor working on a bust of Einstein that now appears outside the Institute for Advanced Study.

Two pieces of evidence revealed Einstein's love affair with Margarita: a photograph of her on display in an exhibition on Russian-Soviet female spies—most of them beautiful—held in St. Petersburg in the summer of 1998, and nine Einstein love letters to Margarita put up for auction at Sotheby's in New York the same year.

After she and her husband had returned to Moscow in 1945, Einstein wrote to her, "Everything reminds me of you. Almar's [a combination of the first letters of their names, referring to their possessions] shawl, the dictionaries, that wonderful pipe that we thought was gone, and all the

Einstein knew he was being investigated by the FBI but had no idea that FBI chief J. Edgar Hoover suspected him of being a dangerous Soviet spy.

other little things in my cell, and also the lonely nest [his office at the Institute for Advanced Study]." He ended another letter, "Write me soon, if you can find the time, and be kissed by your A. Einstein." In a third letter he responded to her enthusiastic account of a May Day celebration, with: "I watch with concern these exaggerated patriotic feelings."

Paul Needham, who translated the letters from the German, said: "In the years I spent at Sotheby's, this is the most interesting discovery story I've ever encountered. They're very open and very different from Einstein's other letters. They reveal both deep emotion and very accessible emotion—the kind anybody who's ever been in love can identify with."

Selby Kiffer, vice president of Sotheby's books and manuscript department, said that there is no evidence that Margarita recruited Einstein: "He essentially refused to fall into that trap." There is also no evidence that he or the FBI suspected that she was a spy. Expert opinion is that although he fell for her, he did not fall into her hands. Einstein was not a traitor.

Her husband Sergei's photo of Einstein taken at Saranac Lake, New York, on August 1, 1945, appears on the cover of this book. It is the only photo of Einstein smiling as an adult among the hundreds, if not thousands, of photos taken of him. He looks like a man in love—with the photographer's wife, in fact—and without a care in the world. Presumably the husbands of Soviet spies accepted cuckoldry as a patriotic duty.

Evidently, Margarita neither turned Einstein into a traitor nor deceived him into believing a false picture of conditions in the Soviet Union.

In the last years of his life Einstein privately criticized Soviet Russia as "politically undeveloped" and as a country where "murder with and without legal accoutrements, has become a commonplace of daily politics," and where "the citizen enjoys no rights." But, as he told the American socialist Norman Thomas, criticism of the Soviet Union, however well-intentioned, was futile.

Afterword

Einstein was a man of remarkable contradictions: The pacifist urged FDR to build the atomic bomb, then urged him not to use it; the absent father devoted a surprising amount of time to entertaining and helping other people's children; the skeptic admired the flamboyant TV evangelist Bishop Fulton Sheen; the man who claimed to have the skin of an elephant and to not care what others thought of him declined to accept a peace prize from the Russians for fear that he'd been taken as a Bolshevik.

Although Einstein was not disturbed by a Californian earthquake, a fierce storm while at sea, or Nazi death threats, he was scared to face an admiring crowd. The scientist who proclaimed his renunciation of the merely human to devote himself to solving the mysteries of the universe showed tender concern for his close friends, his pet parrot, cat, and dog. And the man who was apparently indifferent to his appearance complained that without his mustache he would look like a woman.

One of the greatest scientists of all time had such a poor memory that he once forgot his own name. And the self-confident if not arrogant Einstein, accused by Bohr of trying to tell God what to do, wrote to his friend Solovine, on March 28, 1949, "There is not a single concept of which I am convinced that it will stand up, and I am unsure if I am even on the right road."

However, in a more confident mood, he said that he would

be dead for a long time before his latest work was recognized, and that he was working for future generations. He may well prove prophetic. Today in 2005, fifty years after his death, theoretical physicists are cautiously optimistic that, through string theory, they can complete Einstein's goal of unifying gravity with the other known forces of the universe.

What still remains a mystery are certain incongruous aspects of his life and personality. Those will be a challenge for future generations of his biographers to take on—the Unified Theory of Einstein.

EINSTEIN CHRONOLOGY

1879
- March 14. Born in Ulm, Germany.

1880 • November 18. His sister, Maja, born.

1886 • At seven, starts school in Munich.

1895 • At fifteen, joins family in Italy.

1896 • At seventeen, in Aarau, Switzerland, has his first love affair, with Marie Winteler; obtains high school diploma and enters Zurich Polytechnic. There he meets Michele Angelo Besso, Marcel Grossmann, and his future wife, Mileva Maric.

1900 • At twenty-two, graduates Zurich Polytechnic.

1901 • Becomes a Swiss citizen.

1902 • January. His and Mileva's daughter, Lieserl, is born.

1902 • June 16. At twenty-four, gets job at Bern Patent Office.

1902 • October 16. His father, Hermann, dies.

1903 • January 6. Marries Mileva Maric.

1904 • May 14. His son Hans Albert born.

1905 • At age twenty-six, reveals his genius with papers on light quantum—the photoelectric effect, Brownian motion, and the special theory of relativity, containing the famous equation $E = mc^2$. Produces his Ph.D. thesis at the University of Zurich on molecular dimensions.

1908 • At age twenty-nine, lectures at University of Bern.

1909 • October 15. At age thirty-one, appointed assistant professor, University of Zurich.

1910 • July 28. His son Eduard born.

1911 ◆ March. At age thirty-three, appointed professor at Prague University, Czechoslovakia.

1912 ◆ August. Appointed professor at Zurich Polytechnic, where Grossmann is now a math professor.

1914 ◆ Appointed professor at the University of Berlin. World War I begins.

1915 ◆ November. Reveals his general theory of relativity.

1919 ◆ February. He and Mileva are divorced.

1919 ◆ June. Marries his cousin Elsa, divorced mother of two daughters, Ilse and Margot.

1919 ◆ November. Arthur Eddington says that his experiment confirms Einstein's theory that gravitation bends light.

Einstein in his Berlin study in 1920, shortly after he married Elsa. He was obviously not short of reading matter.

1921 ◆ Fund-raising trip to the United States with Chaim Weizmann.

His host, Lord Haldane, (left) looks on as Einstein, the international celebrity, is photographed in London in 1921.

1921 ◆ Visits Japan, Israel, and Spain with Elsa.

1922 ◆ Receives 1921 Nobel Prize in Physics for the photoelectric effect. Gives the money, as promised, to his former wife, Mileva. Starts work on unified field theory, seeking one fundamental law to unite the forces of nature, gravitation, and electromagnetism.

1923

Einstein in Spain at Escuela Industrial de Barcelona in 1923

1927

At the fifth Solvay Conference in Brussels in 1927, Einstein stands next to Paul Langevin (on his left). Marie Curie sits between Poincaré (on her left) and Perrin.

1928   Strains his heart lugging a heavy case through the snow. Hires Helen Dukas as his secretary.

1929

On vacation near the Baltic in 1928 or 1929.

1930   Eduard has mental breakdown and, diagnosed as a schizo-phrenic, will spend much of his life in a Swiss mental institution.

1933   Einstein visits Winston Churchill at his home in England to discuss the dangerous political situation, especially for Jews in Germany, now that Hitler is in power.

Einstein meets Winston Churchill in England in 1933. Both recognized that Hitler was a threat.

1933 • Leaves Germany for good to work at Princeton's Institute for Advanced Study.

1936 • September 20. His friend Marcel Grossmann dies.

1936 • December 20. His wife, Elsa, dies.

1939 • Start of World War II provoked by Germany's invasion of Poland. Einstein signs letter to President Roosevelt urging him to build an atomic bomb, fearing that Hitler's Germany may have already started on one.

1941 • December 7. Japanese planes bomb Pearl Harbor. United States is at war with both Japan and Germany.

1942 • Einstein's FBI file begins to thicken. FBI chief J. Edgar Hoover suspects him and Helen Dukas of being Soviet spies.

1943 • Despite Hoover's suspicions, Einstein is contracted to advise U.S. Navy on use of new high explosives.

In his Princeton study on July 24, 1943, during World War II, Einstein—admired by many as a pacifist—advises two U.S. Navy officers on how to produce more effective weapons.

1945 • Atomic bombs on Japan end World War II. Einstein promotes idea of a world government to control the atomic bomb.

1948 • His first wife, Mileva, dies.

1951 • His sister, Maja, dies.

1952 • Einstein turns down offer to be President of Israel.

1955 • When asked to join in celebrating the fiftieth anniversary of his special theory of relativity, he declines for reasons of poor health, but adds, "I am not sorry, for anything resembling a personality cult has always been distasteful to me. In the present case, moreover, many people have contributed to the advance of this theory, and it is far from completed."

1955 • March 15. His friend Michele Besso dies.

1955 • April 18. Einstein dies and is cremated. However, his eyes and brain are preserved. His eyes are kept in a bank vault. His brain is sliced up and examined by various scientists hoping in vain to account for his genius. FBI closes the

A magnified section of Einstein's brain.

Einstein file, still not aware that both he and Dukas were loyal American citizens.

1955 • November 21. Thomas Martin, Einstein's first great-grandson, son of Bernhard, is born in Bern, Switzerland.

1965 • Eduard Einstein dies in a Swiss psychiatric hospital.
1965 • Discovery of background microwave radiation that pervades the universe supports Einstein's Big Bang theory of creation.

1973 • Hans Albert dies.

1976 • Laser experiments between earth and moon confirm Einstein's theory of general relativity.

1979 • Centenary of Einstein's birth. To mark the occasion, fifteen hundred people form up on the grounds of Shenandoah Junior High School, Miami, Florida, on November 15, to create the image of $E = mc^2$ as seen and photographed from the air. Helen Dukas and Banesh

Celebrating Einstein's centennial on November 15, 1979, 1,500 people are photographed from above as they gather on the grounds of Shenandoah Junior High School in Miami, Florida, to form "the Equation That Changed the World."

Hoffmann publish their book *Albert Einstein: The Human Side.*

1979 • A three-times-life-size, four-ton bronze informal statue of Einstein by Robert Berks is erected in an elm and holly grove on the grounds of the National Academy of Sciences on Constitution Avenue, Washington, D.C., of which Einstein was a member. It becomes very popular, especially among schoolchildren, who are not discouraged from sitting in the subject's lap. Twenty-one feet from head to toe and twelve feet tall, it cost $1,664,405. Einstein would not have approved. As one of the Academy's 1,250 members representing the elite of American science, Einstein once told a group of them, "When a man after long years of researching chances on a thought which discloses something of the beauty of this mysterious universe, he should not therefore be personally celebrated. He is already sufficiently paid by the experience of seeking and finding." After enduring long-winded speeches at a ceremonial dinner at the Academy when he was guest of honor, he quipped to a table partner, "I have just got a new theory of eternity."

A 12-foot-high statue of Einstein on the grounds of the National Academy of Sciences in Washington, D.C., summer 1996. One-year-old Emma Renee Stockton, posing with the statue, gives an idea of its size. She is the granddaughter of Einstein biographer Denis Brian.

1982 • Helen Dukas dies. All of Einstein's papers are given to Hebrew University, following the instructions in his will. Abraham Pais's *'Subtle Is the Lord': The Science and the Life of Albert Einstein* is published.

1986 • Margot Einstein dies.

1987 • Otto Nathan dies.

1987 • Thirty-two years after Einstein's death, the first volume of his *Collected Papers, The Early Years, 1879–1902*, is published, edited by John Stachel, translated by Anna Beck.

1993 • Instruments on NASA satellite Cosmic Background Explorer confirm Einstein's general relativity theory.

1995 • By cooling atoms to near absolute zero, researchers in Boulder, Colorado, produce a new form of matter, as Einstein and Satyendra Bose had predicted was a possibility.

1996 • This author's *Einstein: A Life* is published by John Wiley & Sons.

1998 • Einstein's summer home in Caputh, Germany, becomes a scholarly retreat, after use as an orphanage, a Nazi youth camp, and a shelter for refugees.

1999 • *Time* magazine names Einstein "Person of the Century," beating FDR, Gandhi, and Churchill for the title.

2004 • Ignaxio Ciufolini of the University of Lecce, Italy, and Erricos Pavlis, from the Joint Center for Earth Systems Technology, Baltimore, Maryland, are the first to measure "frame-dragging," the effect predicted to occur in Einstein's general relativity theory, when a massive body such as the Earth drags space-time around with it as it spins. Another confirmation of Einstein's ideas.

2005 • The one hundredth anniversary of his special relativity theory and the fiftieth anniversary of his death. An unprecedented worldwide celebration by many organizations of Einstein's "miraculous year of 1905." Named variously as "The Year of Physics" and "Einstein's Year."

• The United Nations declares 2005 "The International Year of Physics." Bern, Switzerland, holds a festival and an international physics symposium, and a general meeting of the European Physics Society takes place from July 11 to 15 at the University of Bern. The Institute of Physics adopts 2005 as Einstein's Year, during which the following take place: a series of mass participation experiments; a physics photo exhibition; a pantomime taking the audience on "a trip through the universe"; and a newly choreographed dance based on Einstein's theory of relativity is performed by the Rambert Dance Company at Sadler's Wells, London.

- Worldwide activities to celebrate Einstein also include shining lasers in relay around the planet, the creation of physics toys, and scouting for 2005 youths who show promise as physicists.

- The *Journal of Physics* publishes three issues devoted to Einstein's groundbreaking work. American publisher Harry Abrams publishes *A Hundred Years of Relativity.*

- Berlin holds an exhibition titled "Albert Einstein— Engineer of the Universe." An Einstein Biographical Photo Exposition takes place in his birthplace, Ulm, Germany. France celebrates by cleaning its monuments with lasers. The Korean Physical Society holds an Einstein exhibition in Seoul. Pakistan TV and radio stations air programs about Einstein in local languages.

- In the spring, sculptor Robert Berks donates a bronze bust of Einstein to the town of Princeton, New Jersey. The bust is placed in front of Princeton's Borough Hall.

NOTES

Chapter 1: Was Einstein Dyslexic, a Late Talker, and a "Lazy Dog"?

4 *"The trouble with"* Interview with Wendy Grant, April 21, 2004.

5 *"Most children utter"* Interview with Misty Williams, April 21, 2004.

5 *late talkers as "children"* Interview with Linda Kushner, April 20, 2004.

5 *"sounds quite authentic"* E-mail from Barbara Wolff, April 21, 2004.

5 *"I don't know," he replied* Jamie Sayen, *Einstein in America, The Scientist's Conscience in the Age of Hitler and Hiroshima* (New York: Crown, 1985), 163.

6 *"This could be the behavior"* Williams, April 21, 2004.

8 *He aroused Albert's curiosity* Denis Brian, *Einstein: A Life* (New York: John Wiley & Sons, 1996), 4.

8 *"Albert was profoundly impressed"* Max Talmey, *The Relativity Theory Simplified and the Formative Period of Its Inventor* (New York: Falcon Press, 1932), 163–164.

12 *His sister, Maja, attests* Maja Winteler-Einstein, *Albert Einstein—A Biographical Sketch*, trans. Anna Beck (Princeton, N.J.: Princeton University Press, 1987), xviii.

14 *"His attitude to the world"* Carl Seelig, *Albert Einstein: A Documentary Biography*, trans. Mervyn Savil (London: Staples Press), 1956, 14–15.

17 *After only a few conversations with Einstein* Ibid., 34.

19 *"You're enthusiastic but hopeless"* Ronald W. Clark, *Einstein: His Life and Times* (New York: Avon, 1972), 61.

19 *"You're a clever fellow, Einstein"* Ibid.

19 *"Day and night"* Phillipp Frank, *Einstein: His Life and Times*, trans. George Rosen (New York: Knopf, 1967), 20.

20 *Einstein relished Mach's direct* Banesh Hoffman with Helen Dukas, *Einstein, Creator and Rebel* (New York: Viking, 1972), 78.

23 *"My son Albert Einstein"* Ibid., 33

Chapter 2: Einstein: Woman Hater or Womanizer?

26 *"Einstein's pleasure in the company"* Clark, *Einstein*, 52.

27 *Or as noted biographer* Brenda Maddox, "Einstein in Love," *Library Review*, April 2000.

29 *"as pretty as a picture"* Albrecht Folsing, *Albert Einstein: A Biography,* trans. Ewald Osers (New York: Viking, 1997), 43.

30 *"the kind of male beauty"* Antonina Vallentin, *The Drama of Albert Einstein* (Garden City, N.Y.: Doubleday, 1954), 9.

31 *"perfidious in her hatred"* Roger Highfield and Paul Carter, *The Private Lives of Albert Einstein* (London: Faber and Faber, 1993), 165.

32 *"uncommonly ugly . . . an odious smell"* Highfield and Carter, *Private Lives,* 164, 178.

33 *"Yesterday, suddenly the question"* Michele Zackheim, *Einstein's Daughter: The Search for Lieserl* (New York: Riverhead Books, 2000), 85.

34 *"can be inferred from his reply"* Clark, Einstein, 276.

34 *She told her sons* Peter Michelmore, *Einstein: Profile of the Man* (New York: Dodd Mead, 1962), 79.

34 *"she is healthier"* Max Born, ed., *Born-Einstein Letters* (New York: Walker, 1971), 53.

35 *"It is conceivable that nature"* Alexander Moszkowski, *Einstein the Searcher: His Work Explained from Dialogues with Einstein* (Berlin: Fontane), 1921.

35 *She concluded that* *Born-Einstein Letters,* 39.

36 *"I implore you to do as I say"* Ibid., 40.

36 *"As his mind knows no limits"* John Plesch, *Janos: The Story of a Doctor* (London: Gollancz, 1947), 206.

37 *"a magnet acts on iron filings"* Folsing, *Albert Einstein,* 616.

37 *His biographer Abraham Pais* Interview with Abraham Pais, December 29, 1994.

38 *the niece of a close friend* Highfield and Carter, *Private Lives,* 206.

39 *"like a frog into water"* Einstein to Betty Neumann, January 11, 1924, Einstein Archives.

40 *"when Lenbach came"* Highfield and Carter, *Private Lives,* 208.

41 *"was aroused and shouting"* Dimitri Marianoff and Palma Wayne, *Einstein: An Intimate Study of a Man* (New York: Doubleday Doran, 1944), 129.

41 *"Some managed with stratagems"* Ibid., 205.

42 *"The strongest impression"* Folsing, *Albert Einstein,* 548.

42 *"We do things"* Marianoff and Wayne, *Einstein,* 186.

42 *"an unsuccessful attempt"* Sayen, *Einstein in America,* 70, 80.

44 *"You have gone mad"* Abraham Pais at the memorial ceremony for Helen Dukas, Institute for Advanced Study, March 15, 1982.

45 *She also gave it* Highfield and Carter, *Private Lives,* 211, 329.

45 *"One must not dissect him"* Folsing, *Albert Einstein,* 429.

46 *"Your wife seems to do"* Churchill Eisenhart, "Albert Einstein as I remember him," *Journal of the Washington Academy of Sciences* 54 (1964): 325–328.

46 *"I think you are the most considerate"* Elsa Einstein to Leon Watters, September 10, 1936, Author's collection.

46 *Still she managed to write* Sayen, *Einstein in America*, 75.

47 *"remained serene and worked constantly"* . Leopold Infeld, *Quest: the Evolution of a Scientist* (London: Gollancz, 1941), 282.

47 *she "never lost one iota of respect"* Abraham Pais, *Einstein Lived Here* (New York: Oxford University Press, 1994), 80.

47 *"I didn't think he would ever marry again"* Interview with Alice Kahler, April 15, 1989.

49 *"Perhaps you could tell me"* Interview with Dorothy Commins, August 13, 1988.

49 *"Einstein enjoyed puzzles"* Interview with Alice Kahler, April 15, 1989.

50 *"When it came to Luise"* Margaret Brennan-Gibson, *Clifford Odets* (New York: Atheneum, 1981), 478.

51 *"Her manner of speaking* Frank, *Einstein*, 351.

51 *To their friend* Interview with Kahler, April 13, 1989.

52 *She also cut his hair* Raj Hathirimani, "Memoirs of Einstein's confidante record scientist's political beliefs," *Daily Princetonian*, April 30, 2004.

52 *"a vivid picture"* Interview with Gillett Griffin, July 23, 2004.

52 *"unique collection of books"* Johanna Fantova, "Introduction to 'Gesprache mit Einstein'"[Conversations with Einstein], *Princeton University Library Chronicle* 65, no. 1 (2003): 51.

53 *"Exhausted from a silence long"* Alice Calaprice, "Einstein's Last Musings," *Princeton University Library Chronicle* 65, no. 1 (2003): 66.

54 *"This, though I did not know it"* Marian Anderson, *My Lord, What a Morning: An Autobiography* (New York: Viking, 1956), 267.

54 *"The world has lost its best man"* Kahler to her niece Charlotte, April 20, 1955, author's collection.

55 *"I reminded him of his comment"* Interviews with Dr. Thomas Bucky over the years.

Chapter 3: Was Einstein a Terrible Father? And What Kind of Mother Was Mileva?

58 *"Out of just a little string"* BBC Broadcast, 1966.

62 *"He was expected to act"* Highfield and Carter, *Private Lives*, 223, 224.

62 *"while it was there"* Michelmore, *Einstein*, 124.

64 *"When a blind beetle"* Carl Seelig, *Einstein: A Documentary Biography*, trans. Mervyn Savill (London: Staples Press, 1956), 60.

65 *"one heart and one soul"* Einstein to Ehrenfest, September 1, 1921.

67 *"the dark sides"* Pais, *Einstein Lived Here*, 23.

68 *"Einstein understands as much"* Peter Gay, *Freud: A Life for Our Time* (New York: W. W. Norton), 387.

68 *"Why are you at a Jewish"* Brian, *Einstein*, 183.

68 *"The worst destiny"* Pais, *Einstein Lived Here*, 23.

70 *"In early childhood"* Interview with Elizabeth Roboz Einstein, May 15, 1987.

71 *"It's clear that Einstein"* Interview with Robert Schulmann, November 26, 1991.

72 *"Sometimes my head aches"* Highfield and Carter, *Private Lives*, 237, 238.

73 *"has always tried to stay"* Brian, *Einstein*, 196.

73 *"rejoice in the sky"* Einstein-Besso Correspondence, Besso to Einstein, October 17, 1932, 289.

74 *"Outside circumstances"* Ibid., Einstein to Besso, October 21, 1932, 291.

75 *"There also hangs about him"* Highfield and Carter, *Private Lives*, 240.

76 *"a badly messed-up people"* Sayen, *Einstein in America*, 146.

78 *"a very painful parting"* Highfield and Carter, *Private Lives*, 256.

79 *"the virtually only human problem"* Folsing, *Albert Einstein*, 731.

79 *"We got along great guns"* Interview with Evelyn Einstein, November 13, 1994.

79 *"A dark and dreary dump"* Ibid.

80 *"The boy is nicer than his father"* Einstein, *Princeton University Library Chronicle* 65, no. 1 (2003): 71.

80 *"It tended," he said* Jerry Tallmer, "Sons of the Famous," *New York Post Daily Magazine*, May 23, 1963.

82 *"I never figured out why"* Interview with Elizabeth Roboz Einstein, November 39, 1982.

82 *"Probably the only project"* Pais, *Einstein Lived Here*, 12.

Chapter 4: Whatever Happened to Einstein's Daughter?

83 *"Mileva, an ethnic Serb"* "Einstein Letters Tell of Anguished Love Affair," *New York Times*, May 3, 1987, 88.

88 *"What's more relevant"* E-mail to author from Robert Schulmann, June 29, 2004.

91 *"The matter of your pseudo-daughter"* Zackheim, *Einstein's Daughter*, 242.

92   "*that though he hadn't been following*"   Interview with Robert Schulmann, October 6, 1990.

92   "*a special honor to have*"   Zackheim, *Einstein's Daughter*, 247, 248.

95   "*a mysterious pre-marital incident*"   Michelmore, *Einstein*, 42.

95   "*had opposed the decision*"   Highfield and Carter, *Private Lives*, 94.

98   "*In my family, it was considered*"   Zackheim, *Einstein's Daughter*, 203–204.

98   "*but truthful?*"   E-mail to author from Schulmann, June 29, 2004.

99   "*How can Grete be an honorable witness?*"   Ibid.

99   "*Disappeared?*"   Ibid.

99   "*In addition, Aleckovic*"   Zackheim, *Einstein's Daughter*, 261–262.

99   "*Given to a German woman*"   E-mail to author from Schulmann, June 29, 2004.

100   "*They had no money*"   Zackheim, *Einstein's Daughter*, 246.

100   *After more detective work*   Ibid., 277.

100   "*How in tarnation*"   E-mail to author from Schulmann, June 29, and July 8, 2004.

100   "*Professor Einstein told me*"   Zackheim, *Einstein's Daughter*, 259, 260.

100   "*This is hearsay evidence*"   E-mail to author from Schulmann, June 29, 2004.

101   "*For all his kindness*"   Andrea Gabor, *Einstein's Wife* (New York: Penguin Books, 1996), 25.

101   "*be of a goat*"   Internet reviewer, Manola Sommerfeld.

101   "*withering one-sided portrait*"   Publishers Weekly, October 25, 1999.

101   "*The book is just the latest*"   Associated Press, 1999.

102   "*With grace and conviction*"   Lewis Pyenson, *Isis* 94, no. 1 (2003). Also see, Pyenson, "Just the Facts," *Isis* 80 (1989), 129–135; and Pyenson, "Einstein's Natural Daughter," *History of Science* 28 (1990), 365–379. Michele Zackheim wrote to the author on August 27, 2004, "Mileva traveled to see Lieserl more than was thought. Please see page 45 of my paperback edition. In Serbian society a child was never institutionalized unless it was entirely unmanageable or there were no living family members."

Chapter 5: What Was Einstein Like Face to Face?

103   "*Mileva Maric was no match*"   Seelig, *Albert Einstein*, 12, 17.

104   "*Our first sight*"   Ibid., 101, 103.

104   "*He spoke in the same way*"   Frank, *Life and Times*, 76.

105   "*I was a student at Göttingen*"   Hyman Levy, BBC broadcast, 1966.

105   "*Einstein had already published*"   Earl of Birkenhead, *The Professor and*

the Prime Minister: The Official Life of Professor F. A. Lindemann, Viscount Cherwell (Boston: Houghton Mifflin, 1962), 165.

106 *"Einstein speaks French"* Romain Rolland, *Journal des Années de Guerre 1914–1919* (Paris: Albin Michel, 1952), 510–511.

106 *"He would tease me"* Isle Rosenthal-Schneider, *Reality and the Scientific Truth* (Detroit: Wayne State University Press, 1980), 289.

107 *"I attended one of his"* Interview with I. I. Rabi, October 31, 1980.

107 *"Einstein came to stay"* Felix Ehrenhaft, *My Experiences with Einstein* (Washington, D.C.: Smithsonian Institution Libraries), 5.

108 *"When I visited him"* Hedi Born, *Born-Einstein Letters*, 132.

108 *"I couldn't have had a better patient"* Janos Plesch, *Story of a Doctor* (London: Gollancz, 1947), 167.

109 *"I received a wonderful letter"* L. L. Whyte, BBC broadcast, 1966.

110 *"I live in New York City"* Fulton Oursler, *Behold the Dreamer* (Boston: Little Brown, 1964), 293–299.

111 *"Einstein and I were both"* Herbert Dingle, BBC broadcast, 1966.

112 *"We crossed the Channel"* Marianoff, *Einstein*, 171–172.

113 *"There is a dreamy expression"* B. Kuznetsov, *Einstein* (Moscow: Progress Publishers, 1965), 228, 230.

113 *"Einstein said that no size"* Harry Kessler, *The Diaries*, 137–138.

114 *"Einstein's friend Paul Ehrenfest"* Werner Heisenberg, *Physics and Beyond: Encounters and Conversations* (New York: Harper & Row, 1971), 80–81.

115 *Woolf persuaded Einstein* "Einstein at 50," *New York Times*, August 18, 1929, Section 5, p. 1.

115 *"I was introduced to him"* Otto Frisch, BBC broadcast, 1966.

116 *"Such was the beginning"* Upton Sinclair, *Autobiography* (New York: Harcourt, Brace & World, 1962), 259–260.

116 *"From first to last"* M. C. Sinclair, *Southern Belle* (New York: Crown, 1957), 340.

117 *"When my father was a physician"* Interview with Thomas Bucky, September 7, 1993.

119 *"A kind of wall"* Frida Bucky, "You have to ask forgiveness . . . Albert Einstein as I remember him," *Jewish Quarterly* 15, no. 4 (Winter 1967–1968), 31.

119 *"When I first met Einstein"* Leon Watters memoirs. Author's collection.

120 *"There was light coming"* Hiram Haydn, *Words and Faces* (Harcourt, Brace and Jovanovich, 1974), 164.

121 *"I knew Einstein"* Author's interviews and correspondence with Eugene Wigner; *The Recollections of Eugene P. Wigner*, as told to Andrew Szanton (New York: Plenum, 1992); and a speech by Wigner at the Einstein

Centennial Conference at the Institute for Advanced Study, Princeton, March 8, 1979.

126 *"He seemed to me"* Meyer Weisgal, BBC broadcast, 1966.

127 *"The offer"* Folsing, *Albert Einstein*, 734.

127 *"I climbed"* Alan Richards, *Reminiscences* (Princeton, N.J.: Harvest House Press, 1979), 4.

128 *"I thought I had lost the faculty"* Ilya Ehrenburg, *Post-War Years: 1945–54* (Cleveland, Ohio: World Publishing, 1967), 72, 73, 75, 76, 77, 78.

131 *"I was planning a film"* Interviews with Ashley Montagu, May 5, 1994, and April 5, 1995.

132 *"Frequently, if I brought up"* Ernst Straus, BBC broadcast, 1966.

132 *"I didn't have much personal contact"* Interview with I. F. Stone, May 20, 1987.

133 *"What struck me was"* Interview with Christopher Stone, September 25, 1987.

133 *"Soon after the end of World War II"* Interview with George Wald, October 9, 1985, and correspondence.

139 *"Every time I came to Princeton"* Interview with Linus Pauling, March 14, 1993.

142 *"Einstein was one of the friendliest"* Robert Oppenheimer, "On Albert Einstein," in *Einstein: A Centenary Volume*, ed. A. P. French (Cambridge, Mass.: Harvard University Press, 1979), 47–48.

142 *"My thesis on mathematical logic"* Interview with John Kemeny, September 10, 1988.

146 *"His violin playing"* Interview with Victor Weisskopf, June 14, 1993.

146 *"Whoever said Einstein wasted"* Interview with I. I. Rabi, October 11, 1980; Brian, *Einstein*, 124; and "Albert Einstein: 1879–1955," *Scientific American* 192, no. 6 (June 1955): 2.

147 *"He wasn't like the truly"* Interview with Abraham Pais, January 2, 1992, and correspondence.

148 *"Einstein is a scientist"* David Ben-Gurion, Brian, *Einstein*, 392.

148 *"When I had once pressed"* Maurice Friedman, *Martin Buber's Life and Work: The Later Years, 1945–1965* (New York: Dutton, 1963), 148–149.

148 *"I remember Einstein"* Arthur Komar, from interview with John Wheeler, June 25, 1989.

149 *"Einstein used to walk past my house"* Interview with John Wheeler, June 25, 1989.

149 *"I arrived at Einstein's front door"* BBC broadcast, 1966, and author's interview with I. Bernard Cohen, October 9, 1985.

154 *"Einstein's intervention on my behalf"* Philippe Halsman, letter to the editor, *New York Review of Books*, May 26, 1955.

154 *"One day in April 1955,"* Abba Eban, *Abba Eban: An Autobiography* (New York: Random House, 1977), 190–191.

156 *"I got to know him"* Bertrand Russell, BBC broadcast, 1966.

157 *"During the summer heat wave"* Interview with Dorothy Commins, August 13, 1988.

157 *"My mother would show him letters"* Interview with Clair Gilbert, December 14, 1991.

158 *"In 1954, when I was a curator"* Interview with Gillett Griffin, July 23, 2004.

Chapter 6: Einstein's Food for Thought: Was He a Gourmet or a Gourmand?

162 *Because Einstein had never tasted* Brian, *Einstein*, 56.

164 *"Things downstairs were all neat"* Interview with Jane Leonard Swing Chapman, May 10, 1988.

165 *"Einstein was planning to write"* Interview with Dorothy Commins, August 13, 1988.

Chapter 7: Did Einstein Believe in God?

166 *"What I seek to accomplish"* Peter Michelmore, *Nobel Prizes*, Encyclopaedia Brittanica, 1997, 7.

167 *"Conceptions which had dimly"* Reiser, *Albert Einstein*, 70–71.

167 *"years of anxious searching"* Mozkowski, *Einstein the Searcher*, 4.

168 *"whispered feverishly"* Reiser, *Albert Einstein*, 71.

170 *"Simply impossible," Einstein said.* Moszkowski, *Einstein the Searcher*, and Brian, *Einstein*, 115.

170 *Had he been "an oversized quantum"* E-mail to author from Dr. Robert Schulmann, July 8, 2003.

170 *This aspect of the special theory* Interview with Banesh Hoffmann, October 29, 1982.

171 *"Almighty is laughing at it"* Seelig, *Albert Einstein*, 126.

171 *Einstein said to him, "Can we get another idea"* Interview with Hoffmann, October 23, 1982.

172 *"He believed it was a fatal mistake"* Sayen, *Einstein in America*, 156.

173 *"freed of their myths"* Max Jammer, *Einstein and Religion, Physics and Theology* (Princeton, N.J.: Princeton University Press, 1999), 116.

174 *"It is quite clear"* Gerald Holton, *Einstein, History and Other Passions* (Woodbury, N.Y.: Perseus Press, 1996), 172.

174 *"Strenuous labor"* Pais, *Einstein Lived Here*, 113.

174 *"Can the energy quanta"* Folsing, *Einstein*, 265.

174 *"God should punish the English."* Alice Calaprice, ed., *The Expanded Quotable Einstein* (Princeton, N.J.: Princeton University Press, 2000), 201.

175 *"An inner voice tells me"* *The Born-Einstein Letters*, 91.

175 *"Raffiniert ist der Herr Gott"* Lewis S. Feuer, *Einstein and the Generations of Science* (New York: Basic Books, 1974), 104.

175 *"God is slick"* Michael Gilmore, *Skeptic* 5, no. 2 (1997), 62ff.

177 *"One can view the world"* Folsing, *Einstein*, 585.

177 *"A good joke"* Feuer, *Einstein and the Generations*, 83–84.

177 *"God does not play dice"* *London Observer*, April 5, 1964; and Irene Born, *The Born-Einstein Correspondence*, 180.

177 *Responding to someone* In the Twenties: *The Diaries of Henry Kessler* (New York: Holt, Rinehart and Winston, 1971), 321, 322.

178 *Interviewed by George Sylvester Viereck* Brian, *Einstein*, 185, 186.

179 *Yet in a conversation* Alice Calaprice, "A Talk with Einstein," *Princeton University Library Chronicle*, October 1943, 215.

179 *In 1929 Einstein wrote* Gerald Holton, "Mach, Einstein, and the Search for Reality," *Daedalus* (Spring 1986), 658–659.

180 *"to one formula all laws"* Clark, *Einstein*, 495.

180 *Disappointed that Einstein* Ibid., 413–414.

180 *Anxious to defend Einstein* Ibid., 414.

181 *Einstein's first sentence* *New York Times Magazine*, November 9, 1930, 1.

181 *Rabbi Dr. Nathan Krass* *New York Times Magazine*, November 16, 1930.

181 *"If I had been able"* Ibid.

181 *"the more Einstein became"* Bernstein, *Einstein*, 17.

182 *"Now I know there is a God"* Yehudi Menuhin, *Unfinished Journey* (New York: Knopf, 1976), 96.

182 *"One may not ask that"* Abraham Pais, *Einstein Lived Here*, 37.

182 *"Every one of us appears here"* Brian, *Einstein*, 233, 234.

183 *"since our inner experiences"* Helen Dukas and Banesh Hoffmann, *Albert Einstein, the Human Side* (Princeton, N.J.: Princeton University Press, 1981), 4.

183 *The Einsteins had lost their Bible* Interview with James Blackwood, September 7, 1994, and correspondence.

184 *But serious scientific study* Dukas and Hoffman, *Albert Einstein*, 117.

184 *"Does it ever get monotonous"* Interview with James Blackwood, September 7, 1994, and correspondence.

185 *But "I don't think you are really religious"* Max Eastman, *Einstein, Trotsky, Hemingway, Freud and Other Companions* (New York: Collier, 1962), 25.

185 *"Scientific method can teach us"* *Christian Register*, June 1948, 49.

186 *"Only the church stood squarely"* *Baltimore Evening News*, April 13, 1979.

187 *Einstein replied that he had never* G. H. Raner and L. S. Lerner, "Einstein's Beliefs," *Nature* 358:102.

187 *Though seriously ill* Folsing, *Albert Einstein*, 730–731.

188 *In his last few years* Ibid., 736.

188 *"The Jewish religion is, more"* *Forum*, 1930, 373.

189 *"super-personal objects"* Pais, *Subtle Is the Lord*, 319; and Thomas Torrance, *Einstein and God*, Center of Theological Enquiry, 1.

189 *Einstein's former student* Gerald Holton, "What Precisely Is Thinking," *Einstein: A Centenary Volume*, ed. A. P. French (Cambridge, Mass: Harvard University Press, 1979), 162, 163.

189 *"which we try to formulate"* Jammer, *Einstein and Religion*, 121, 122.

190 *"C. P. Snow called Einstein"* Interview with Banesh Hoffmann, September 2, 1985.

190 *When the Israeli leader* David Ben-Gurion, *Ben Gurion Looks Back in Talks with Moshe Pearlman* (New York: Schocken Books, 1970), 216, 217.

191 *Einstein regarded him* Alice Calaprice, "Einstein's Last Musings," *Princeton University Library Chronicle* 65, no. 1 (2003): 74.

191 *"People keep writing to me"* Interview with George Wald; Brian, *Einstein*, 415.

192 *Theologian Torrance thought that* Torrance, *Einstein and God*, 2.

192 *He also agreed with Spinoza* Jammer, *Einstein and Religion*, 148–149.

192 *And this was also in line with the rationalist* Ibid., 143–145, 149–150.

193 *"When I am judging a theory"* Folsing, *Alfred Einstein*, 703.

193 *"It would be perfectly consistent"* Stephen Hawking, "The Edge of Space-Time," *American Scientist* 72 (1984): 355–359.

193 *"Why is there a universe?"* Hawking, *A Brief History of Time* (New York: Bantam, 1988), 174.

Chapter 8: Einstein under Attack: Was He a Plagiarist and Was Mileva His Scientific Partner?

195 *"The Jew conspicuously lacks"* Wiliam L. Shirer, *The Nightmare Years, 1930–1940* (Boston: Little, Brown & Co., 1984), 185.

196   *He said that he admired Lenard*   Folsing, *Albert Einstein*, 465.

196   *"Apart from Einstein's relativistic"*   Ibid., 463.

197   *In 1919 he wrote*   Clark, *Einstein*, 130–131.

197   *"Dear Friends, I have come among men"*   Brian, *Einstein*, 211.

197   *Physicist Gerald Holton*   Communication to author from Gerald Holton, September 2004.

198   *"was quite aware that his way"*   John Stachel, *Einstein from 'B' to 'Z'* (Boston: Birkhauser, 2002), 4.

198   *"despite the contrary evidence"*   Gerald Holton, *Thematic Origins of Scientific Thought: Kepler to Einstein* (Cambridge, Mass.: Harvard University Press, 1988), 344, 345.

198   *"After nearly half a century"*   Folsing, *Albert Einstein*, 214.

199   *"Einstein said, 'This is not just'"*   Melvyn Bragg, *On Giants' Shoulders: Great Scientists and Their Discoveries—From Archimedes to DNA* (New York: John Wiley, 1998), 204.

199   *"This does not preclude the fact"*   Ibid.

199   *"That Einstein's work in 1905"*   Holton, *Thematic Origins*, 204.

200   *"It has always hurt me"*   I. Bernard Cohen, "An Interview with Einstein," *Scientific American* 193 (1955), 73.

200   *Einstein biographer Folsing*   Folsing, *Albert Einstein*, 375, 376.

202   *"All serious Einstein scholarship"*   Robert Schulmann and Gerald Holton, *New York Times Book Review*, September 20, 1995.

203   *"In one of his most widely"*   Pyenson, *Isis* 94, no. 1 (March 2003).

204   *"There is his legendary"*   Holton, *Thematic Origins*, 356.

Chapter 9: Einstein's FBI File and the Soviet Spy He Loved

207   *Then, obviously referring to*   *New York Times*, April 18, 1938.

209   *"Perhaps most perplexing"*   Richard Alan Schwartz, "The F.B.I. and Dr. Einstein," *The Nation*, September 3–10, 1983.

212   *"Are you a Communist or anarchist?"*   *New York Times*, December 6, 1932, 1.

212   *"At first," wrote Sayen*   Sayen, *Einstein in America*, 204.

215   *"Dear Mr. Stalin, as an old Jew"*   Ibid., 207.

215   *"Overall, the FBI's dossier"*   Fred Jerome, *The Einstein File: J. Edgar Hoover's Secret War against the World's Most Famous Scientist* (New York: St. Martin's Press, 2000), 144.

215   *"The Navy gave its assent"*   Ibid., 42.

216   *"During the interview"*   FBI memo. Internal Security, To Director, FBI. From SAC, Newark (100-29614), March 9, 1955.

219 *"A review of this file"* Ibid., May 2, 1955.

220 *had he known* Brian, *Einstein*, 422; interview with Bucky, October 2, 1988.

220 *"I suppose you must realize"* Jerome, *Einstein File*, 93; Einstein file, Section 8, 75.

220 *Abraham Pais implies* Sayen, *Einstein in America*, 256.

220 *"Everything reminds me of you"* Einstein to Margarita, *Standard-Times*, June 2, 1998.

222 *"In the years I spent"* Paul Needham, Sotheby's.

222 *"He essentially refused"* Selby Kiffer, *Standard-Times*, June 2, 1998.

223 *"politically undeveloped"* Sayen, *Einstein in America*, 210.

Einstein Chronology

228 *When asked to join in celebrating* Daniel Greenberg. "A Statue without Stature," *Washington Post*, December 12, 1978.

230 *"When a man after long years"* Ibid.

SELECTED BIBLIOGRAPHY

Anderson, Marian. *My Lord, What a Morning: An Autobiography.* New York: Viking, 1956.

Besso, Michele. *Albert Einstein—Michele Besso, Correspondence, 1903–1955.* Ed., Pierre Speziali. Paris: Hermann, 1972.

Birkenhead, Earl of. *The Professor and the Prime Minister: The Official Life of Professor F. A. Lindemann, Viscount Cherwell.* Boston: Houghton Mifflin, 1962.

Born, Max. *My Life: Recollections of a Nobel Laureate.* New York: Scribner's, 1978.

Born–Einstein Letters. Commentary by Max Born, trans., Irene Born. New York: Walker, 1971.

Clark, Ronald W. *Einstein: The Life and Times.* New York: Avon, 1971.

Cohen, I. Bernard. "An Interview with Einstein." *Scientific American* 193 (1955): 68–73.

Curie, Eve. *Madame Curie.* New York: Pocket Books, 1964.

Dukas, Helen, with Banesh Hoffmann. *Albert Einstein: The Human Side, New Glimpses from His Archives.* Princeton, N.J.: Princeton University Press, 1979.

Eban, Abba. *Abba Eban: An Autobiography.* New York: Random House, 1977.

Einstein's FBI File.

Folsing, Albrecht. *Albert Einstein: A Biography.* Trans. Ewald Osers. New York: Viking, 1997.

Frank, Philipp. *Einstein: His Life and Times.* Trans. George Rosen. New York: Knopf, 1947.

Halsman, Philippe. *Sight and Insight.* New York: Doubleday, 1972.

Haydn, Hiram. *Words and Faces.* New York: Harcourt Brace and Jovanovich, 1974.

Herneck, Friedrich. *Einstein privat.* Berlin: Buchverlag der Morgen, 1978.

Highfield, Roger, and Paul Carter. *The Private Lives of Albert Einstein.* London: Faber & Faber, 1993.

Hoffmann, Banesh, and Helen Dukas. *Albert Einstein: Creator and Rebel.* New York: Viking, 1972.

Holton, Gerard. *Einstein, History and Other Passions.* New York: American Institute of Physics Press, 1995.

———. *Thematic Origins of Scientific Thought: Kepler to Einstein.* Cambridge, Mass.: Harvard University Press, 1988.

Jaffe, Bernard. *Michelson and the Speed of Light.* New York: Doubleday, 1960.

Jerome, Fred. *The Einstein File: J. Edgar Hoover's Secret War against the World's Most Famous Scientist.* New York: St. Martin's Press, 2000.

Kessler, Count Harry. *The Diaries of a Cosmopolitan: Count Harry Kessler, 1918–1937.* London: Weidenfeld & Nicolson, 1971.

Laurence, Dan H., ed. *Bernard Shaw: Collected Letters 1926–1950.* New York: Viking, 1988.

Marianoff, Dimitri, and Palm Wayne. *Einstein: An Intimate Study of a Great Man.* New York: Doubleday, Doran & Co., 1944.

Michelmore, Peter. *Einstein: Profile of the Man.* New York: Dodd, Mead, 1962.

Moszkowski, Alex. *Einstein the Searcher: His Work Explained from Dialogues with Einstein.* Berlin: Fontana, 1921.

Oursler, Fulton. *Behold the Dreamer.* Boston: Little, Brown, 1964.

Pais, Abraham. *Einstein Lived Here.* New York: Oxford University Press, 1994.

Patner, Andrew. *I. F. Stone, A Portrait: Conversations with a Nonconformist.* New York: Doubleday/Anchor, 1990.

Plesch, Janos. *Janos: The Story of a Doctor.* London: Gollancz, 1947.

Reiser, Anton. *Albert Einstein: A Biographical Portrait.* New York: Albert & Charles Boni, 1930.

Rolland, Romain. *Journal des Années de Guerre 1914–1919.* Paris: Albin Michel, 1952.

Rosenthal-Schneider, Ilse. *Reality and Scientific Truth.* Detroit: Wayne State University Press, 1980.

Rubel, Eduard. *Eduard Einstein.* Bern, Switz.: Paul Haupt, 1986.

Russell, Bertrand. *The Autobiography of Bertrand Russell: 1944–1969.* New York: Simon and Schuster, 1969.

Sayen, Jamie. *Einstein in America: The Scientist's Conscience in the Age of Hitler and Hiroshima.* New York: Crown, 1985.

Schulmann, Robert, and Jurgen Renn, eds. *Albert Einstein/Mileva Maric: Love Letters.* Princeton, N.J.: Princeton University Press, 1992.

Schwartz, Richard Alan. "The F.B.I. and Dr. Einstein." *Nation* 237, no. 6 (September 3–10, 1983): 168–173.

Seelig, Carl. *Albert Einstein: A Documentary Biography.* Trans. Mervyn Savill. London: Staples Press, 1956.

Sinclair, Mary Craig. *Southern Belle.* New York: Crown, 1957.

Solovine, Maurice. *Albert Einstein: Lettres à Maurice Solovine.* Ed. M. Solovine. Paris, 1956.

Talmey, Max. *The Relativity Theory Simplified and the Formative Period of Its Inventor.* New York: Falcon Press, 1932.

Trbuhovic-Gjuric, Desanka. *Das tragische Leben der Mileva Einstein-Maric.* Bern, Switz.: Paul Haupt, 1983.

Watters, Leon. "Comments on the Letters of Professor and Mrs. Einstein to Dr. Leon L. Watters." The Leon Watters Collection, Jewish American Archives, Hebrew Union College, Jewish Institute of Religion, Cincinnati, Ohio. n.d.

SELECTED BIBLIOGRAPHY 247

Whitrow, G. J., ed. *Einstein: The Man and His Achievement.* New York: Dover, 1973.

Wigner, Eugene P., as told to Andrew Szanton. *The Recollections of Eugene P. Wigner.* New York: Plenum Press, 1992.

Zackheim, Michele. *Einstein's Daughter: The Search for Lieserl.* New York: Riverhead Books, 1999.

INDEX

NOTE: Page numbers in *italics* refer to photos.